GAFF GODDESS

www.penguin.co.uk

SILICONE
FILLER
SILICONE REMOVER
SALT

Laura de Barra

GAFF GODDESS

SIMPLE TIPS & TRICKS TO HELP YOU RUN YOUR HOME

TRANSWORLD IRELAND

TRANSWORLD IRELAND
Penguin Random House Ireland, Morrison Chambers, 32 Nassau Street, Dublin 2, Ireland
www.transworldireland.ie

Transworld Ireland is part of the Penguin Random House group of companies
whose addresses can be found at global.penguinrandomhouse.com

First published in the UK and Ireland in 2020
by Transworld Ireland
an imprint of Transworld Publishers

The information in this book has been compiled by way of general guidance in relation to the specific subjects addressed, but is not a substitute and not to be relied on for construction, plumbing, electric or other professional advice on specific circumstances and in specific locations. So far as the author is aware the information given is correct and up to date as at 30 August 2019. Practice, laws and regulations all change, and the reader should obtain up-to-date professional advice on any such issues. The author and publishers disclaim, as far as the law allows, any liability arising directly or indirectly from the use, or misuse, of the information contained in this book.

A CIP catalogue record for this book
is available from the British Library.

ISBN 9781848272620

Design by Bobby Birchall, Bobby&Co
Typeset in Avenir LT Std 10 pt
Printed and bound in China by Toppan Leefung Ltd

Penguin Random House is committed to a sustainable
future for our business, our readers and our planet. This book
is made from Forest Stewardship Council® certified paper.

1 3 5 7 9 10 8 6 4 2

For Shane, the one I dared to dream for

Contents

INTRODUCTION

utopia (n.)
An imagined place or state of things where everything is so perfect there is complete contentment.

What's my utopia? It's somewhere where, whether tenant or homeowner, we are all goddesses of our own gaff. Reigning supreme, tools in hand and lipstick game strong, we are independent, knowledgeable, and in Chanel RTW S/S 95 at the weekend and anything by The Row during downtime. How fabulous.

In this utopia, where wine flows liberally, we recognize the importance of our home and her role in our lives. We recognize how much calmer and freer we feel when she is working as she should.

Although we're not experts and know when to call one, repairs and replacements are within our capabilities and we tackle them with the confidence of someone who just knows she can. When something happens out of the blue, we're able to identify and tackle the issue because we're prepared and informed.

We reap the benefits of a well-zoned space. One that is laid out to make performing even our most mundane tasks feel like a breeze, where our favourite moments will be enhanced and are easy to slip into. We have switching-on and switching-off down to a fine art, and the calm it brings pays forward the Zen into our days and nights. We are more time-efficient, satisfied and appreciative of our home as she works to help our day run well. She's a sanctuary for the bad days and a delight on the good days.

We treat our home like the queen that she is and we tend to her in times of need. We are aware of all her requirements and how we can help her serve us to her full potential. We are prepared, we are poised, we are privy.

While this utopia might not be entirely possible for everyone – there's not enough S/S 95 for all of us, after all – we can all work towards it. I feel we've forgotten the value of a well-functioning home and how important she is to the way our lives work and run.

What we have, what we buy and how we store it has taken over from lovingly caring for and maintaining our appliances, creating a calm space, and having a set-up that suits our individual routines.

I want to revisit the days when things in the home lasted – because they were valued – and where carrying out repairs ourselves was a must. I want us to be prepared for life's accidents and emergencies. But I want us to do it with a modern approach, of course – some fabulous She-IY.

I hope that reading this book will help to enhance your relationship with your home, to rediscover your space, to make repairs less stressful and your home work for you and your lifestyle. I hope it will make you feel powerful and confident and, above all, like the Gaff Goddess you are.

1. SHE'S HOME

A home is like anything else of great value you will own in life, be it a car, a boat (shriek), a Prada handbag (double shriek) … Correct handling and treatment along with a little love will ensure it lives a much longer life and will need fewer repairs. I'm not talking simply about cleaning and tidying, and your home's general appearance here – this runs a little deeper. Whether you're a tenant, a homeowner or a landlord, it's important to be aware of how and why your home works the way she does.

Once you've got to grips with her condition and any potential niggles, you'll be able to anticipate various issues that might crop up in the future. You'll also be able to enhance her safely and confidently if you know her limits. While there will always be surprises beyond your control, the more you know about her, the more you'll be able to prevent the preventable – easily, efficiently and more cost-effectively. In this chapter we'll cover getting to know your home, how to check her vitals and learn all about her emergency buttons.

Checking Her Vitals

Taking a deeper look into your home's health on the day you move in is a great thing to do, but it's also fabulous to do at any time of the year. Think of it as you would a medical check-up for yourself – there's never a bad time to have one. In my opinion it's essential, even if you're a tenant. Most people think that if an inventory has been carried out, that means the property is in full working order. Actually, inventories only cover the appearance and condition of the rooms, and will rarely give an indication of how the property functions, how the white goods operate, and so on. An inventory clerk will check if a sink is clean, for example, but they won't state whether the drain is fully functional.

At the end of this chapter on pages 24–8 you'll find a checklist to help you take your home's vitals. Once completed, you'll have a go-to page to keep track of any necessary repairs and future decorating tasks you might want to sink your teeth into. If you're renting, it's a good opportunity to highlight anything you think your landlord might need to know about, such as a dripping tap or signs of damp. It will give them an opportunity to address the issue before it gets worse. It will also give you a good idea of which jobs you could bundle together for a contractor. You'll be able to see all the electrical work, for example, that you could get a quote for and get done in one appointment. Your list will also become a great go-to excuse to cancel plans. 'I have to re-silicone my shower' is the new 'I'm washing my hair.'

When assessing your home, you might find some issues initially cause you great alarm. I, for one, used to shriek internally at the sight of cracks in walls or mould in the bathroom because my brain was trained to see them as disastrous and a sign of huge costs ahead. However, these 'red flags' might not be as serious as they at first appear. Here are a few things I've learned during my time preparing properties for the rental market, to help you distinguish between issues needing urgent attention, those that are an easy fix, and those that can wait until you're ready to tackle them.

Cracking up

Wall cracks are super common, especially in new builds. When they're of the tiny variety seen near windows and doors, it's usually the building settling into itself and they can continue to appear for a few years after the property has been built. They are easily repaired with some filler and a coat of paint. I'll cover how to do this later in the book (see pages 45–9), so you can rest assured it's on the easy-to-repair list!

The more sinister cracks are the ones that don't tend to run in a straight line and are wider. They're more common in older properties and can sometimes be a sign of the foundations moving. I would have a professional check out any that are over 2 mm wide.

The joy of paint

If, once you've filled all your cracks, you still find that there are other issues with your property's walls – marks, stains, discolouration and so on – you'll find that a simple coat of paint can cover these easily. If you have an older home, I'd advise using a matt paint which won't bounce light from dents and imperfections, thus highlighting them. It will instead create a smoother look to the walls and woodwork.

Ventilation

Poor or inadequate ventilation in a bathroom can lead to a world of pain. If there's black mould on your walls or ceiling, the paint is peeling and it takes a long time for steam to clear after a shower, you might need to install an extractor fan or you might have an underperforming one in place. The easiest way to see whether it's in full working order is to hold some tissue paper against it when it's on. Remove your hand and if the power of the fan alone can hold the tissue against it, it's working fine. When I'm inspecting a new property, I like to put a length of four squares of tissue against the fan to really put it through its paces. If it fails this test, it's time to call in an electrician to assess whether it can be repaired.

If you do find mould growing in your home, I outline the reasons for it, how to deal with it and how to prevent it from coming back on pages 224–31. Mould can be super dangerous for anyone with asthma or allergies, and it should be dealt with as soon as you notice it appear.

Leaks

If you spot any damp patches on walls, ceilings or floors, I'd advise acting on these immediately – leaking water can cause a lot of damage very quickly. Leaks from an adjacent property can also affect your home and your neighbours might not be aware of the problem. So, if you can't find the source of the leak within your own home, check if it could be coming from your neighbours' pipe, or even an external one.

Smaller leaks are usually caused

by loose or worn fittings and can be fixed easily there and then. One of the most common leaks I see is under the kitchen sink. It's almost always the result of the pipes having been knocked during use of the cupboard underneath, or someone having unscrewed them to unblock the sink and not tightened them enough afterwards. In fact, it's one of the first areas I look for signs of trouble when I get to a new property. If I see water sitting on the floor of the cupboard under the sink, I tighten all the fittings, put down some kitchen towel or a cloth and run the tap full blast. If the towel or cloth stays dry I know the fittings are back to working as they should.

If it doesn't stay dry and water is still escaping from the joints of the pipes, it could mean a washer needs to be replaced. A plumbing washer is essentially a rubber seal that prevents water from leaking through a threaded fastener. So when you see a screw-in part in a pipe, which is a nut, there will always be a washer present inside. Replacing a washer in a pipe is a super-straightforward process and you can find some simple instructions on pages 110–13.

Dripping taps and shower issues

I can't tell you how many times I've come across a dripping tap, or a shower head or a shower hose not working as it should. Usually, these problems are – again – down to a worn-out washer in need of replacement. On pages 111–13 you can find detailed instructions on how to change a tap washer and how to deal with pesky shower hose and head issues on pages 117–18. Many people are unaware of how to carry out these repairs but some are surprisingly easy to sort!

Flooring

If, as you do your assessment, you find yourself staring at a long list of issues and losing your mind a little, do not fear. One thing that can make a huge difference to your home is flooring. A large inexpensive rug can cover a host of issues, such as ugly old carpets or worn-out floorboards, and give you some time to focus on the more pressing and less expensive jobs at hand. Rugs are also a quick fix if you find yourself renting and stuck with carpets you hate. Remember, if you're placing a rug on a laminate or slippery floor, make sure it is secured firmly with a rug grip.

Keep these potential 'red flags' in mind along with the goddess attitude of 'can do' when filling out the checklist at the end of this chapter. Remember, you're getting to know your home, which will ultimately lead only to good things. You'll also be surprised at how many jobs you'll be able to do yourself and how many jobs one contractor could fit in during an appointment.

Perfect Timing

If you do find yourself with a looming to-do list and wish you'd never started, do not fear – just because you have a list doesn't mean everything on it has to get done right away. Thankfully, there are better times of the year than others to take care of certain tasks. While I'd always encourage people to deal with anything that affects comfortable and safe living as soon as possible (such as hot-water supply, broken windows or trip hazards), I'd also encourage tackling each task at the most suitable time of year for it. Doing this can save you money and ensure the job is carried out more effectively.

Here's some advice on the best times to take care of specific tasks, which will help you to decide when to do them. You can then colour-code your to-do list into 'urgent', 'any time' and '[specific time of year]'. Approaching it in this way means you can tackle each job at the ideal moment, with enough time to plan, shop for and learn more about it, rather than having to confront one long list head-on (grim).

Early spring

Interior painting

People tend to think that painting is best done during the summer months. You can fling open the windows, throw on a pair of vintage hot-pant dungarees and a Moschino-style headscarf, turn up Dolly Parton and let the glorious weather aid the drying process, right? Wrong. (Although that does sound fabulous.) The humidity of the summer months can actually mean that the walls dry unevenly.

Air is at its driest in early winter and early spring. I tend to prefer painting during the spring as you can take advantage of the longer days and continue into the evening in natural light. Glorious.

Tiling

Buy your tiles in bulk in late winter and early spring for the best deals. This is just after the Christmas rush and right before retailers bring in new stock for the busy spring/summer period. Much like fashion retailers, homeware stores have main lines (think of plain white tiles as the white T-shirts of the bathroom world) and trend-led ranges which represent what is currently popular in the world of interiors. Again, as in the fashion industry, these usually derive from high-end designer ranges and trickle down to high-street stores in a more pared-back, commercial style. Here, the bonus for you is that every season, chances are at least one trend will suit your taste if the main lines are too plain for you. At the end of the season this trend will be being phased out and you'll find prices greatly reduced.

Tiles are usually priced per square metre and not per tile. Most online retailers have a calculator on their website to help you figure out how many tiles you'll need for your whole job, so don't feel too overwhelmed at the thought of costing your tiled space. You'll just need to know the measurements, and don't forget to add 10 per cent extra to cover any breakages or spares that might be needed.

If you're moving in to a new place and need to replace a tile on an existing floor or wall, it's worth checking behind the bath panel or behind the kitchen kick board (the panel that looks like a skirting board under the base cupboards), as contractors tend to store spares here after a job. I've had success here many times before (and hope you do too!).

Spring/summer

Chimneys and gutters

Unless you're faced with an urgent issue, I'd always avoid undertaking any replacement or deep-cleaning work to a part of your property during the season it is most in use. It's best to tend to your chimney's needs, for example, during the warmer months of the year because the chimney contractor is likely to be more available then and you won't be needing to use the chimney.

When a contractor comes round to take care of things such as chimneys and gutters, I'd advise clearing a path for them to ensure ease of access and the removal of any rubbish. I'd also always suggest removing anything breakable from the area where work is being carried out and putting down an old sheet or tarpaulin to protect your flooring from work carried out inside. These kinds of jobs are messy and it's your responsibility to limit what can get in the way.

Early autumn

Boiler and central heating system maintenance

It's always best to sort any hot-water or heating issues as soon as they arise, but if you're in the market for a new boiler or central heating system, the best time of year to get one installed is early autumn. This gives you time to shop around, suss out the best deals and book in the most suitable contractor. These kind of decisions taken in haste (and cold weather!) can result in some costly lessons. No one wants a hefty bill from an out-of-hours call-out after a week of cold showers, because don't forget that not all boiler issues are solvable in one appointment – spare parts might need to be ordered or you might need a new system altogether.

While we're on the topic of boilers, you should be getting yours serviced annually. Not only should this result in lower costs because preventable repairs will be picked up, it will also prolong the boiler's life and protect those in the house – from a gas leak, for example.

Winter

Buying appliances

From Black Friday to the January sales, you'll get the most bang for your buck when purchasing home appliances during the winter months, if you can hold on until then. If I'm planning on investing in an appliance during the sales, I like to read up on makes and models on comparison sites ahead of time and take in some reviews. I feel this gives me a more thorough understanding of the deal I'm getting, as well as making sure I'm buying what I need rather than having my decision swayed by some epic discount.

Many poor performers are heavily discounted during these sales so it's key to know what is truly a bargain and what is simply bad stock. So shop around for a few weeks before the sales begin and be aware of your needs and wants before being dazzled by a 70 per cent off sticker. When it comes to discounts, I always think it's only a bargain if you were going to buy it anyway as opposed to buying something simply because it's dramatically discounted.

Emergency Buttons

Your home is constantly switched on in one way or another. Even if you've turned off the TV and all the lights, some utilities are still running in the background. It's important to know what they are and how to shut them off completely should there be an emergency.

Would you know how to cut off the water supply in your home if you needed to? The longer a leaking or burst pipe is allowed to flow in your home, the worse the damage will be. Would you know what to do in the event of a gas leak or a power cut? Speed is key when facing issues such as these.

Mains water

Delivered to our homes from our local water provider, we use this water for everything from washing our clothes to brushing our teeth. It's a good idea to learn how to switch it off.

Enter the stopcock!

You never know when you may need her so it's important to be aware of where she is and how she works. It's also worth checking your buildings insurance policy to check whether water damage claims are affected by a faulty stopcock. This all sounds a little scary but turning your water supply on and off is something that is super easy to be in control of with a little know-how.

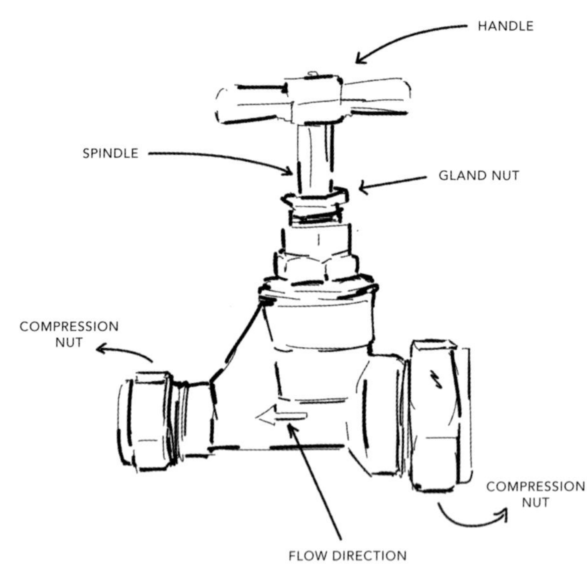

Who is she? In short, a stopcock looks like a tap connecting two pipes which, when switched off, cuts the mains water supply to your home, thus stopping the waterflow in its tracks before it can further damage your nest. Her main role is to regulate the flow of mains water, but she can also be a great help to you or your plumber when carrying out any work, adjusting water pressure and, of course, in case of an emergency.

Where is she? In most modern homes the stopcock is under the kitchen sink. In some older buildings they're located in the front or back garden near where the water pipes enter the property. If you can't locate yours, ask the previous owner, a neighbour, your landlord or the building management company.

If your home has undergone a renovation in recent years and you're struggling to track down your stopcock, try the room that originally housed the kitchen, or the wall the kitchen sink used to be on. I've also seen stopcocks moved to some odd places during a remodel – here are some common locations:

- Downstairs toilet
- Utility room
- Under floorboards in entrance hall
- Storage or boiler cupboard
- Under the stairs
- Cupboard in communal hall (newer apartment blocks)

Some stopcocks are concealed by screw-on panels. If you can't change this to a hinged one, I'd advise picking up a cheap screwdriver that matches the screw heads and tape it to a hidden spot near by. If you ever need to access your stopcock in an emergency, you'll be glad you did this. You could also ask your plumber to fit a stopcock switch in an easy-to-use location. It wouldn't cost an extortionate amount to do so and may save you in the future as you'll be able to turn off the water quicker during an emergency, thus reducing water damage.

(If you find some taps still run after you've turned off your stopcock, you may have two of them. This is usually the case in larger, older properties but isn't that common.)

How does she work? Once you've located your stopcock, you need to make sure she's in full working order. This means ensuring she's carrying out her day-to-day work well but can also switch to the 'off' position when needed. There is an arrow on all stopcocks to let you know which direction the water is flowing. This is what a plumber will note to ensure it is the right way up when installing, replacing or repairing. Inside, there is a watertight seal that, simply put, is locked into place by the turning of the tap.

Fortunately, we shouldn't need to use the stopcock often, but this brings some issues in itself. Over time, the handle can seize up, making her impossible to turn. If she's just a little stiff, WD-40 can be applied to loosen her. If a full replacement is needed, I'd always advise getting a qualified plumber to carry out the work, unless you're super confident.

Usually, a leaking stopcock is the result of a worn part, such as a washer (see diagram on page 113) that needs to be replaced – a very straightforward job – or the nut (see diagram on page 14) at the base is a little loose. I'd always ensure this nut is tightened before you pay a plumber to visit as it's one of the main reasons for call-outs to a leaking stopcock.

What is 'off' and 'on'? To check your stopcock is in full working order, you need to set it to 'off' to see if the water stops. If you're lucky enough to have a modern stopcock installed, you may have a switch mechanism, which is far easier to use – a simple click and you're sorted. Otherwise you'll have an older model, which looks like a brass tap. Gorge.

To turn a brass tap-style stopcock to 'off', remember this: **c**lockwise = **c**losed; **a**nticlockwise = **a**jar. Or, lefty loosey, righty tighty! Once it's off, turn on a tap, which should run for a short while and then gradually stop. This will show you that your stopcock is working as it should be – the water that came out was what was left in the pipes after you turned the stopcock off. To ensure you have only one stopcock controlling your water, check all your other taps aren't running.

Some poor water-pressure issues can be caused by a stopcock not being fully 'open'. People can sometimes knock their stopcock by accident and reduce their pressure without realizing it. Ensuring it's fully 'open' isn't a guaranteed fix but worth checking out.

If your water pressure is fine and you're just checking whether your stopcock is working, make sure that you count the number of turns it takes to reach the 'off' position. When turning it back on, make the same number of turns in the opposite direction to make sure it goes back to its original position. You essentially don't want to affect your water pressure. I'd also recommend not twisting the handle too tightly closed (I like to leave a quarter of a turn from the final off position), as you're then leaving some wiggle room should it seize up.

Flooding

If you notice a major leak or flooding, inside your home or out, you should call the water board that services your area to notify them. If it's a non-emergency and there's no danger to anyone, you can also visit your water board's website where there are usually some forms you can fill out quickly to make them aware of the issue. As with the power network, the water board takes care of your area's supply and you can report and follow up any issues via them.

Their website will also include information about pipe responsibility, so you should familiarize yourself with this and have a quick list jotted down for your reference. It's essential to be in the know about what you might be responsible for so you can react quickly in the event of a problem. The rule of thumb is that the water board takes care of the pipes up to the boundary of your home; you are responsible for any problems on your property and in your building.

If there is flooding in your area due to natural causes such as a storm, your local authority will sometimes handle the repairs. The water authority will only take care of leaks and flooding caused by their pipework but it's really useful to have this info to hand when you need it.

Mains power

Power is something we rely on heavily in our homes. She provides all we need to charge our phones, keep our food fresh, allow us to cook, have light … The list goes on. She's the queen who serves us every day and it's easy for us never to realize her true importance, until something goes wrong. This is why I feel it's important to shine a light back on power for a moment and cover some bases so that you're more equipped should something fail in the future. To the fuse box!

#SAFEISCHIC

My goddess note here on safety is a very serious one and not to be ignored. When it comes to dealing with electricity, I would never advise carrying out jobs you are not super confident or comfortable doing. Always call an electrician if you're unsure and never open up an appliance or plug on something that has caused a circuit breaker to trip. Accidents happen but 99.9 per cent of them are preventable.

The fuse box

The fuse box is also known as the circuit board or consumer board. Technically, these days, there are no more old-school fuses – we now have circuit breakers – but we still tend to refer to her as a fuse box.

Who is she? She's essentially a service panel and if the stopcock is the goddess of water in your home, the fuse box is the goddess of power.

What is she serving? Aside from visual overload realness, she serves your entire home and has three main parts.

The first is the mains switch (in reality, this can be one or two switches), which can cut your electricity off in one flick. It's usually the largest on the board and is always labelled clearly. Find out where this is and make sure to test it. This has to be switched off before beginning any electrical work so it is essential to know she is in full working order.

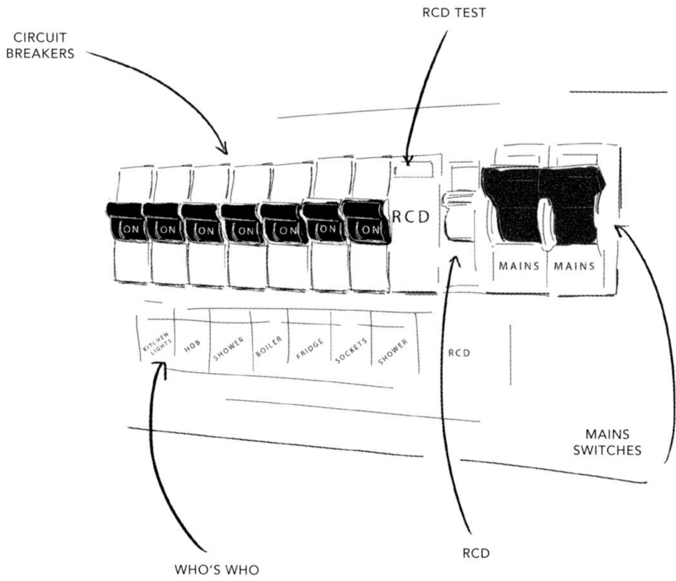

Next are the RCDs (residual current devices). Like the mains switch, these are usually labelled clearly and are a bit larger than the circuit breakers, which protect each circuit in your home from damage caused by excess current. An RCD can protect more than one circuit and her main job is to monitor the current running through a circuit and notice when the flow of electricity is irregular. If it's not doing what it should, she cuts the electricity to it. She can even tell when electricity is flowing through a person – someone who has touched an exposed wire, for example. She essentially saves lives.

Finally, the circuit breakers. Each one is dedicated to a circuit of power – this means one circuit breaker can be responsible for multiple lights and sockets. Individual labels or a list on your box should tell you which one each switch relates to. If this hasn't been done, ensure you apply your own labels, as you never know when you'll need to know this information.

To find out which switch or socket corresponds to which circuit, I'd recommend going through your home, room by room. To avoid overloading, plug one item max into each socket and turn on the lights. Back at the fuse box, each time you flick off a circuit, note which sockets or lights it affects – this will be the circuit that controls that socket or switch.

So, what do you do if a switch trips? When a circuit becomes overloaded or something goes wrong, the switch will trip – it will flick down and cut the electricity supply to the circuit in question. The simple fix is to switch it back to 'on'. It could have been that the circuit couldn't handle a temporary surge of power, such as an overloaded extension lead, but is now OK.

If it trips again, go to the area of your home powered by that circuit. Turn off everything and unplug all appliances, then flick the switch on your fuse box back on again. Next, start plugging everything back in and turning each item back on, one by one. I'd start with the very last item you switched on in that area as it will usually be the cause of the tripped switch. When the switch trips again, the last thing you plugged in or switched on will be the offender. She will need to be checked over by an electrician to bring her back to full health before being used again.

If all circuit breakers are on but the RCD switch is off, this means this RCD has used her overriding powers to cut the power supply to all the circuits she oversees. You now need to figure out which circuit is actually causing the problem. To do this, switch your RCD back on – she'll usually trip again straight away – then turn all the circuit breakers linked to that RCD off. One by one start to turn them back on. The faulty circuit will be obvious as it will trip the RCD switch when you switch the circuit on. Switch off the faulty circuit, but you may turn on the others. Call an electrician or figure out the faulty appliance in that circuit. Many times it will be something with a heating element or something that uses water.

Power cuts

Should your power suddenly cut out, follow these few simple guidelines. First of all, check whether your fuse box is showing any signs that something in your own home is causing the problem. If not, you need to find out whether the issue is confined to your property or if your area is affected. This is pretty easy to do if the power cut happens at night: just check if your street lights are out. If it happens during the day, ask a neighbour if they're experiencing similar problems.

Each country has its own freefone number and website pages to help you log a power failure and also find out more information about your power cut. You don't need to call your energy provider. Even though you pay them for your energy, they are not responsible for the supply – this is all down to the distributor. You'll find the Irish and UK numbers in the box on the following page, but should you ever experience a power cut when abroad, you can easily find similar numbers online for any country. You can also usually follow the situation online where live updates are available for faults and also any planned power outages.

Gas leaks

If you smell gas, *never* ignore it. A gas leak is a serious risk to you and others, and must be dealt with urgently. First, ensure that your gas appliances are not running unlit. Strict rules apply when you smell gas, such as do not smoke, use a naked flame, or unplug or turn off anything electrical.

These rules (and more) can all be found online with numbers to call in an emergency and for further advice. The website of your gas supplier will have great advice on what to do if you need to turn off your gas or contact someone. I'd recommend that everyone in your household is aware of the protocol when they smell gas and have the relevant numbers readily available – store them in your phone, email, or stick them to the fridge.

At some point, you're likely to face the issues of water and power cuts, as well as some gas issues in your home. Here are some handy numbers and websites to save in your phone or you can take a photo instead and save to your favourites or share with your flatmates.

Power
Ireland: 1850 372 999; esbnetworks.ie
UK: 105; powercut105.com will direct you to your local distribution network operator.

Water
Ireland: 1850 278 278; water.ie
UK: water.org.uk will direct you to your local water authority.

Gas
Ireland: 1850 205 050; gasnetworks.ie
UK: 0800 111 999 (Northern Ireland: 0800 002 001);
findmysupplier.energy will direct you to your local gas network.

In the event of an emergency, always dial 999.

The Goddess Checklist

On my first day in any new property I follow a checklist which gives me an idea of where things are at in all rooms. It's also a very handy thing to bring along to any viewings you make of potential new properties. You'll be surprised at how noting the condition of parts of each room can lead you to see the bigger picture of underlying issues in the whole property. Filling in the checklist could highlight how many to-dos could be knocked off with a simple deep clean or cosmetic improvements, such as a coat of paint. It can also provide you with a complete list of tasks for specific contractors so you can take care of some items in bulk and incur fewer costs overall.

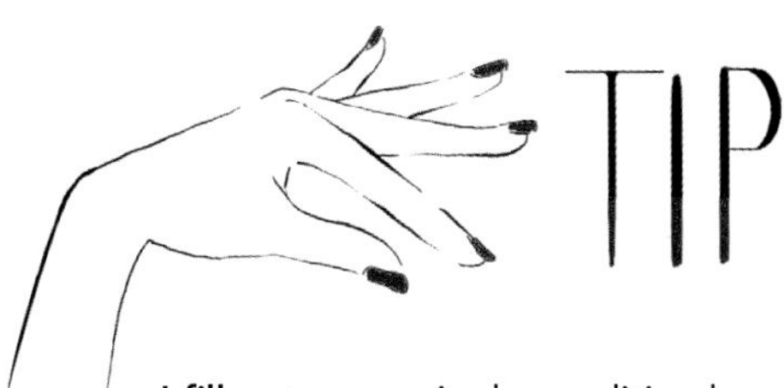

I fill out every single condition box on my list, even if it is a freshly painted area. This means that if, for example, I notice a damp patch in that room a few months later, I can go back to my checklist and see I had noted it as being fine. I then can work out the period of time for which there was zero water damage.

When filling out the list, I annotate all the jobs with E for electrician, PL for plumber, PD for painter/decorator and DC for deep clean. This saves me going back through the list time and time again – I can just pluck out all the Es for a quick and easy quote from an electrician or tick all the DCs as I deep clean so that I don't miss anything.

Where there's more than one of something in a room, such as a window or a door, I will give them numbers so that they're easily identifiable. E.g. window 1: faulty lock; window 2: working fine but needs a clean, and so on.

If there's a lot of work to do I also colour code: one colour for things to be taken care of immediately now, one for the near future and one for later down the line.

Making your own list

The list on the following pages is an insight into the areas and items I assess in each space. They could be useful to include in your own checklist and you can add as many rooms as you need for your home.

To start with, here's a sample checklist for two of the trickiest rooms: the bathroom and kitchen. There are so many elements to consider in each of these spaces that it can be hard to know where to start. The list also includes the front door and entrance – vital things to assess if you're viewing a property. The front door is often forgotten once we've walked through it at a viewing, so it's important to note how secure it is.

Date:

	Current condition	Notes	WWAGD – What would a Goddess do?	WWSDI – When would she do it?
Example: ***KITCHEN WALLS***	*Need to be painted*	*Must be cleaned first – a lot of grease*	*Clean and add to quote for PD*	*Clean ASAP*
BATHROOM				
Shower unit, head and hose				
Shower tray and/or bath				
Shower/bath and sink plug and drainage				
Shower curtain/ doors				
Sink and taps				
Water pressure (taps and shower – any leaks?)				
Toilet (including handle and flush)				
Toilet seat				
Wall fittings (such as towel rails and mirrors)				
Extractor fan				

Date:

	Current condition	Notes	WWAGD – What would a Goddess do?	WWSDI – When would she do it?
KITCHEN				
Cupboards – top/bottom (fittings, doors and interiors)				
Drawers (including fittings)				
Worktops				
Splashbacks				
Fridge/freezer				
Oven				
Hob (including knobs, etc.)				
Extractor fan and filters				
Washing machine				
Dishwasher				
White goods manuals				
Sink and draining board				
Under-sink cupboard – pipes dripping?				
Sink taps, drain and plug				
All switches/ controls				

Date:

	Current condition	Notes	WWAGD – What would a Goddess do?	WWSDI – When would she do it?
FRONT DOOR				
Front door handle and any locks				
Door (front, back and fittings (e.g. spy hole)				
Architrave, door strip, frame				

No matter which room you are assessing, below is a general list that should cover everything in there when unfurnished.

Date:

	Current condition	Notes	WWAGD – What would a Goddess do?	WWSDI – When would she do it?
EVERY ROOM				
Flooring/ walls/ ceiling				
Skirting/ architraves/ door frames				
Door(s) (inside and out (hinges, handles and locks))				
Door strips				
Window(s) (hinges, handles and locks)				
Window dressings				
Light fitting(s)				
Radiators				
All sockets (check with phone charger)				
All switches/ controls				
Built-in storage				

Finally, here's a list of things which are great to note while you're carrying out your assessment. It's also a brilliant thing to have if you are or have a tenant as it's all super important info to have a note of. You can add as many alarms or meters as you need.

Date:

	Full working order?	**Comments**	**WWAGD?**	**WWSDI?**
GENERAL				
Heating and boiler				
Smoke/heat detectors				
Carbon monoxide alarm				
Meters	**Type of meter and supplier**	**Meter location**	**Meter reading**	**Meter condition**
Meter 1				
Meter 2				
Meter 3				

FILLER
SILICONE
SILICONE REMOVER

2. TOOLS

Your toolkit. Every home should have one, but how do you decide what should be in it? When I say I have a functional toolkit, people think that I must own a large toolbox brimming with an extensive selection of screwdrivers, pliers, spanners and a range of tools I never use. I'm glad to declare this is not the case and it's because most tasks around the home usually require the same few tools. These days, there are so many great devices out there with interchangeable parts, that even the smallest of kits can do the mightiest of jobs.

In this chapter you'll find the tools I think are essential to own and which will make sure you're covered for the majority of repairs and DIY tasks you might need to carry out at home.

Screwdriver

The hand-operated screwdriver is, in my opinion, a simple but effective, long-lasting, high-performance piece which is often overlooked and overshadowed by more fearsome-looking tools. Not to be confused with the popular cocktail (sigh), screwdrivers are used either to remove or insert screws into furniture and walls. They're usually made of steel so that they don't bend or damage during use and will have an ergonomic handle, usually with a grip.

How should you shop for your screwdriver? Let's look at how they differ. There are two main types of screw heads found in the

home, and a different screwdriver tip is needed for each. The first has an indentation running all the way across its head shaped like a lowercase L and requires a flathead screwdriver; the second has an X shape across its head and requires a cross-tip one. The cross-tip screwdrivers are more commonly known as Phillips screwdrivers, named after Henry Phillips who invented crosshead screws in the 1930s to improve car manufacturing. They enabled the assembly line to increase the torque applied (due to the grip), which meant the fittings were tighter. Fabulous. #safeischic after all.

Both types of screw heads come in many different sizes, as do screwdrivers. To ensure you have the best chance at inserting or removing a screw, you'll need to make sure that you have the correct size tip to your screwdriver. One that is too big simply won't fit into the screw head or can damage it when turning. One that is too small will not only give you the worst torque ever (I know 'torque' sounds like a headpiece for formal events – it actually means the force that causes the rotation), it can also damage the screw head.

Fear not. Just like make-up brushes, although there are loads of different ones out there, you will only need to use a few regularly. It's better to have a small number of useful ones than a large set that goes mostly untouched.

There are usually four sizes of Phillips tips, but numbers 1 and 2 are the most common.

Flathead sizes are determined by the width of their tip. It's best to own a small set of different sizes – two to three will do – so you have options, even though flathead screws aren't used that much in flat-pack assembly or household tasks.

You could always buy a screwdriver handle with a set of interchangeable tips, which can be super useful and save you time if you need to switch between different head sizes. You can even buy super tiny-sized kits for electronics. These kinds of screwdriver sets are really common now, widely available, and can be a more economical purchase than buying individually. Although not widely used by trades people (electricians don't always use them in case a tip falls out and into an unsafe area), they are ideal for DIY and for storing in your home.

Ratchet Screwdriver

I *live* for a ratchet screwdriver. OMG, come through with all your fabulous time- and energy-saving realness, girl! Let's count the ways in which she can serve:

- She saves your wrists! With a regular screwdriver, once your tip is snugly in the screw head, you need to twist, then reset your hand position and repeat until the screw is fully in or out. With a ratchet screwdriver, she does all the work so your hands and wrists are under less pressure. She also saves time – once the tip is in, it will stay in place and the handle can twist as it pleases.
- She comes with interchangeable heads. The ratchet screwdriver I carry in my work handbag has ten tip options, all stored neatly in the base of the handle.
- She can be set to turn clockwise or anticlockwise, depending on whether you're inserting or removing a screw. Remember, left is loose and right is tight.
- She can also be switched to the 'locked' position to function like a traditional screwdriver (living).

Hammer

Use it to drive in or extract nails from a surface. (Don't forget a hammer is fabulous for fixing shoes too! You can do a quick heel-tip replacement with the help of a claw hammer.)

When selecting your new hammer, it's good to keep some things in mind:

- A mid-weight hammer (16 oz) is best for DIY tasks. You won't need anything too heavy unless you're knocking down walls, so go for this size if you're carrying out jobs such as hanging pictures, building furniture and so on. This size hammer is ideal to have in your home toolbox as it can apply a good whack without wearing out your arm or causing a tremendous amount of damage should you miss the nail. If you can't bear that kind of weight for too long, a lighter-weight head with a longer handle can actually apply a fabulous strike and so be a good option for you. It can just be a little harder to aim and not as easy to store.
- Wooden-handled hammers are usually the cheapest and can absorb shock better, but I'd always choose a steel-handled one. This means the entire hammer is one solid piece of metal and is therefore likely to last longer. The rubber grips fitted to the handles of these hammers usually do a great shock-absorbing job.
- I'd also select a hammer with a claw as you'll need her should you wish to rip out a nail.
- If you want to get super luxe, look for a hammer with a 'nail starter'. This is a good feature to have

should you need an extra bit of help when starting to hammer in the nail – if you need to place the nail somewhere not at eye level, for example, or if you have to use one hand and can't hold the nail in place. The nail starter is essentially a groove above the hammer head, which is usually magnetic, where you sit your nail to rest hands-free. With one hit it pops the nail straight in or, in DIY terms, starts it off. You can then tap it into place further. Lovely.

Spanner

A spanner set is an essential item for any toolkit. Not all jobs will involve screws or nails – should you find yourself needing to tighten or loosen nuts, bolts or similar fastenings, you'll find a spanner is the ideal tool.

As with screws, nuts and bolts require different sizes of spanner, so an adjustable one is very useful to have. These spanners are also sometimes called adjustable wrenches (there's much debate over the difference between the two, but you basically want something that looks like the illustration here). This one tool can fit many different fastenings and is perfect for jobs such as loosening shower hoses.

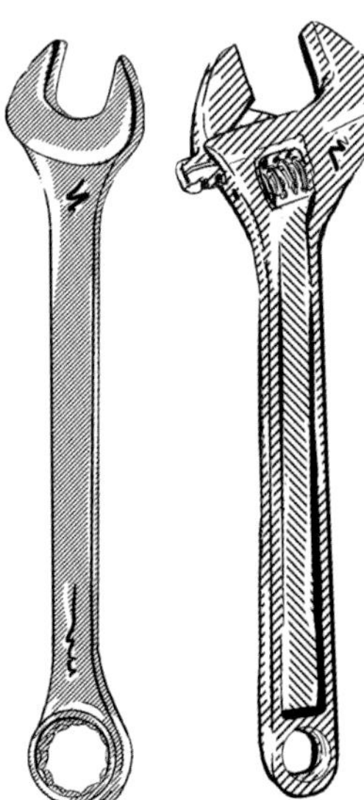

However, when it comes to tightening fastenings, I don't find adjustable spanners as good as fixed ones. If you're planning on carrying out a lot of flat-pack assembly around your home, I'd strongly advise getting your hands on a good-quality spanner set. The cheap ones supplied with flat packs will often take double the time and effort as I always find they dent and bend, making them less effective as you go. Very frustrating.

Allen Key Set

Allen keys are L-shaped tools with hexagonal heads that fit into screws with a hexagonal socket. If you've ever assembled flat-pack furniture, you'll have probably used an Allen key that came in the box – and thrown it away after.

My first piece of advice is that should you ever build a piece of furniture that comes with a tool, tape that tool to an inconspicuous area of the item you've just assembled. I guarantee you'll need to use it at some point in the future to tighten anything that's become loose, and it will save you searching for the right-sized tool for a small job. If you rent a property to tenants, you can also quickly do this small job at the end of each tenancy to ensure your furniture lasts longer.

Second, I'd invest separately in a high-quality Allen key set to use for flat-pack assembly and other DIY jobs. They're usually stronger than the cheap ones that come in the flat packs and so the torque is greater, which will speed up the job. Heaven!

Drill

I love a good drill. The time they save, the ease they bring to a job, their sound, the way they feel in your hand … I could go on. There are so many factors that come into play when buying a drill, but budget is the main one when purchasing for DIY tasks. All I can say here, without leaning towards one brand or another, is 'buy cheap buy twice'. I'd always encourage having a chat with someone at your local DIY store to find out the highest quality brand and model that will cover your needs and sit within your budget. Things to consider are: whether your drill comes with a battery and charger or whether she will be 'bare' (just the drill body), how she feels in your hand (heavy is never great), and what her functions are.

Toolbag/box

Storing your tools safely is a must! As your toolkit grows, you'll need to ensure that everything is easily accessible as well as safe. Tools have lots of pointed and sharp edges, so ensuring they're out of harm's way is important and easy to do with the correct box or bag.

Personally, I love a toolbag as it means I can carry my tools easily and comfortably on my shoulder. Large toolbags have a hard shell base and protective internal pockets, which mean both I and the tools are safe from damage when carrying and using it. Although a toolbox can provide you with the space for optimum organization and

protection of your tools, it's not always very portable. If you have to carry it a lot, you'll hit two issues: the more tools you acquire the more difficult the box will be to carry, and I've found that because these boxes are made of plastic they break more easily. However, if you're just looking to store your tools under the stairs and want a neat option that won't be leaving the house, a rigid box is a great choice.

How to Care for Your Tools

The first step in making good-quality tools last a lifetime is to store them correctly. This isn't just about choosing the right box or bag, it's also about the environment in which they're kept. Just like many things around the home, moisture is our enemy. Moisture means rust and rust means . . . goodbye, tools.

You know those little packs of silica you get in a box of new shoes? The ones that say 'DO NOT EAT'? Well, let me tell you, these are a ready-made solution for keeping rust at bay. Although these pouches were designed to absorb any moisture in a box of new Ferragamos, they'll do exactly the same job in your toolbox. I like to make sure there are a few in there to be on the safe side.

When it comes to power tools such as drills, always store them in their hard case. Never leave the battery sitting in its charging dock for longer than it needs to as, much like with a phone battery, heat generated during unnecessary charging will shorten its life.

When you're finished using your tools, a clean rag is fine for giving them a wipe-down but remember, if you do need to wash them, use warm water and washing-up liquid (this will remove any grease and won't strip off protective coatings like harsher cleaning products would) and dry them thoroughly. Never put tools away wet.

Finally, think about where your tools will be kept when not in use. I've seen many rusting tools stored loosely under kitchen sinks, an area of high moisture. It's best to keep your toolkit in a dry, sealed bag or box.

#SAFEISCHIC

Tools are fabulous but can cause injury. Make sure you are always using the right tool for the job. Ensure you are wearing the necessary safety equipment and are confident you know how to operate the tool you are using correctly.

3. OOPS

This chapter is dedicated to everyone who has ever stood back and thought, *WTF* ...

I believe that in life, it's not what is thrown at us that affects us most, it is how we respond and react. This is why I feel it's important to dedicate a chapter to the moments where something goes wrong unexpectedly. No matter how careful we are, we can never prevent it all; pipes leak, toilets get blocked and best friends kick over glasses of red wine while lip-syncing the full 'Single Ladies' routine at your house-warming (making like a ghost has damaged many a carpet and friendship, I'm sure). Buckle up for a brief run-down of what can be useful to have to hand for the less fun parts of being an adult.

She's Got It Under Control

For those times when something disastrous happens out of the blue, it's important to be as prepared as you can. This can help to keep any damage caused to a minimum and ensure life returns to normal sooner.

Most government websites will have great advice on what to have ready in an emergency kit in the event of a disaster, such as a flood, natural disaster or fire: everything from food and water, to what you'll need to construct a makeshift shelter, and so on. This is great stuff to read up on and chances are you'll have a lot of the items already, so it could prompt you to get organized and store them together.

Repairs and spares

But what if an emergency happens within the home? What if you need to make a quick repair, take a temporary measure or if a spare of something is needed? While we can't be prepared for every scenario, we can try our very best to make a stressful or uncomfortable situation easier. In my opinion, here's a list of things it's ideal to have handy in a kit for should the unexpected happen …

Start by thinking about what will hold your entire kit:

A **metal bucket** not only looks *great*, it's more environmentally friendly and durable than a plastic one. It can last a lifetime! It can house and protect your kit when you're not using it and if there's a leak, or if you need to store water, it will come in handy. It could also double up as your mop bucket, holding water while

you're cleaning, or be used to transport broken glass and sharps when you need to dispose of them. In this bucket, I'd keep a separate plastic box for any items of your kit that could be damaged by water – just in case.

What goes inside:

- **Head torch.** These are inexpensive to buy, and easy to store because they're so small. If the power goes when it's dark outside, this is a fantastic piece of kit to have, as your hands will be free should you need to carry out any work. I also use mine whenever we go camping or if I need to search for something under the stairs – it's a win–win purchase, really. One of my favourite head-torch hacks is to secure it around a large bottle full of water, with the light facing in – it becomes a much larger light instantly. Great for night-time garden parties or during a blackout.

- **Two pillar candles and a box of matches.** I prefer larger candles that I don't have to hold and that can stand alone during power cuts. They're also handy to have if your windowless bathroom light goes and you can't change the bulb right away.
- **Batteries.** Make sure you've got a few spares for smoke alarm units as well as for your TV remote controls or any other battery-operated devices you use a lot.
- **Lightbulbs.** Familiarize yourself with the bulbs used in your home and keep a stash of the most important ones in your kit – those that would be a total pain not to have on hand should one blow (ones that light a windowless room such as an en suite or dark stairwell, for example).

- **Plumber's tape.** If something has a small leak that you can't fix immediately but need to keep using (a shower hose or a pipe under the sink, for example), plumber's tape can be applied around the leaky fitting as a temporary measure. It's a waterproof tape that acts like a wee plaster.
- **Washers.** On the subject of leaks, one of the main causes of leaky pipework is a worn-out washer (see pages 110–113). You can save a lot of money by replacing these yourself instead of a tap or pipe.
- **Glue.** Superglue or any strong adhesive is handy to have in your kit to take care of any breakages.
- **Heavy-duty rubber gloves.** Get the extra-long ones! These can be used for so many tasks, such as opening tight jars and cleaning up broken glass or blockages (grim, but a fact of life). They basically protect your hands and give you a great grip.
- **Swiss army knife.** You may have all the tools you need in your tool kit, but this will serve as an easy-to-reach smaller version.
- **Rags.** Before you throw out an old tea towel, cut it into two rags and pop them in your kit. They will be super useful if there's ever a spillage or if you need to apply a product and don't want to ruin anything nice.
- **Rope.** A bundle of thin rope is reusable, durable and can be useful to have to hand. You can use it to make a washing line, tie together anything you're gluing … The list is endless. 
- **Twine.** Yes, a thinner rope but just as useful.

- **Stain remover.** A spray or foam that will work on a range of stains and is suitable to use on most of your furnishings and carpets. I'd take a moment to read up on the remover's small print and put a sticker with any warnings on the bottle for when you go to use it. 'Don't use on bedroom carpet', for example.
- **Plunger.** Look, life's not easy but it's even harder if you don't have a plunger when you need one. I think storing them in your bathroom next to your toilet should be outlawed. It screams, 'I block this toilet on the reg.' So my advice is to keep them in this kit. I also like to have two plungers. Aside from the obvious need to keep one separate for the toilet, it's good to have two types: one for the toilet and one for unblocking sinks. Sink plungers don't need to be as wide – they just need to cover the circumference of the plug hole.
- **Plastic tarp.** These take up barely any space but can be used again and again. They're useful when there's a leak, to protect your flooring if you're painting or decorating, to catch any debris when you're carrying out repairs, or even to go under your blanket at the park. Chic.

Holes in Walls

When you move into a property, it's likely the previous owner will have had some artwork or mirrors hanging on the walls, or – worse – a TV. There may be some small damage to those surfaces, which will need to be repaired. Little holes left by picture-hanging fixtures can also affect a tenancy deposit so be sure that any of these are noted when you move in. If you cause them during your rental period, make sure to repair them before you move out.

For simple repairs to a white wall where a thin nail has left a neat hole, one fab hack is to rub some white chalk against it, then wipe away the excess. You'll be left with the hole filled in nicely, making it barely noticeable.

If there are small holes or cracks left from a thicker fixture, here is how you can make them good …

Fixing holes or cracks

Before you begin, wipe down the surface with a warm damp cloth to make sure that there is no debris or grease on the area that will prevent the filler from sticking. Make sure the surface is fully dry before you get started.

You will need:

- **Filling knife.** If you don't have one, you could use an old plastic loyalty card.
- **Tube of filler.** This is the easiest product to use for repairing small holes as it's premixed and designed for easy use. Make sure you massage the tube first to smooth out the mixture inside. You can buy a range of fillers for different jobs but

those packaged in tubes are the easiest to use and usually come in quick-dry varieties.

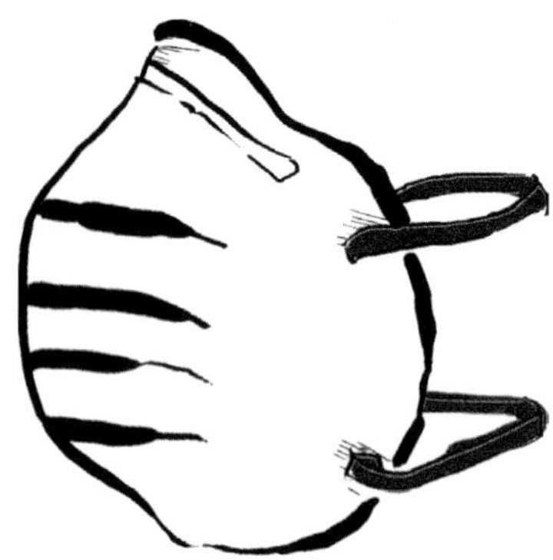

- **Sandpaper.** When buying sandpaper, remember: the lower the number, the coarser the paper will be; the higher the number, the finer. Coarser paper is ideal for wood but you'll need fine sandpaper for this job.
- **Safety glasses** and a **mask** #safeischic
- **Tub of water.** (It'll make sense, I promise – just make sure the water is deep enough to dip your knife into.)

1. First, smooth out the area surrounding the hole. It may have some raised cracks around the edges and be a little lumpy, as the hanging fixture might have been pulled out with some force. Run your filling knife over the area, kind of like you would do shaving your legs. Be just as gentle here and you should be able to chip off any excess plaster. If the hole protrudes slightly from where the fitting was yanked out, flip the filling knife round and use the bottom of the handle to tap the plaster very gently so that it recesses into the wall a little. It's better to fill in a dent than to layer filler on top of something sticking out, thus making an even bigger bump.

2. Squeeze some filler on to your knife. How much you need will, of course, depend on the size of the hole you are filling. The best rule of thumb is to use more than you need, as any excess can be wiped away with your knife. The texture of it will be like a clay face mask. How fabulous.

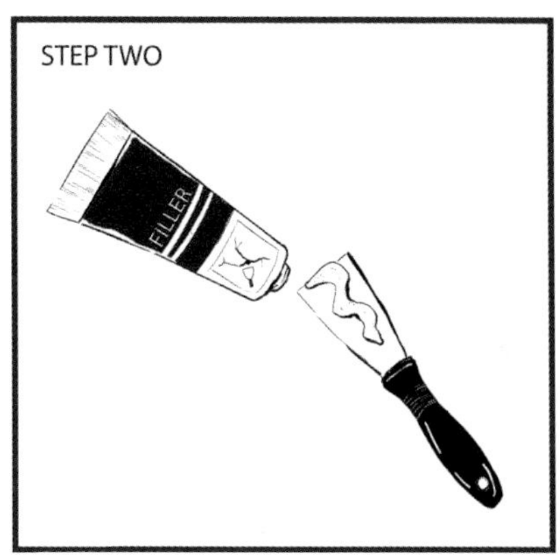

3. Use the knife to smear the paste over the hole so that it becomes filled, then start to smooth it outward. Like applying a foundation, you want to make sure there are no harsh lines. A great tip to ensure this is to dip the knife in your tub of water to wet it after the first smooth out and repeat the process from the centre again outward. This will help to get rid of any bumps or uneven bits. The filler will taper off across the wall with no hard lines or edges. It always reminds me of a good ombre.

4. Allow the filler to dry as per the instructions on the pack. This could take anywhere from 5 minutes to 5 hours.

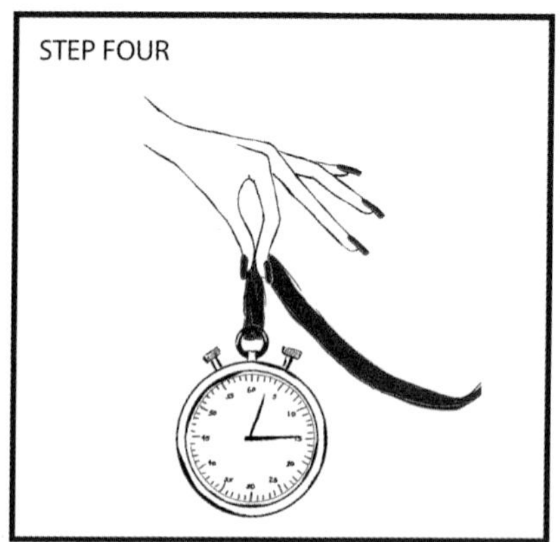

5. When dry, sand gently over the filled patch to even out the area. I love a sanding block on a flat area – I feel its firmness helps you achieve a smoother surface. Think about it like this: would you use a floppy nail file? No, you need a firm, flat one. Keep running your hand over the surface as you go to see how it's feeling. You'll notice any uneven part better this way than you will through sandpaper. Remember to wear goggles and a mask! Lots of fine particles will be released into the air and you are precious.

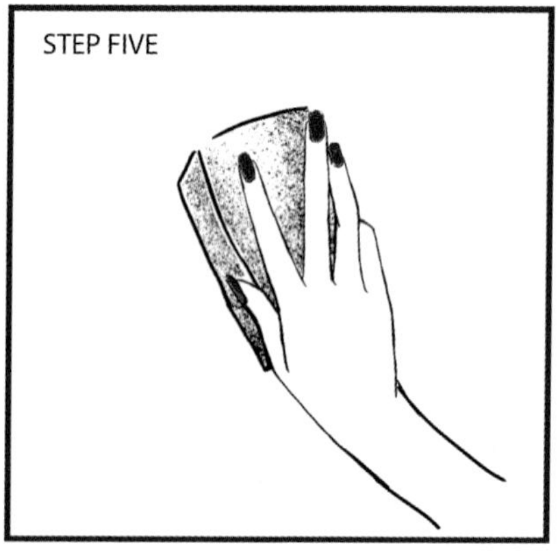

6. Now the surface is ready to paint. Sometimes it's best to re-paint the whole wall once you've made your repair, unless you know you have the exact same colour. This applies even to white walls, as a touch-up in the wrong shade can leave a really obvious mark. If you've just moved in, look around for tins of paint. Really sound people leave behind any leftover tins for the next owner, as they know they might be needed for touch-ups and it would be a waste to dump them. For some reason I always find them either under the sink or by the washing machine. You'll most likely need two coats of paint for a great finish so don't hesitate to throw on a second if it's not looking amazing.

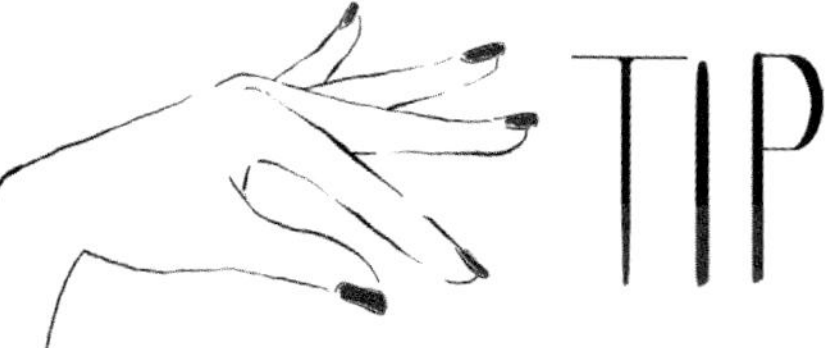

A final note here: if you're making a repair to a textured wall, a lovely smooth filled patch will stand out like a bad shoe. The trick is not to go too wide with the filler and go thick – when your filler is still wet, take a clean paintbrush and use it to stipple the filler into a similar texture of the wall. Gorge.

Stains

No matter how careful we are, stains just happen. I find that once you're armed with some basic knowledge, you're halfway there to removing the stain – the rest is about using the right product and some elbow grease.

Luckily, most stain removers you pick up in the supermarket these days can tackle even the worst stains. They work by using:

- Enzymes that literally eat the stain and break it down. They love protein stains and oily stains.
- Surfactants that help make it more difficult for the stain to be on the surface of the fabric.
- Oxidizers that remove the colour from the stain so that it basically becomes invisible.

Know your stain

In order to successfully remove a stain, first figure out what type it is. There are four main groups:

1. Proteins **2.** Oils **3.** Tannins **4.** Dyes

Treating fabric stains

- Act quickly. The longer a stain is left to sit and dry out, the tougher it is to remove. Identify the type of stain as well as your fabric and its requirements. Check out the care label explanation on page 97 if you need some guidance.
- Get rid of any excess as soon as you can. You can blot (never rub!) wet stains and scrape anything raised or dried with a

spoon (nothing that can cause the fabric any damage). If it's an oil stain and you're out for dinner, ask for a sugar substitute sachet or grab some loose translucent face powder and sprinkle them over the stain to help draw the oil out.

- It's important to add water and dampen the fabric right away so the stain doesn't set. Make sure you've scraped off or blotted any excess so you're not spreading more of the stain through the fabric. Don't soak it, just apply some water with a napkin or cloth.
- If you can, work the stain from the reverse of the fabric to stop it soaking through. You're then working on lifting the stain off the fabric rather than moving it through it.
- If not, slide a plate or saucer under the stain when treating it, to avoid it reaching another layer of fabric.
- If you're going to apply a stain-removal treatment, test an unseen small area first. You need to be certain the fabric can take it and that you're not risking the fabric discolouring or disintegrating.
- It's especially important not to apply heat until you know the stain is gone for sure. Always let the stain air-dry after you have treated it.

Aside from fabrics, here are some of the main stains I encounter in the home and how I deal with them.

Red wine on carpets

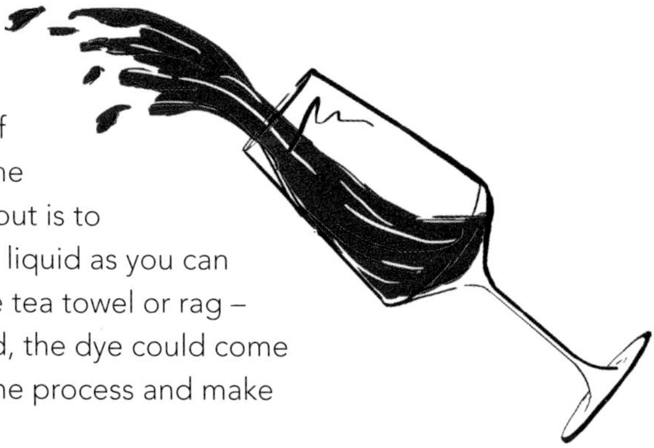

Dealing with this dilemma is almost a rite of passage, if you ask me! The best way to get this stain out is to immediately blot as much liquid as you can off the carpet. Use a white tea towel or rag – if you use something dyed, the dye could come off on the carpet during the process and make

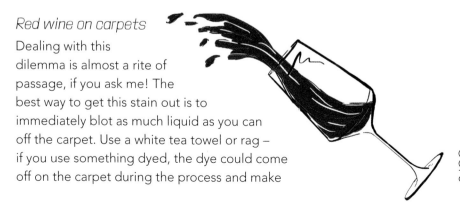

Stain type	What is it ?	Type of stain remover required	DIY stain removal	OMG. Stop!
PROTEIN				
	These stains come from something biological – milk, sweat, blood, etc.	Enzymes love to digest anything protein-based and will chomp through these.	Most regular washing detergents contain these enzymes – if they are biological ones. Non-bio detergents* won't contain them, but these days they are usually strong enough to remove protein stains. * *Non-bio is more commonly used if someone in the household has allergies, sensitive skin, or if you wash a lot of natural fibres.*	Heat sets protein stains, so avoid using hot water when removing them and, most importantly, let the garment dry naturally. Don't apply heat at the drying stage without being sure the stain is completely gone as it could in fact set it. Natural fibres such as silk and wool can be damaged by enzymes so double check your fabric first.
OIL				
	Oil and grease stains come from cooking, cosmetic oils or greasy items such as bike chains.	A degreaser is perfect here as it's a cleaner designed to remove grease from the fabric and dissolve it.	Washing-up liquid is the best, least harmful degreaser in your home. It can help lift an oily stain better than most things. You can pre-treat the stained item before a wash: just rub the liquid into the mark beforehand. Good old brown paper – shiny side up – and a hot iron works here too.	Don't let the stain dry. Soak it in water to keep it wet until you can treat it.

Stain type	What is it ?	Type of stain remover required	DIY stain removal	OMG. Stop!
TANNIN				
	These stains come from natural dyes such as plants, fruits and vegetables: wine, blackcurrant juice, tea, etc.	An oxidizing agent will help to remove the colour from spills. As these stains are water soluble they can usually be blotted, flushed out and treated.	The sooner you act with a tannin stain, the better. It can be a case of fighting fire with fire – a liquid with a liquid – so blot and rinse the stain out with water (always rinse from the back). You can also steam tannin stains off fabrics. Vinegar can help remove a lot of tannin stains, such as tea and coffee, as it's so acidic.	Do not use soap as it will set the stain and it will be extremely hard to remove. Salt can actually set some tannins so avoid entirely!
DYE				
	These are stains from things such as grass, or something that contains a strong pigment, such as make-up or mustard. These are a 'mare to get rid of and usually need a strong remover.	Biological washing detergents can help remove dye stains as can dye removers. Vinegar, non-chlorine bleach and rubbing alcohol can all help remove this type of stain.	Make sure you act straight away while the stain is still wet. Use a stain remover formulated for dye stains, and follow all instructions carefully as water temperature and so on matter here.	Dye stains are the worst to apply heat to as this will lock the dye into the fabric. Use cool water and allow to dry naturally.

things worse than they already are. The less wine you are left with after blotting, the less you'll have to actually deal with later, so be patient and keep blotting. Move the rag around every few blots so that a fresh piece gets used.

Remember to work from the outer edge of the stain inwards so that you're catching the stain before it can spread.

Now, water down the stain so it's not as concentrated. To do this, add a little water to the stain. Soak a clean white rag and apply gently. If you pour water straight on the stain, it will flow through your carpet, so concentrate your efforts on the stain and have more control over the water. If you haven't blotted thoroughly as per the first step, the stain will become even bigger now, so be careful! Start blotting again with a fresh white rag. You'll notice how the liquid being picked up isn't as dark as before because it's diluted. Fabulous.

Take a teaspoon of washing-up liquid and a teaspoon of distilled white vinegar (no other type of vinegar here, please!). Mix them together in 2–3 cups of warm water to create a really good mixture to wash out the stain. Use a clean cloth or sponge to douse the stain with the mixture, starting from the outer edges and working inwards. Don't rub, just massage it. Now, start blotting again with another fresh rag and the colour should come

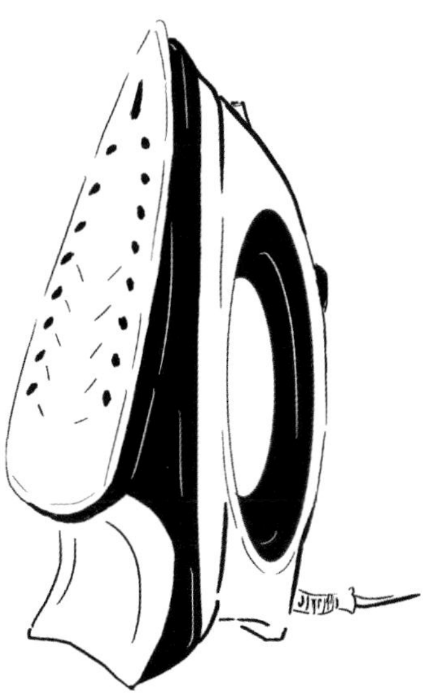

away entirely. If it's a large stain (from a particularly dramatic spillage), double up on the quantities given here.

Finally, wash the vinegar/washing-up liquid mix out of the carpet. Use a wet cloth to work fresh, clean water into the carpet and dry well by blotting. Never leave liquid to sit on a carpet without blotting it out as it can cause water marks and mould to develop.

Candle wax or oil

Your dinner party has ended, your guests are gone and you're feeling glorious. Until you notice the candle wax on your limited edition printed tablecloth. Cripes.

Peel off any excess wax. If it's yet to harden, you might be able to scrape it off lightly with a spoon or something blunt, such as a butter knife. As with the wine stain, the less of the stain you have left over at this stage, the less you have to tackle.

Grab an iron and some brown paper – the type where one side is shiny. Place the paper, shiny side up, over the stain. Make sure your iron is on a medium setting – you don't want it too high, just hot enough that the wax will melt. Now, run the iron over the brown paper. As the wax melts, the paper will absorb it, so move the paper around so that you have a fresh piece over the stain every few seconds.

This way you'll avoid scorching the fabric and getting too much wax on the iron.

Once you're satisfied that the wax has been removed, dab some washing-up liquid into the stain to remove any more oils or dyes and pop the fabric in the wash. Make sure you clean your iron after using it, as any wax on it may damage your clothing next time you use it.

Collar or armpit stains on shirts and white tees

These can be so annoying as they can be pretty obvious and make the garment look unclean, even after a wash. As these are protein stains, they need to be lifted with something acidic – vinegar is great! Another reason the underarm area of your clothes may be discoloured is because some deodorants have mighty staying power and can cling to fabrics as well as your skin. Vinegar is ideal for removing these kinds of stains too.

Soak the neckline or armpit with distilled white vinegar and leave for around 30 minutes. Then, pop on a cool wash with detergent as normal. Heat sets protein stains, so don't dry the item using heat unless you're sure the stain is gone.

Now that we've learned enough to deal calmly with a wine spillage at a soirée, I'm going to give you a break from things that go wrong so I can introduce you to white goods. In this glorious chapter we'll look at how these fabulous appliances carry out their duties and I'll share some advice to help you get the most out of them.

4. WHITE GOODS

Let's hear it for the girls! The main goddesses at work in our home. The white goods that reduce our daily toil by keeping our dishes washed, our food fresh and our clothes clean. Their presence means we have more time to focus on being fabulous and living well.

These days, we consume more of everything – and this includes white goods. Our relationship with them has become less of a long-term romance and more of a fling. Appliances that once would last and serve us well are now discarded at the first sign of trouble. Trouble that is often the result of misuse or a lack of knowledge about how to treat these godsends.

From shopping for white goods and caring for them, to resolving minor issues, by the end of this chapter you'll be armed with a greater insight into the gals who help keep our homes going, and how to keep them around for longer. After all, white-good lifespans are maximized with a little know-how and a lot of love.

The Dishwasher

A glorious piece of domestic kit, the dishwasher affords us an easy life and does a fantastic job if taken care of properly. Most dishwashers have an average lifespan of ten years – slightly less if you live in a hard-water area. However, if you clean and maintain yours well, you can make her last years longer. I know people who have functioning dishwashers that are well into their teens. These owners have taken care of their machine and don't test it to its limits. They've also probably read their manual from cover to cover.

Shopping for a dishwasher

Before taking a look at dishwasher maintenance, I should first talk to you about buying one. As well as your budget for the machine itself, you should take into account the running, installation and delivery costs for your new appliance. A slightly more expensive model with better features could cost you less to run annually and come with bonuses such as free delivery, thus saving you money overall.

Most price comparison sites feature calculators that can tell you the running cost of a machine quickly and easily. If you have a specific model in mind, make sure to shop around. Some sites may offer a lower price for the machine, delivery and installation bundled together, and some may even offer the option of taking away your old machine. A well-informed shopper bags the real bargains!

While budget alone will whittle down your search considerably, there are some other factors to consider when choosing the right model of dishwasher for you.

Style

As with almost all white goods, there are two main types of dishwasher: integrated and free-standing, as well as slimline versions of both for smaller kitchens. Integrated means that the appliance is installed under a counter and concealed by a cupboard door. As these models are essentially hidden from view, they have a more unfinished appearance. A fitted door in the style of the other cupboards in your kitchen will give it a sleek look. It will live there permanently – integrated appliances are rarely taken with the owner when they move house. If you have room for an integrated dishwasher, or are replacing one, make sure you know all the measurements your new machine needs to fit the space.

A free-standing dishwasher is usually a more basic version of an integrated one in terms of looks, price and features. As these are usually in full view, they always come with a fully finished exterior. It doesn't need to be fitted into your kitchen units in the same way as an integrated model, but you have the option to should you have the space. Many people opt for free-standing when there isn't sufficient under-counter space or if they wish to take the machine with them when they move.

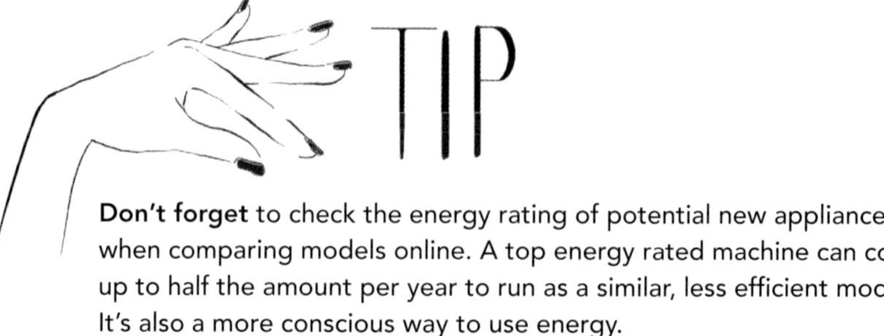

Don't forget to check the energy rating of potential new appliances when comparing models online. A top energy rated machine can cost up to half the amount per year to run as a similar, less efficient model. It's also a more conscious way to use energy.

Your needs

When it comes to appliance features, consider the items you clean most often in your dishwasher. My wine consumption and love of a dinner party means I live for the option to adjust the height of my dishwasher rack and fold-down parts so that wineglasses, flutes and large serving dishes can be placed easily and safely in the machine. If you'll be washing baby bottles a lot, you might consider a rack design

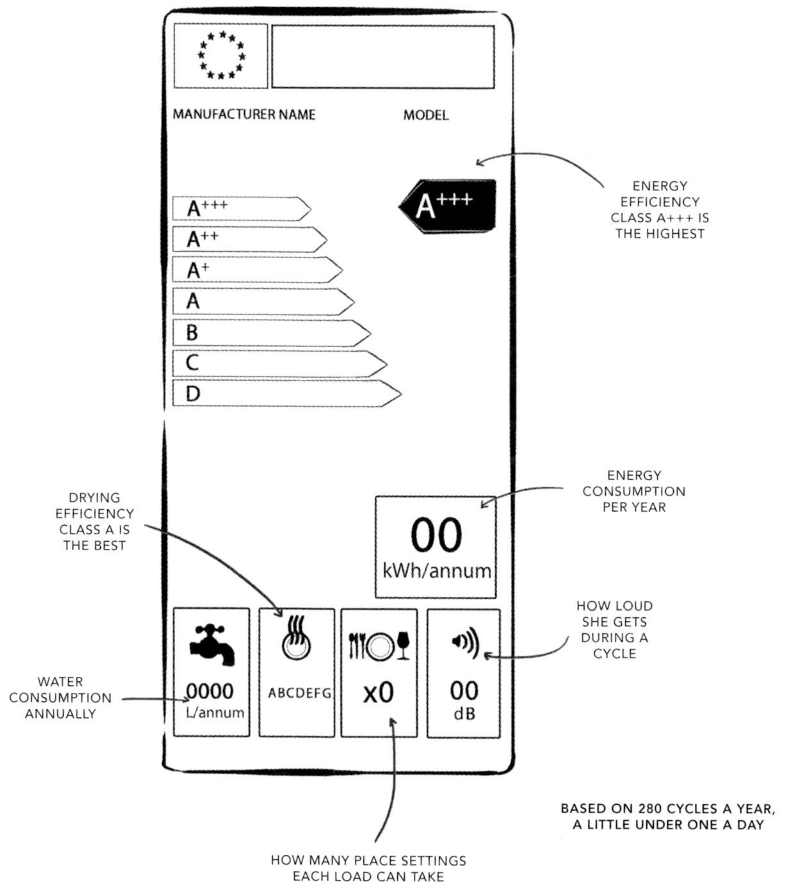

that allows the bottle parts to sit at angles that will ensure the deepest clean and best drying. I also prefer a delay timer so that I can set my wash to come on during an off-peak electricity period or when I'm not in the shower.

When reading reviews and looking at comparison sites, keep an eye out for info on how loud the machine is. Usually, the more expensive models barely let you know they are washing; the cheaper ones make the most racket. This isn't always the case but make sure you suss it out. I find there is very little difference in the wash quality of cheaper models – any price difference mainly comes down to additional features, lower running costs and lower noise levels.

Finally, the cycle options are important. I like to have lighter wash cycles for glassware and longer, heavier ones for dinner- and cookware. Eco washes are a great choice for energy efficiency and some dishwashers even have a 'baby' setting for washing your child's bottles.

If price were no object, my ideal machine would be integrated with a stainless-steel interior, silent, have a flat cutlery rack, three adjustable trays and feature a projector on the bottom of the door that beams the remaining timing of the wash on to the floor (yes, this is really a thing! No more opening mid-wash and getting sprayed in the face). HEAVEN.

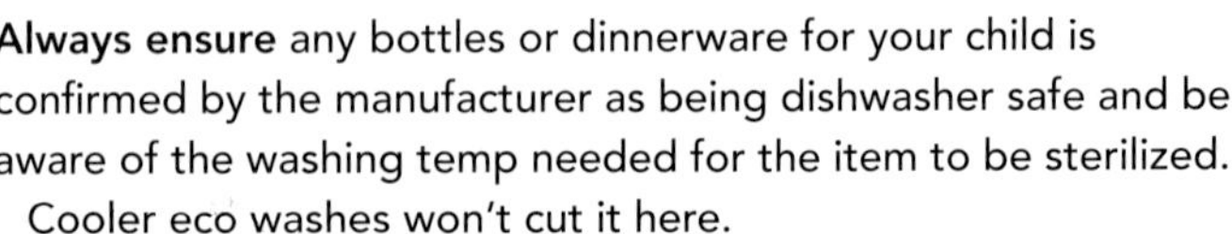

Always ensure any bottles or dinnerware for your child is confirmed by the manufacturer as being dishwasher safe and be aware of the washing temp needed for the item to be sterilized. Cooler eco washes won't cut it here.

Dishwasher maintenance

If you've just moved in to a property and there's already a dishwasher in place, find out how old she is. The easiest way to do this is to look at the stickers that should be on the side of the door. There will be a manufacturer's helpline number, which can help you determine the machine's age and warranty status – when you call them up simply give them the codes located on the same sticker. The manufacturer might also know if it's been serviced by them recently. Most importantly, before you wash your dishes in this machine for the first time, make sure you follow the cleaning tips on pages 71–3.

Let's take a closer look at how and why she works the way she does. It's important to understand how a cycle works in order to clean, maintain and troubleshoot any issues you might encounter.

Her cycle

During a dishwashing cycle, water is sprayed over the dishes to clean them. The water is then drained and the dishes are dried with the help of some heat. There will always be a little water in your machine, under the filter, to prevent the seals from drying out when it's not in use. It's why you'll usually hear a gurgling sound at the start of a cycle, which is when this stagnant water gets drained away.

Washing

Clean water comes into the machine through her inlet valve. This can be hot or cold depending on your set-up, but it's usually cold and fills up the water reservoir at the base of the machine. The float you see inside lets the machine know when the correct water level has been reached. There's also an element in the base of the machine to heat this ready for washing.

Beneath the reservoir of the machine is a pump, which draws in the heated water and then pumps it into the upper and lower spray arms. These arms rotate and gloriously dispense the hot water evenly, washing each and every dish and glass.

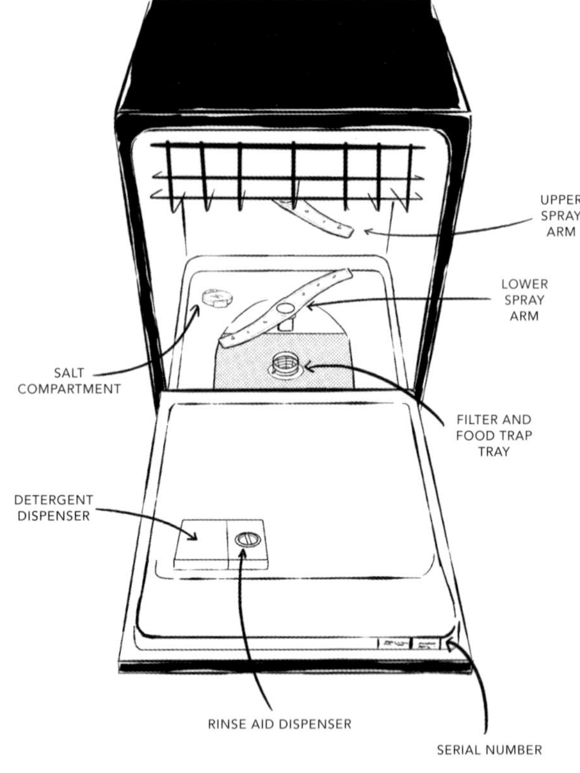

To make sure that any food washed off during this first wash doesn't come back around again, the water runs through the filter at the base of the machine before it reaches the pump for round two. This filter holds on to any food or debris and prevents it re-entering the unit. Depending on which cycle you've selected, there will be one or many washing stages. Once these stages are completed, the water exits stage left through the drain hose.

Rinsing

Next come the rinse cycle(s). Fresh water is pumped and sprayed over the dishes and rinse aid is applied on the final rinse (more on this on pages 69–70 – it's fabulous!). This water is then drained and the drying stage can begin.

Drying

Here comes the heating element, cha-cha-ing her way to centre stage. She heats up to warm the air inside the unit, which speeds up the drying process. This isn't a feature of some settings – your manual will help you decide whether you want to have it or not. Not all dishwashers have this element either – in many new models a hot rinse is the final stage of the cycle.

Manufacturers are constantly developing more ways to wash and dry things efficiently while using less energy. In the future, we'll likely see more of the style of dishwasher that pops open the door at the end to aid the air-drying process.

Loading a dishwasher

Now you know how a dishwasher cycle works, you can see why it's great to take the time to load items correctly. Doing so means not only will the cycle run well, but there will also be less to damage your machine.

- To rinse or not to rinse? (Hands up if you've fought with someone you've lived with about this.) My view is: if you wouldn't put it in a basin of water like that when washing up by hand, don't put it in the dishwasher like that either. Scrape everything off your dishes before you stack them so that the water being circulated has the best chance of cleaning them.
- Stack dishes face down. As the arms are under each rack, the water is sprayed upwards. Any dishes face up will miss the powerful cleaning action of the water on its way up and gather dirty water on the way down. Not good.
- Now you know the water is heated in the reservoir at the base of the unit, it will make sense that the water dispersed from the upper arm will be cooler than that from the bottom one. It also means the water pressure up there will be a little weaker. For this reason, it's best to place the dirtiest dishes at the bottom and glassware at the top.

- Try not to overstack the dishwasher. If it's overloaded, the spray arms will be prevented from getting water to the full surface of the dishes. A lightly stacked machine will also mean the drying process will be a dream.
- Cutlery should be stood upright in the cutlery basket – unless it's a sharp knife – so that any food is washed away easily. This also prevents food from gathering in the base of the basket. I prefer to put the same type of cutlery in each compartment so that when I'm unloading I can take out all the forks at once, for example.
- Before you shut the door, give the spray arms an aul' spin to see if anything prevents them from rotating properly.

Products for a better cycle and longer life

There's no escaping the fact that a dishwasher needs three products present in every wash to live a long and happy life.

Detergent

Never use washing-up liquid in your dishwasher. It's highly concentrated and will create a hard-to-control situation. It can also bubble into areas of your machine that moisture should never reach, which could cause damage. If you're reading this because you've just done it, turn the machine off at the wall ASAP and then skip to the troubleshooting section on page 74. Stay calm, I've got you.

Dishwasher detergent mostly comes in tablet form now. During the washing cycle, this tablet drops from its compartment in the door into the hot water where it then dissolves. Your tablet is made up of different elements that will perform different functions during the washing stage.

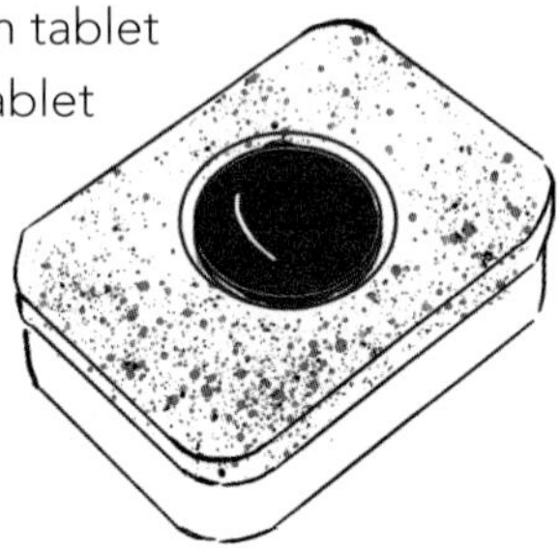

One component will tackle grease and oils, another will neutralize odours; some tablets will contain anti-corrosion ingredients to protect your machine, or enzymes to get rid of any proteins and so on. Choose a detergent that is most suited to what items you wash most frequently.

Some 'all-in-one' dishwasher tablets contain dishwasher salt and rinse aid. However, this doesn't necessarily mean that they provide the correct levels of each, so I'd recommend using both products as well as a tablet. Here's why.

Dishwasher salt

You're probably wondering what the water softening unit at the bottom of the machine is for. Water flows through it before it enters the reservoir and becomes softened on its way through. Hard water is a nightmare in general, but even more so when it comes to white goods such as dishwashers and washing machines. Not only can it cause limescale build-up in the unit itself, it can also cause poor washing performance and drying, resulting in dirty dishes and water marks on glassware.

When it comes to hard water, two gals run the show: calcium and magnesium ions. Both need to be removed from water for a really great wash. Come through, dishwasher salt, whose sodium chloride level can eradicate these and ensure the water becomes wonderful and soft.

'Can I use any salt? Table salt?' No. Dishwasher salt is a specific grade and the grains are of a particular size so that it doesn't clog or sneak into the dishwasher's reservoir. It's large and coarse and won't damage your machine as other regular salt would. Also, without getting too technical, the magnesium found in table salt would actually defeat the whole softening process. I prefer to buy dishwasher salt that comes in a box rather than a bag as it's easier to store. It's inexpensive and a medium-sized pack can last 6–12 months.

How to add salt to your machine

Basically, you need to fill up your water softening unit. If your machine is brand new, run a wash so it fills with water – if your machine is already in use, there will already be water in there. Water softening units usually have a screw top – unfasten it and pour your salt straight inside. You may need a funnel to help with this. I usually fill it to a couple of centimetres from the rim.

As you pour the salts in, the excess water that is not needed in the water softening unit will drain out into the reservoir. Don't panic, this is OK – it's meant to do this. Remember how the dishwasher usually drains before a cycle? Well, this water will be drained away the next time you run a cycle.

Screw the cap back on and wipe away any spilled salt with a damp cloth. Now, water coming in to wash your dishes will be full of deliciously saline goodness and will help you avoid water marks on your glassware and limescale in your machine.

Newer dishwasher models with advanced functions will let you know when your salt levels are low. I usually top up mine quarterly, as opposed to letting it run out completely before filling it up. If you live in a hard-water area, you may need to do this more frequently, particularly if you see evidence of hard water appearing on glasses.

Rinse aid

Rinse aid is the forgotten gem of the whole dishwasher process. She often slips our mind but can ensure handing a glass to a guest isn't accompanied by the panic of worrying it looks unclean. No marks, no spots, no fog. Don't be fooled by her name, she has little to do with the rinsing process; she is simply introduced to the dishes at that point. She works her magic during the drying stage, helping to speed up the whole process, thus preventing water marks from forming on dishes and glassware.

How does she carry out her work? By reducing the surface tension! Rinse aid contains surfactants, which make the water run off the item in thin sheets so the drying process happens much faster. This rapid movement of water means it doesn't have the opportunity to form into droplets or stay on the item for long. Any chance of watermarks or spotting is removed. Glorious!

To use rinse aid, simply fill the rinse-aid dispenser. This is usually right next to the detergent compartment on the door of the dishwasher. The key thing to remember here is that you don't need to do this for every wash as you would with detergent. Open the dispenser and top up to the guide level. Don't over-fill (you'll see why in the troubleshooting section on page 75). If you do, just wipe away any excess with a damp cloth.

Your machine will have either a dial or a digital function to set how much rinse aid you want to add to each wash. Your manual should include a guide to which setting is best for areas with hard water, if that applies to you. New machines will tell you when you're low on rinse aid; others you will have to check yourself. I'd suggest doing so once a week.

A little eco note here: there are some amazing natural rinse aid brands out there. As it's a product that can last a long time, research and find one that is kind to everything it comes into contact with, from the manufacturing stage to after it has done its job in your home.

Other things to consider for a longer machine life

Daily

- Try to run full loads. The machine's parts will wear the more often you use them. Fewer loads are also better on your pocket and for the environment.
- Only ever wash items that are dishwasher safe. If they're not labelled so, there's a good reason for that. Don't risk it.

Monthly

- Run a dishwasher cleaner through your machine once a month. This will clean all the parts you see but also those you can't. A cup of distilled white vinegar is a great alternative should you wish to be more eco-conscious with your cleaning products.

Long term

- Deep clean your machine seasonally.
- Book a service for your dishwasher if you feel it isn't running smoothly and you've already carried out any troubleshooting your manual recommends. Running cycles with missing or broken parts can, over time, damage your machine and lead to bigger issues long term.

- Inlet and outlet hoses should be changed roughly every five years as there can be a lot of build-up in them. In fact, most detachable pieces can be replaced easily. You'll find the parts for your dishwasher model online.

Cleaning your machine

What you'll need:

- Heavy-duty gloves
- A 'goddess bath': a sink of lovely, hot soapy water
- Washing-up liquid
- Basin/mop bucket/large plastic bowl with warm water (to have next to you while washing the machine's interior)
- Microfibre/regular cloth for cleaning
- Another cloth for drying and buffing
- Distilled white vinegar

1. Make sure your machine has cooled down before you start cleaning it (parts can be hot if it's just finished a cycle).
2. Prepare your 'goddess bath' if you haven't already done so. Washing-up liquid is a great product to use here – it will cut through any grease and is also far safer than using lots of cleaning chemicals and sprays. I'd never clean a dishwasher, or any of its parts, with anything I wouldn't use to clean a plate.
3. Remove the dishwasher's racks, cutlery basket and spray arms. If you're unsure how to remove any parts, consult your manual. Set these to one side – they won't need to soak as long as these next parts …
4. Remove the filter and food trap tray (your manual will also have details on how to do this), pop them in your 'goddess bath' and allow them to soak while you get on with cleaning the machine.

These parts come into contact with the most food and dirt, and deserve some bathing time.

5. Your dishwasher should be completely empty now. With gloved hands, clean out and dump anything that's sitting in the nook for the filter, or anything that may be lurking in the bottom of your machine. There may be broken glass or other sharp items so please be careful – you have beautiful hands and we want to make sure they don't get injured.
6. Next, wash the interior. Soak your cloth in the warm water next to you and pay particular attention to corners and fittings where food can hide. You can use a dishwasher cleaner or I like to add 2 cups of vinegar to the bucket of water.
7. The rubber seals around the door are next on the list. These stop the machine from flooding your kitchen during a wash, so be super careful when cleaning them and take care not to damage them. Rinse your cloth and add a little vinegar to wipe them down. If you've not cleaned your dishwasher in a while, this might be a slightly stomach-churning task, but stay strong. Allowing any food or debris to sit on these seals, as well as using harsh cleaning products, can actually weaken the rubber over time and lead to numerous issues.
8. Moving on to the door, you might find residue around the dispensers and door, so give these a thorough clean. The sides of the door and hinges also tend to gather fallen food, so don't forget them. The top of the door, where the buttons sometimes are, can be particularly dirty, so pay extra attention here. As these parts are on the exterior of the machine, it's OK to use a small bit of surface spray or cleaner here if they're particularly grimy.
9. Rinse out your cloth, removing any dirt, then wet soak with fresh, warm water and wipe down the entire interior, door and seals, ensuring that any cleaning product and debris is now removed. If you've used washing-up liquid as your cleaning agent here,

wipe down twice with a wet cloth as it can bubble up in later washes – you want to make sure every last trace is gone. Use a fresh, dry cloth to dry all surfaces and remove any last traces.

10. Now, back to the soaking filter and food trap tray. Give these a good scrub and rinse well. You'll also need to wash the racks, cutlery tray and spray arms in the sink. This can be a little tricky as they're quite large items – I find tackling them in the sink corner by corner can help.
11. Pop all these pieces back in place. Now it's time to clean the parts that haven't been seen to, or are not seen at all. Enter, vinegar! Place one cup in a sturdy, dishwasher-safe container on the top rack. I usually use a large mug and fill it with two cups of distilled white vinegar. Run a long, hot cycle. The vinegar will remove odours and build-up in the pipes and any areas you can't get to. It will also disinfect the machine, which is great if you've just moved in!
12. If your machine is in particularly bad condition and hasn't been cleaned for a while, run another short, hot-water cycle – put a cup of bicarbonate of soda in the mug this time and place on the bottom rack for an extra-thorough cleanse.

Troubleshooting

'There's a grainy residue on my dishes after every wash'

If you find little flecks of food on plates or glasses after a wash, your filter needs to be cleaned. If it's the first time you've done this, consult your manual on how to remove it (usually an anticlockwise twist). I'd clean her using washing-up liquid and warm water, as you would a plate. To maximize the life of your machine, filters should really be rinsed every week. If you find your filter is cracked or broken, you can usually buy a replacement from the manufacturer's website.

'I've put washing-up liquid in my dishwasher and now it's bubbling out of control'

Good god. This can be quite frightening as there can be a *lot* of bubbles filling your machine and seeping on to your floor. Turn off the machine at the wall ASAP – never mess with any appliance that still has power. Spread some towels over any overspill first. Protect your flooring, especially if it's wood or laminate, by mopping up this water and preventing it from sitting and spreading. You don't want a slippery floor at this time of crisis either.

Next, take everything out, including racks (these can be placed on towels, if needed). If your machine has a heating element, this could still be quite hot, so be careful. Wait for it and any water left inside to cool down – tend to any areas outside the machine during this time. Now you're free to scoop out the bubbles using a large plastic bowl (nothing breakable, please). It might take a while but keep going. Once you're done, wipe down all surfaces inside the machine with a wet tea towel. Do this twice to remove as much washing-up liquid as possible.

Even if you can't see any more washing-up liquid, it could all kick off again during the next cycle as it can be really difficult to remove all traces of it. You might need something to literally deaden the bubbling energy of the liquid. Advice I've come across includes using sticks of butter, ice cubes and salt. One thing that might be easier on the machine and its parts is a cup of distilled white vinegar in a mug on the top rack. On the next cycle, open the door after a couple of minutes to see if any bubbling has started to build up. If it has, throw in another cup, then a third if it still persists. Once this cycle has finished, I'd run one more empty one with a fresh cup of vinegar before you wash a full load again.

Tell this story at dinner parties, save a kitchen floor.

'My dishes aren't being cleaned properly'

Have you loaded your machine correctly, followed all guidelines and cleaned your filter but are still experiencing dirty dishes? You might have a blocked spray arm and the washing and rinsing stages are not completing as they should. Your manual will tell you whether you need to pull or twist your spray arms to remove them – always check first. Then pop them into a goddess bath of warm soapy water and scrub with a washing-up brush. If you find some are still clogged, a cocktail stick can help clear them free of debris. Rinse, dry and refit them to your machine.

'My glasses are cloudy'

If you find your glasses are cloudy or have a light blue tinge to them, too much rinse aid is being released during the rinse cycle. Sometimes this happens if you've overfilled the dispenser. If the problem persists, turn down the setting – consult your dishwasher's manual for how to do this.

'My dishwasher isn't filling at the start of a cycle'

This is one of the most complicated issues to resolve and you may need to enlist the help of a plumber if it's an issue with the inlet valve, water pressure or float. Your manual should give you some troubleshooting guidelines here, but the simplest fix could be to do with your water supply. Check your stopcock is in the right position (see pages 15–17). Sometimes previous tenants, owners or contractors will turn this off when the property is vacant, or you could have knocked it recently.

'My dishwasher isn't draining'

This could be the result of a clogged filter (see pages 71–3). Your manual will contain the exact troubleshooting steps you'll need to take for your specific model of dishwasher, but one thing to check is whether the drainage hose is kinked. Sometimes large items shoved under the sink can cause a kink in the hose, which stops it working. Other issues can be a faulty pump or a blockage in the waste hose. In which case, your best bet is to consult a plumber.

The Fridge

Designed to keep items at a consistent temperature between 0 and 5 degrees Celsius, where bacteria cannot thrive and grow rapidly, our fridges circulate cool air around our food to keep it fresh. The process, simply put, works through evaporation, depressurization and compression. You know that humming you hear? That's her turning a liquid coolant into a gas, circulating it as cool air, then turning that cool air back into a liquid, before repeating the process.

Shopping for a fridge

Here are some tips on finding the right fridge for you.

Style

As with dishwashers, fridges can be integrated or free-standing. When it comes to integrated models, there's usually less choice and they cost a little more. You also need to consider whether you need to go for a fridge-freezer or if the small ice-box that comes in a standard fridge would be sufficient. You can also opt for the American-style fridges.

Most fridges give you the option of being able to open from the right or left, as they have adjustable doors. Don't be turned off a fridge if it looks like it's opening out the wrong way, this could just be for display reasons in the store.

Size

Like most white goods, there is a standard width for fridges of 600 mm. However, if you're opting for an American-style model, double doors, or a tall fridge-freezer, it's super important to ensure you leave enough space around your machine to allow it to breathe. Although it's a cooling appliance, it actually generates a lot of heat.

If you're not tied to a certain size or are building your kitchen from scratch, consider how big your fridge needs to be and base your choice on what you consume. There's no point buying a huge model if you won't use all the space inside. Don't forget: a fridge works better with more in it.

As well as leaving adequate space around your fridge, never use an extension lead to plug it in – always plug directly into the wall. A fridge uses a lot of power and this can pose a fire risk.

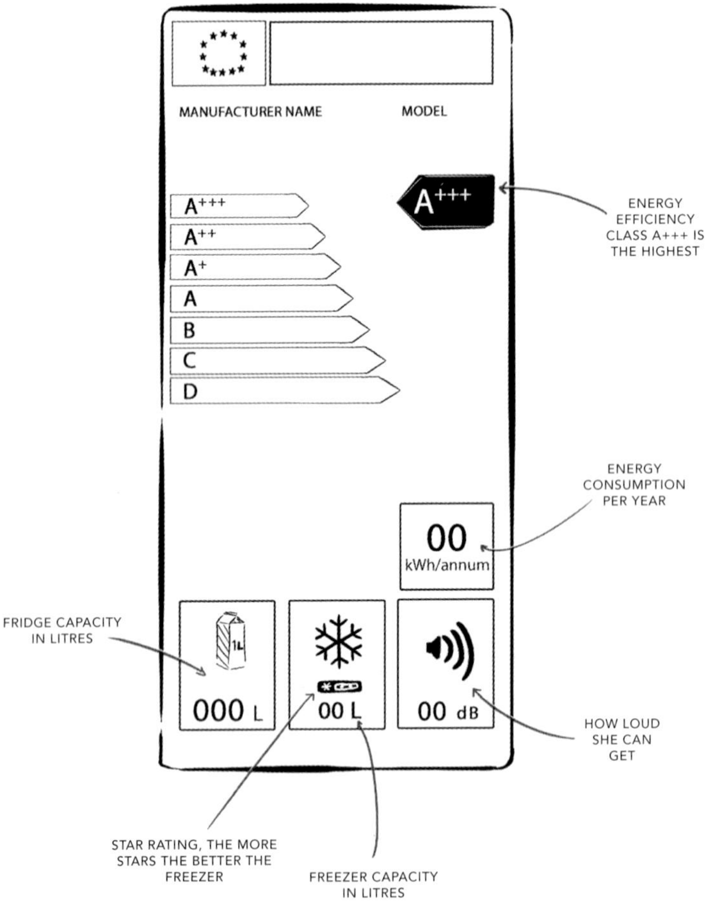

MANUFACTURER NAME
MODEL
A^{+++}
A^{++}
A^{+}
A
B
C
D
ENERGY EFFICIENCY CLASS A+++ IS THE HIGHEST
ENERGY CONSUMPTION PER YEAR
00 kWh/annum
FRIDGE CAPACITY IN LITRES
1L
000 L
00 L
00 dB
HOW LOUD SHE CAN GET
STAR RATING, THE MORE STARS THE BETTER THE FREEZER
FREEZER CAPACITY IN LITRES

Your needs

The most basic of fridges will chill your food, but you also need to consider any extra features you might need. If you eat a lot of fresh food and buy this in bulk shops (say, weekly), you will need several shelves to keep this on and larger crisper boxes. If you buy your food on more of a day-to-day basis and store more wine (hi, friend!), you might find an extra wine rack more useful and fewer shelves.

Setting her up

Always read your manual the day you set up your fridge. Every manufacturer knows how to get the best from their units and their advice is golden. Sit for a moment to take it all in and learn more about her.

Inside your fridge, at one end in the drain hole on the back wall, you'll probably find a stick (usually green) with a circle at the end. Many people think this is to be disposed of, but it's actually a tool to help keep the drain free. Store it in your cutlery drawer or toolbox, as it's a really useful thing to hold on to. It's designed to help you safely keep the drain free from anything that may block it, but because of its shape it won't fall in or get stuck.

Bacteria cannot thrive between 0 and 5 degrees Celsius. Your manual will tell you which setting on your appliance will achieve the perfect temperature. Be sure to follow the manufacturer's advice as it's super important. Some fridges' temperature settings will be in degrees, others will use a system of numbers or letters. You may have a digital thermometer.

If you're going to ever leave your fridge empty and for a period of time – for example, if you're going on a long holiday or when you move out – make sure you clean it thoroughly beforehand, and leave the door open if you're turning it off. When you view an empty property, you might see the door of the fridge open if it's off or it may be left on even if it's empty. This is because the bacteria and mould growth is pretty intense in a warm, closed environment. I can't even tell you what I've experienced when a fridge was turned off, barely wiped down and left shut. Shudder.

Cleaning your fridge

When it comes to fridges, cleanliness is super important. Not only because the food you are going to eat will be stored in there first, but because it will help prolong the life of the appliance.

Daily

It's important to clean any leaks or spills as they happen. Some spillages, such as those from packets containing meat, can be dangerous and others, such as milk, can smell horrendous if left for days. Keep all items in sealed packets or airtight containers to keep odours to a minimum and freshness to a maximum.

Weekly

Ensure you clear out old food and leftovers regularly. This is the easiest way to keep a fridge clean and sanitary. Each time you do a shop, make sure you chuck anything out of date before you put in new stuff. A fridge actually works best when it's full, but make sure there's always enough air to circulate around all your items.

Deep clean

This should be done at the start of a season, when you move in, or if you haven't done it in a while (or, ever!).

What you'll need:

- Cool bag/box and ice (or ice packs)
- A 'goddess bath': a sink of lovely, hot soapy water (with washing-up liquid)
- Rubber gloves
- Two clean cloths: one for cleaning, one for drying. Microfibre are great here but don't break a sweat if you don't have them, any cloth is grand
- 1 tbsp bicarbonate of soda
- Empty spray bottle (to hold the water-and-bicarbonate mix, so you'll need about half a litre capacity)
- Distilled white vinegar

TIP

As with a dishwasher, I don't like to clean a fridge with anything I wouldn't use to clean a plate. In my opinion, harsh chemicals have no place here. Bicarbonate of soda is great for eliminating odours, washing-up liquid is fab for tackling grease and food stains, and vinegar is brilliant for killing bacteria. What more could a gal want?

Step 1: Cull

- First of all, dump everything that needs to go. Keep the door closed as much as you can while you do this – to conserve energy and keep cool what's staying inside. Anything that's past its sell-by date, looks off, or you have no idea when it was opened, needs to go. We have a habit of storing lots of opened condiments in our fridge, but we should be realistic about whether or not they are usable. Your fridge isn't an appliance for display purposes, it's for storing what you're actually going to eat.

Step 2: Cool

- Prep a cool bag/box with some ice (or ice packs) inside and transfer any food and drink items to here that need to be kept cold while you clean. It can be dangerous to keep meat and poultry at inconsistent temperatures so I try to clean my fridge when I'm not storing any. Vegetables and dairy can handle temperature changes better.

Step 3: Clean

- Now that your fridge is empty, turn it off at the wall for safety and to conserve energy. As you'll have to keep the door open while you're cleaning, if you don't switch it off, the cooling mechanism will work overtime to try to maintain a low temp while you're letting in lots of warm air.
- Take out all the removable parts and check the manual if you're unsure about anything. Most of the main shelves, crisper drawers, shelves inside the door and so on should slide out easily. The plastic strips on the main shelves usually come off too. As a lot of dirt can hide here, remember to remove them. Soak the dirtiest parts in the goddess bath – they can bathe nicely while you clean the interior.
- For the interior walls of the fridge, mix 1 tablespoon of bicarbonate of soda in half a litre of warm water. Decant to a spray bottle and squirt on the inside walls. Create a good mist to ensure any dirt is encouraged to leave the surface when you wipe it down. For tougher stains, rub a little bicarb directly on to them, which should help to loosen them.

- At the back of most fridges is a drain: a hole at the bottom of the V-shaped groove on the back wall. Condensation runs down here before evaporating. Be sure to clean this well. Run a cloth over the V first and then use the drain-cleaner tool to ensure the drain is clear. If you don't have the tool, use a drinking straw instead. Tie a knot in the middle of it first to act as a stopper should it go in too far.
- Splash some vinegar on to a damp cloth and wipe down all surfaces again to kill bacteria. Then, rinse your cloth well and use it to remove any vinegar or dirt left on the interior surfaces. Afterwards, give them one last wipe with a clean, dry cloth.
- Clean the door seals separately. The rubber of the door seal is one of the most important parts of the fridge so I leave this until last and only wipe it with a clean damp cloth. If you damage this rubber, it can prevent the door from sealing properly and will let warm air into the fridge. The seals are made up of folds, so be sure to clean in between them. Warning: rubber loves to trap dirt and moisture … and pet hair.
- Time to wash down the removable parts that have been soaking. These items can be quite large, so be careful – particularly with glass shelves. Sometimes, if my sink isn't big enough, I'll position these items on a tea towel on the draining board and clean them one side at a time. Dry them all and place back inside the fridge.
- Don't forget to clean the exterior of your fridge too – especially the parts of door handles we don't see … Remember, you touch these before you touch your food.

Storing your food

Two things to remember about airflow in your fridge: the coldest air will travel to the bottom, and warmer air will rise. You shouldn't over-fill your fridge so air can circulate. Leave some space around items to allow this to happen. Here's the lowdown on what food should go where …

Door

While not *warm*, the door is the warmest area of the fridge. This means it's not actually the best place for storing milk as it's a difficult area to maintain at a constant temperature when it gets hit with warm air every time it's opened. It's ideal for storing juices and condiments, however – they're high in acidity so can all handle the change in temperature every time the door is opened.

Top shelf

This is the warmest of the shelves so is perfect for storing ready-to-eat food, such as hummus, and leftovers.

Middle shelf/shelves

Store dairy products and cooked meat here. Remember, the back of the fridge is colder than the front, so put the riskiest produce to the rear of the shelves.

Bottom shelf

She's the coldest so can happily keep raw meat, poultry and fish safe. Store all these items in sealed containers. Dripping meat juice can be very dangerous.

Fruit/vegetable drawers

At the bottom of your fridge, these are also called crisper drawers. They're located in the most humid part of the fridge so that fruit and vegetables can stay fresher for longer.

Ethylene is a plant hormone that gets released as a gas. It has no taste or smell and is completely harmless to humans. It is basically nature's ripening agent but can cause harm to certain fruit and veg, as it speeds up their ageing process and they go off quicker. Be careful which items you store together: lettuce, for example, can't cope with being near to apples. Knowing what to store where – and why – will mean your fruit and veg will stay fresher for longer. It's a great thing to learn about and read up on but an easy rule of thumb is that fruit and veg sensitive to ethylene won't have holes in their packaging. Next time you're in a supermarket, note what sits together: you'll see the ethylene-sensitive foods aren't displayed next to the ethylene-producing produce.

Most fridges have two crisper drawers. You can usually alter the humidity in them by using slider clips that will make them suitable for what's inside. They also give you the option to have a high-humidity drawer and a low-humidity one. These clips slide over holes in the drawer, much like trickle vents on windows. When closed, nothing gets out (your high-humidity drawer) and when all holes are exposed, the air can be released (your low-humidity drawer). Check your fridge manual to find out how to alter your drawers.

The drawer with the higher humidity is best for girls who need a moisture-rich environment but are sensitive to ethylene. These include:

- Leafy greens
- Peppers
- Broccoli
- Cauliflower
- Green beans
- Strawberries

The low-humidity drawer should be used for items that don't love a lot of moisture but do produce ethylene, including:

- Apples
- Pears
- Avocados
- Any stone fruits

You should always keep these fruits and veg separate so they can't affect each other. Also, most vegetables need a high-moisture environment to stay fresh. Finally, crisper drawers are most efficient when two-thirds full rather than close to empty or over-packed.

Storing herbs

Leafy herbs such as coriander and parsley can have a tough time when stored. Often, we'll buy a pack, use a meal's worth and the remainder will yellow and wilt in the fridge within days. These packets of fresh herbs should last ages and here's how to help them along …

Treat them like flowers. Trim their stems, pop them in a jar of cool water, then place their original packaging over the top. Hello, greenhouse. You can still keep them in the fridge – I like to put them in the shelf at the bottom of the door so they have loads of room.

Don't store basil in the fridge – she's more of a countertop, out-of-direct-sunlight kind of girl. Cold temps will make this sensitive gal wilt.

Woody herbs, such as rosemary and thyme, last longest when wrapped in damp kitchen towel and kept in a sealed container once they've been cut, to retain their moisture.

Food that doesn't belong in the fridge

Not all food needs to be kept at the same temperature and not all foods thrive in a cold environment. Here are some items that are better stored outside the fridge:

- Tomatoes. I prefer them out of the fridge and stored stems down, at room temp, out of direct sunlight. If you do prefer them chilled, make sure to keep them away from ethylene-sensitive vegetables.
- Garlic. Store in a cool dry place. No plastic for this girl and definitely not in a sealed container as it will sprout as a result of the humidity. While safe to eat, it will taste bitter!
- Bread. Although many argue it will stay fresher for longer in the fridge, the cold temperatures will actually dry it out.

- Onions. First, they will absorb any odours in your fridge so won't really be ideal to cook with. Second, the atmosphere of a fridge isn't right for them – it's too cold and humid – so they won't keep for as long. They need space to breathe, so an open basket in a cool space, away from sunlight, is ideal. It's fine to store them with garlic.
- Potatoes. Cold temperatures turn the starch in potatoes into sugar – this alters their taste and changes their colour. This is why old-school potato sacks are made out of heavy brown paper – they do a great job of keeping out the light and moisture. Be mindful not to store onions and potatoes together as they can spoil each other.
- Jams and marmalade. With their high fruit content and therefore high acidity levels, these sweet treats can actually live outside the fridge. Make sure always to use a clean knife each time you use them to avoid baddies getting in.
- Bananas. They grow and thrive in hot climates and so hate the cold. Store them next to ethylene-releasing tomatoes if you'd like to speed up their ripening process.
- Chocolate. Tastes best at room temp so store out of sunlight and out of the fridge!
- Eggs. They're not stored in a refrigerated aisle in the supermarket because their packaging is perfect for keeping them safe and fresh! Don't keep them in the fridge, especially not in the tray in the door. Every time the door is opened, you risk damaging them. Keep them safe in their original packaging in a cupboard instead.
- Avocados. If not yet ripe, the best way to store an avocado is in an open brown paper bag in a cool dry place. Ripened avocados *can* go in the fridge. If you are storing

half an avocado, keep the stone in and sprinkle with lemon juice. The acid will prevent it from ripening any further. Avocado products such as guacamole contain a high lemon content to prevent the avocado from browning.

Troubleshooting

'Water keeps gathering at the bottom of my fridge'

Check your drain! A blocked drain means the build-up of condensation has nowhere to go and will collect at the bottom of the fridge, usually under the crisper drawers. Sometimes it can gather unnoticed for some time and leak out when you open the door. If your fridge seems to be leaking, check your drain before you call an engineer. See page 83 for advice on how best to clean it.

'It's like ice, ice, baby'

Are the more delicate items in your fridge, such as lettuce, freezing? Are some foods attracting a thin layer of ice? Check your fridge's thermostat. Use a thermometer to make doubly sure your in-built one isn't out of whack. Also, check that its setting is what is recommended by your manual.

'Everything is in the dark'

Is the inside light not coming on when you open the door? Check there is power to the fridge – sometimes a tripped switch or a knock to the plug will have cut the supply without you realizing. If there *is* power but the light still isn't working, you could try replacing the lightbulb before calling an engineer. This is such an easy thing to do and full details will be in your manual! Find out what type you need by unscrewing the current one and finding a match online or looking locally for a replacement.

'My fridge stinks'

Does a bad smell escape whenever you open the door? The first port of call is to dump whatever might be causing this odour. If it doesn't fade in a few days, or there was nothing bad to start with, you might need some extra help.

- Deep clean the fridge, as per the instructions on pages 80–3, and add some lemon juice to your bicarb spray to help neutralize the odour. It might be that a spillage you can't see is causing the problem.
- Clean the drain at the back of the fridge. If it's become clogged with some rotting food, this can cause quite the stench.
- If it's more of a lingering smell, place a cup of bicarbonate of soda in the fridge for a few days. Alkaline in its make-up, bicarb can be a great odour-buster. If this still doesn't work, add some coffee granules, which can also dispel strong smells.

The Washing Machine

This is one white good that has added valuable time to our lives. At the flick of a switch a whole load of washing can be washed, rinsed and wrung out.

Just like the dishwasher and fridge, she can be cared for to last longer, but in general her average life span is around ten years. Depending on how often she's used and how well you care for her, she can still break down and need some vital parts replaced after as little as just three years. It's true that white goods are not lasting as long as they used to, but the trade-off is that we are now able to buy them cheaper than ever before. As with all major purchases, I'd make sure to do as much research as you can before you buy. Cheaper machines can end up costing more in the long run. As with my notes on purchasing a new dishwasher, you might be able to increase your budget if you can work out how to reduce other costs involved, such as delivery and installation.

Shopping for a washing machine

As with all white goods, budget will be the main factor here. However, given the front of your washing machine is generally on show, its appearance will often be a consideration. I'd suggest taking into account the following before you make your final decision.

Style

There are two main types of washing machines: top-loading ones and those we mainly use in this part of the world – front loaders. Front loaders are actually more economical to run as they use less water and you can fit larger loads inside. Hurrah! Just like dishwashers and fridges, they can be integrated or free-standing.

Size

Standard washing machines measure 850 mm × 600 mm and usually have a depth of about 600 mm. If you have a small space, consider a slimline appliance, which can be up to 150 mm slimmer. Don't forget that there will be parts at the back of the machine that you will need to leave room for, such as a drain hose and power cable, so make sure the space isn't too snug.

Your needs

The first thing to consider is capacity. Think about the size of your household and the weight of the loads you'll be doing on a regular basis, as this will have an impact on the size of the drum you'll need.

When shopping around, take a look at the load capacity, which will be given in kilograms. It should be on the machine somewhere, usually near the model name, and states how heavy a load can be *when dry* for the best and safest wash.

So, if you have a one-bed flat with two occupants you won't need the same capacity as a family of six. Knowing that five T-shirts weigh roughly 1 kg, I've found that a machine with a 5–7 kg load capacity is good for two people, a family of four can opt for 7 kg, but the larger 9+ kg machines would be needed for families larger than that. To give a further sense of scale, you can wash king-size duvets in an 11 kg drum. If you aren't using the full capacity of the machine on a regular basis, it will waste water and electricity so it's worth figuring out your household needs.

The next factor to consider is the spin speed, which is measured in rpm (revolutions per minute). Domestic machines usually have an rpm of 1,200–1,600 but the average is closer to 1,200 rpm. The higher the spin speed, the more water will be extracted from your clothes, thus decreasing drying time.

The rpm can affect the noise your machine makes, but cheaper machines are usually the loudest. If your washing machine is in an open-plan kitchen or living room, or you love a late-night wash, you may need to do a bit more research into how loud your machine is. Most websites will note the noise level of the machine in dB in the product specification section.

When it comes to assessing the myriad cycle options available, think about what kind of clothes you will be washing most. A quick wash is a great option to have if you wash lightly soiled clothes often and don't need a long heavy wash. 'Baby', 'sportswear' and 'hand wash' are also great programmes to have as they ensure the job is done correctly. Half-load settings are great as they are more energy-efficient and eco washes are brilliant too: lower temperatures are used but for longer so you still get a thorough wash. However, I'd encourage using your machine for hot washes every now and then to keep limescale – and any other build-up in your machine and its outlets – to a minimum.

As with dishwashers, the more you're willing to pay the more functions your machine will likely have: delay start, digital display, child lock, anti-allergy cycles and extra rinse are all now more readily available features in mid-priced machines. Higher-priced units can even be controlled from your phone these days.

Finally, you should consider the machine's energy rating. Each appliance will have an EU energy label to state clearly how efficient it is when it comes to water usage and energy consumption. The energy rating goes from A to A+++, with A+++ being the best in terms of energy efficiency. Cross-reference this information with the cost to run the machine annually as the most energy-efficient machines are not always the cheapest to run.

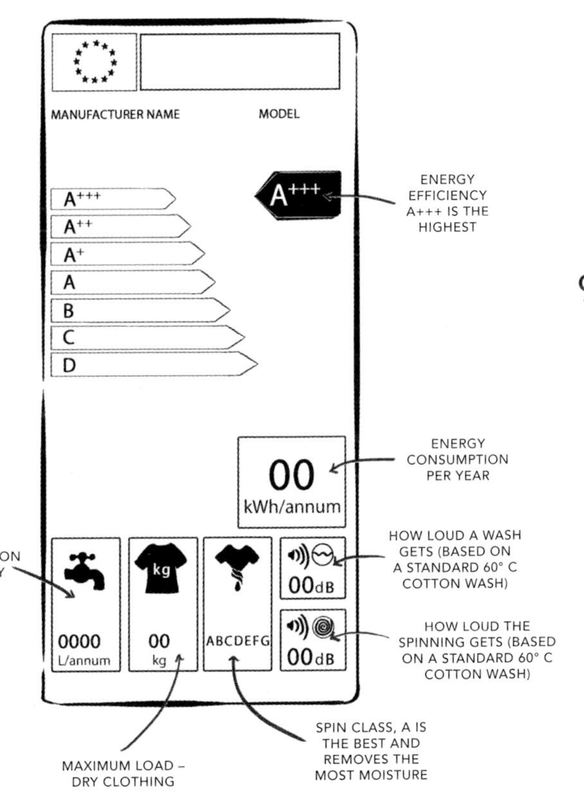

MANUFACTURER NAME
MODEL
A+++
A++
A+
A
B
C
D
A+++
ENERGY EFFICIENCY A+++ IS THE HIGHEST
00
kWh/annum
ENERGY CONSUMPTION PER YEAR
WATER CONSUMPTION ANNUALLY
0000
L/annum
kg
00
kg
ABCDEFG
00dB
00dB
HOW LOUD A WASH GETS (BASED ON A STANDARD 60° C COTTON WASH)
HOW LOUD THE SPINNING GETS (BASED ON A STANDARD 60° C COTTON WASH)
MAXIMUM LOAD – DRY CLOTHING
SPIN CLASS, A IS THE BEST AND REMOVES THE MOST MOISTURE
BASED ON 220 COTTON CYCLES PER YEAR, MADE UP OF BOTH 40° C AND 60° C, FULL AND HALF-LOAD CYCLES BUT DOESN'T TAKE INTO ACCOUNT VARYING FACTORS SUCH AS COLD WATER TEMPERATURES IN VARYING REGIONS, ETC.

Most comparison websites now show the yearly running cost of a machine, basing their calculations on the EEI (energy efficiency index) on the energy label. This states how many kilowatts per hour the machine would use for 220 washes – the estimated yearly use. As most machines are in the A+ category and above, the difference may be minimal but it's always worth knowing.

Her parts

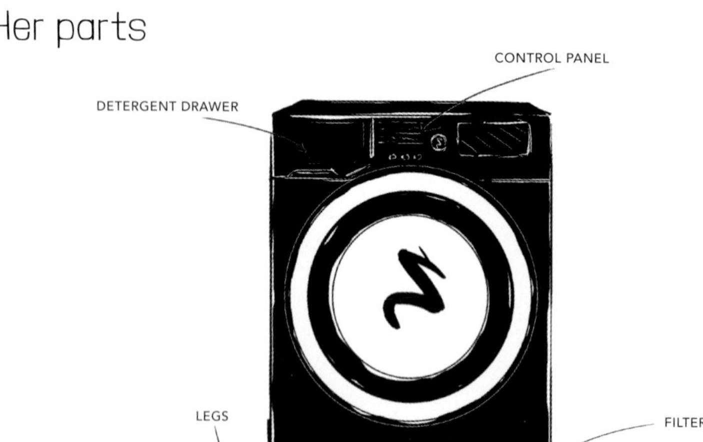

Her cycle

Simply put: during a washing cycle, clothes are washed in detergent and water to remove stains and odours, then rinsed and spun to remove the water. Little-known fact: in order to do the best cleaning job it can, there are two drums in the machine. One is a hidden, watertight tub that holds the perforated drum you can see when you look inside. The large tub is usually made of plastic and allows water to flow in and out of the holes in the metal drum.

Washing

Once you've selected your cycle, water runs from the inlet valves through the detergent drawer. You'll hear it! Here, the water mixes with the detergent and they enter the drum together. As the drum fills up, an element beneath heats up the water.

First, your clothes are soaked in a prewash. This is the perfect time for the enzymes and stain-busters in your detergent to get to work on stains and odours. Next, the real washing commences. A motor attached to the back of the machine rotates the drum, causing vital agitation to work the water and detergent through the clothes, ensuring a thorough wash. Hand-wash cycles aren't as intense, so as to minimize damage to delicate garments, while more deep-cleaning cycles will agitate more and for longer.

Rinsing

Next, the machine rids the drum of the soapy, dirty water so it can start to rinse the garments. The water drains away through the drainpipe which is controlled by the drain pump, in much the same way as the dishwasher operates. Before this water hits the pump it passes through a filter, which traps excess fluff, hairclips, buttons – you name it. I even found a fake eyelash during a repair once.

Fresh cold water then enters the machine and as the drum rotates again it rinses the clothes of any detergent or dirt. Depending on the cycle, this process may happen a few times. On the last rinse, your machine will release the fabric-softener dispenser so that the softener enters the drum for the final stage of rinsing.

Spinning

A great deal of spinning is needed to remove as much water as possible from the washed clothes. Consequently, the machine needs to be weighted in the correct places so it doesn't take off. This is why there is concrete casing in your machine – to make it more stable. It's usually at the top of the machine and around the drums, along with some cleverly placed heavier parts, to ensure the vibrations don't cause the machine to move out of place.

The drum will spin at speed – a set number of revolutions per minute (rpm) – until the water has left the clothing through the holes in the drum. Your machine won't start spinning at full speed right away, it will rotate slowly and self-balance the load, ensuring the even distribution of the clothes. Once it senses there is no imbalance, it will crack on to full spin. She's a genius!

Selecting your cycle

What cycle should you use and at what temperature? There are some general rules for clothing: what it needs and what it can endure when being washed. Some fabrics have particular needs to be aware of. Here are some of them:

Hot wash – 90° C

Great for any light-coloured cottons that come into close contact with the body, such as bedlinen, towels, underwear and socks. It's also good for durable fabrics which get heavily stained, like workwear, but washing at this temperature will cause garments to fade.

Warm wash – 40–50° C

Good for coloured or printed synthetic garments. The temperature is not too taxing on the dyes used but warm enough to take out any stains. Don't forget, if you have a monster stain you can pre-treat it before the wash (see pages 52–3).

Remember, fabric softener adds a silky feel to fabrics by almost coating them, so it's not great for anything you rely on for absorption, such as towels.

LAUNDRY CARE LABELS

WASH

TEMPERATURE GUIDE FOR MACHINE WASH CYCLES

SYNTHETICS CYCLE

DELICATE CYCLE

DO NOT WASH

GRAND TO USE A DETERGENT WITH BLEACH IN IT

USE A BLEACH THAT HAS NO CHLORINE

DON'T EVEN THINK ABOUT USING BLEACH ON THIS

WASH WITH YOUR GORGEOUS HANDS ONLY

THIS LOOKS LIKE A DELICIOUS SWEET BUT IT MEANS DO NOT WRING THE GARMENT

DRY

TUMBLE DRY AWAY AS YOU PLEASE, SHE'S WELL ABLE FOR IT

TUMBLE DRY ON A LOW HEAT

TUMBLE DRY ON A HIGH HEAT

DO NOT TUMBLE DRY

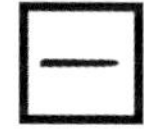

DELICATE

SYNTHETICS

HANG DRY

DRY FLAT

PRESS

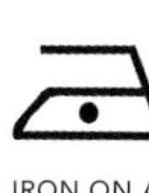

IRON ON A COOL HEAT

IRON ON A MEDIUM HEAT

IRON ON A HIGH HEAT

DO NOT IRON

DO NOT STEAM

DRY CLEAN

DRY CLEAN ONLY

DO NOT DRY CLEAN

THESE NOTES ARE FOR YOUR DRY CLEANER AND INDICATE WHICH CHEMICALS ARE OK TO USE

Cold wash 20–30° C

Perfect for delicates, such as lingerie, silk, wool and so on. Just remember, some natural fibres don't take well to the enzymes in some detergents and fabric conditioners, so check the care label first!

CARE LABEL

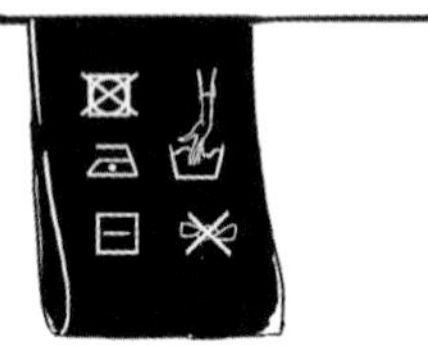

ENSURE YOU FOLLOW THE CARE LABEL, ALWAYS DOUBLE CHECK ANYTHING YOU ARE UNSURE OF

STAINING

PRE-TREAT ANY HEAVY STAINS AND REMOVE AS MUCH OF A DRIED-IN STAIN AS POSSIBLE BEFORE WASHING

COLOUR FASTNESS

WASH LIGHT COLOURS SEPARATELY WASH SIMILAR COLOURS TOGETHER AND CHECK IF THE FABRIC IS LIKELY TO RUN

How to ensure a great wash and longer machine life

- Read the manual thoroughly to familiarize yourself with the products she cannot handle, some golden rules and other instructions that will differ from your previous machine.
- Before you load her up, check nothing is lurking in the pockets of clothes to be washed that could damage her or clog her filter. Gently scrape off as much dirt from any heavily soiled items as you can – use a spoon – and shake off any mud.
- Don't overload your machine. You should be able to fit a hand on top of the load once it's in the drum. This will reduce the pressure the machine is under during a wash cycle and your clothes will wash better too.
- If you live in a hard-water region, use a de-scaling product on a monthly basis. In soft-water areas, quarterly de-scaling is sufficient. A de-scaler keeps all the machine parts that would suffer from a build-up of limescale in good working order.
- As washing machines use so much heat and water, closing the door straight after a wash is quite bad for it. All the moisture needs to go somewhere, so leave the door open as long as you can after a wash so that it can evaporate. I also like to pull open the detergent drawer a bit. Don't forget this is where the water goes first before the drum and also needs to dry!

Cleaning your machine

Another thing you can do to make sure she leads the longest, strongest life possible, is to clean her regularly. Here's how ...

You'll need:

- Rubber gloves – I know you have nice hands so protect them
- Washing-up liquid
- A basin/mop bucket/large plastic bowl to have next to you while washing the interior
- A 'goddess bath': a sink of lovely, hot soapy water
- A microfibre or regular cloth for cleaning
- Another cloth for drying and buffing
- 1 cup distilled white vinegar
- ¼ cup bicarbonate of soda

When cleaning any electrical appliance, the first step is always to unplug her or turn her off at the wall.

1. Check your manual to find out how to remove your detergent drawer, then pop it in the goddess bath and leave to soak. There will be a lot of build-up on it, from detergent and fabric softener, which can stop the machine from filling up correctly or starting cycles. Make sure that the casing where the drawer is housed is cleaned too. This can become really mouldy if you use washing tablets that go in the drum and not the drawer, or if you keep the drawer and door closed after washes.
2. Once the drawer has had time to soak, scrub her down, dry her off and pop her back into place.

3. Next, wipe down the drum. Deeper drum-cleaning will happen a few steps on – right now focus on removing any dirt or hair that's stuck in the drum.
4. On to the door seal … If you pull back the folds, you might see some mould. Rubber loves moisture and trapping it, so any water remaining after washes will be drawn to the seal. Don't use any cleaning products or implements that can damage it, or you'll be left with a leaking machine during every cycle. I simply wipe it down with a damp cloth or a product that is OK to use, such as a washing-machine cleaner.
5. Pour 1 cup of vinegar into the drum and close the door. Mix ¼ cup of water and ¼ cup of bicarbonate of soda together and pop into the detergent part of the drawer.
6. Set a hot wash and the vinegar and bicarb will do their thing to give the inside of the machine a great deep clean. When the cycle has finished and the drum has cooled down enough to touch, wipe down the seal again, making sure to work into the folds. Finally, leave the door and drawer open so that the machine air-dries.

   C'est bon.

Troubleshooting

'There's product on my clothes after a wash'

Late introduction of detergent If you've put detergent in the wrong part of the drawer, it might have been released too late in the cycle – possibly at the rinse stage – and hasn't washed off properly. Consult your manual to check you're using the right part of the drawer.

Excess detergent On the other hand, it could be because you're using too much product. While you might think more is better, you could have overloaded the wash with detergent – especially if you've chosen a quick-wash cycle – and there wasn't enough water to rinse it off the clothes. Double-check your dosage.

Hard water You might have very hard water, which means the detergent can't foam sufficiently. Try adding a water-softening product to the wash or make sure you buy a detergent that is designed for use in hard-water areas.

Blocked filter There's a chance your filter might be blocked slightly and the soapy water isn't draining sufficiently at the right time. See the clogged filter section on pages 106–7 to find out how to fix this.

Overload If you overload the drum, the garments can't move around enough to be rinsed properly. Too many clothes could be the issue so make sure your drum is only two-thirds full.

'My clothes don't smell like I've used any detergent'

Dirty machine When a machine needs to be cleaned it can start to smell damp. Try giving it a deep clean as per the instructions on pages 100–1 to rid it of any odours. This damp smell could also be the result of using short wash cycles and lower temperatures. Wash items such as towels and bed linen on a higher temperature setting so that you're not only killing bacteria and odours, you're technically washing the machine's insides thoroughly as well.

Clogged dispenser drawer Your dispenser drawer could be clogged with old detergent. This can happen if you overfill a drawer or fill the wrong compartment with the wrong product. Pull out the drawer, clean it, and also clean down the recess where it sits.

Excess detergent More means even cleaner, right? Wrong. There won't be enough water present to wash it all away and so the detergent can end up coating stains instead of removing them.

Sitting time If you tend to leave your clothes to hang around in the drum for a while after the cycle ends, they can end up smelling damp. Leaving them for up to 6–8 hours can be fine, but taking them out as soon as possible is better.

Overload If you've put too many clothes in a load, there won't be enough detergent for them all. A full drum is one where you can still fit your hand on top of the clothes inside. If you can't, then there won't be enough room for the product to disperse evenly.

Stubborn odours It may not be your machine's fault. We now use wash cycles at lower temperatures and with less water, so odours such as sweat can linger. If the fabric can take it, wash items on a higher temp or add a cup of vinegar to the wash, making sure you pour it in the fabric softener drawer to be used at the rinse stage. This can neutralize any stubborn smells.

'My machine is mouldy'

Look, it happens, eh. You're definitely not the only one to experience it, but now you're going to be in the club that knows how to prevent it. Geddit, girl!

Detergent In case you haven't gathered by now, the overuse of detergent is a waste of time and money. Here's another downside: less water and more detergent means you're more likely to be left with soapy water at the end of a cycle. This water doesn't evaporate the same way clear water does, so it tends to sit in the machine, especially along the rubber seal, attracting and feeding mould. Stick to the recommended quantities of detergent given on the packet, and if you're doing a quick wash use even less.

Temperature A machine tends to dry off quicker after a hot wash than a cold wash, so lower-temperature washes can mean we need to help the machine a little more to dry out after cycles. You can do this by keeping the door (and dispenser drawer) open after washes.

Back in the day, cycles were hotter, longer and used more water. This meant they would do a great job of killing mould spores, keeping limescale at bay and washing away detergent entirely during the rinse cycle. Now, our machines are far more efficient appliances but we need to work with them to prevent mould. You can still keep up the eco washes, just make sure you run a hot wash every so often.

'Holy mother of god, my machine is walking'

This is up there with one of the more scary things I've encountered when dealing with white goods. When a washing machine goes walkabout, there can also be a great deal of movement and jumping within its confined space and lots of horrendous noise. It is terrifying. The reason your machine may be moving as it vibrates is because of an imbalance.

Balancing When washing machines are installed, they are balanced – using the adjustable legs at the bottom of the appliance – to make sure they are level. A level is placed on the top of the machine and the legs are adjusted until the machine sits evenly. This prevents the drum from tilting, which can make it move when it's spinning at a high speed. Hence the walking.

I'm sure you're wondering how your machine might have suddenly moved from its level position. It's usually the result of one of the reasons below. You'll mostly likely need a level and a wrench to fix it, but it's not a tough job. The movement required is minimal and you won't even need to lift the machine.

- Sometimes people will unintentionally move their machine by sticking something like an ironing board down the side and this may unbalance it, if the floor is uneven. Once nudged back to its original place, it will be level again.
- Your machine's legs may have come loose over time and you'll need to tighten them. Check your manual for instructions, and keep a level on top of the appliance to ensure it's just right. It's simply a case of twisting them in or out until it shows as level.
- The machine was incorrectly balanced to begin with. To rebalance it, you'll need to adjust all the legs. Always make sure you consult the manual, take in all instructions and safety advice, and don't forget your level!

Uneven loads If your machine is level, it could be an uneven load that is making your machine move when it starts to spin. This can happen when you put something really heavy – even a soaking-wet towel – in the drum alone. Always wring out anything sopping before you place it in a machine, and it's advisable to have a minimum of half a load in the drum. It can also happen when you pack a load in so there's not enough space for it to move around and one part of the drum becomes super heavy.

'The machine isn't draining'

Oh, cripes. Another problem that can be stressful. Thankfully, newer models of washing machine won't allow you to open the door when there's still water inside, so you'll avoid finding out there's an issue *after* you've soaked the floor.

Water not leaving the machine is usually the result of a clogged filter or drainage hose. Before we get into how to remedy this, double-check that the outlet pipe to your machine isn't kinked, preventing water from draining correctly.

Clogged drainage hose

If you disconnect the drain hose at the back of your machine (that's the hose that takes the water away from the machine and out of your home), you can empty the water much easier than through the filter at the front of the machine. When the end of the hose is placed below the level of the water in the machine, water will pour out, so be sure to hold the end above this level until you have a bucket ready. The water should start flowing into the bucket, and will mean the route from the top of the drain pipe to the machine is clear. If it doesn't, it means this pipe is blocked. This could mean it needs replacing because there's a limescale build-up, or a drain snake could help dislodge anything that might be stuck in it. Just remember to be careful and not make a hole in the pipe.

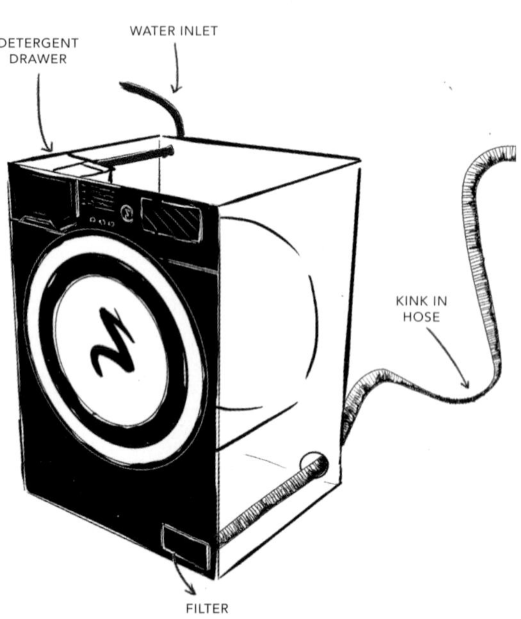

Clogged filter Every machine has a filter – it's usually in the bottom right-hand corner at the front of the appliance, covered by a little flap or door. Open this and you will see a twist cap. Tilt the machine back slightly so you can fit a shallow bucket or basin under the filter. Don't use anything that could break and have someone keep a hold of the machine while it's tilted back. Slowly twist open the filter. Water will start pouring out quickly. If the bucket you're using is nearly full and you need to empty it, simply twist the filter closed and the water flow will stop. Empty the bucket and repeat the process until the water has stopped and you can pull the filter out fully to inspect what could be blocking it. I've seen so many different things: from hair clips to Lego to jewellery.

It's worth checking the filter monthly to make sure there is no build-up of lint, hair or coins that could end up stopping a wash.

Takeaways for Your White Goods

- Be aware of your budget for the running costs of the appliance as well as the machine itself. You could end up buying a more expensive model with cheaper running costs and still save money overall. BE THAT GIRL.
- When troubleshooting, use common sense. Always turn the machine off at the wall first, and know when to call in the professionals!
- Your manual is extremely important. Take time to read and understand it before you use your appliance for the first time, and keep it handy for issues you may encounter. It's also worth remembering that most manuals are available online if yours does go astray.
- Rubber seals must be cleaned very carefully with a warm damp cloth. No harsh products or scouring pads!
- Don't overuse detergents – they are designed to work well in the prescribed quantities and overuse can cause damage to your machine.

5. SHE-IY

This important chapter will arm you with info and a host of tips to help you keep on top of minor repairs and replacements in your home. We often live with things not working as they should because we don't have the knowledge to fix them ourselves, and hiring a contractor for such small tasks can feel like a waste of money and time. Dripping taps, slowly draining water, blown lightbulbs, mouldy silicone ...

So I've taken some of the most common issues we face around the home and put together some easy-to-follow how-to guides. What you'll learn will hopefully give you enough knowledge and confidence to feel even more powerful within your home and help you deal with these issues as and when they arise.

The Kitchen Sink

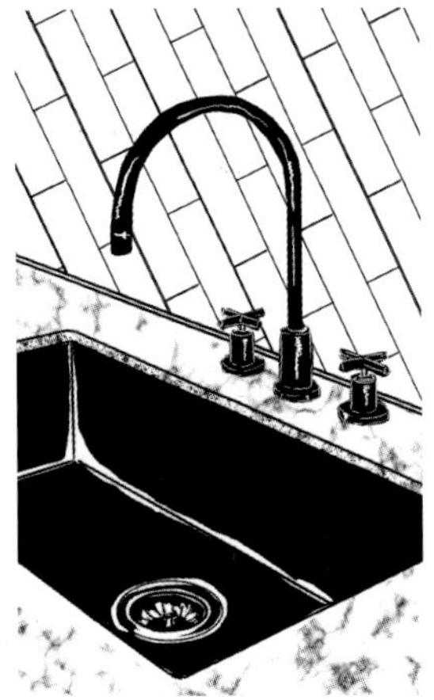

It's not surprising that one of the most used items in the home is one that can have the most things go wrong with it. The three main problems you'll likely encounter are:

- A leak in the pipe under the sink
- A dripping tap
- A blocked drain

They're usually easy to sort out by yourself without having to call a plumber. Here are some possible solutions:

A leak in the pipe under the sink

If you've discovered a pool of water under the sink, it can look like a much bigger issue than it actually is. If you're sure the sink, taps and draining board are all sealed and watertight, then it's going to be the pipes underneath that are to blame.

These pipes are made up of sections – some bent, some straight – all screwed together, and any leak here is usually caused by water coming through one of the joints. First things first: identify which joint is leaking. This isn't always easy to figure out because, thanks to gravity, any escaping water will run and collect at the bottom of the bend and drip from there no matter which connection is at fault. I find the quickest way to determine which joint isn't watertight is to wrap a couple of sheets of kitchen paper, or a cloth, around each one and run the tap. Whichever tissue soaks first is the culprit.

The next step is to tighten the joint in question. It doesn't hurt to tighten them all while you're at it. The area under the kitchen sink is one that gets knocked about more than others so sometimes we can bump these pipes and loosen the fittings without realizing. When you're done, run the taps and hopefully you'll find that everything is watertight.

If it hasn't worked and you're not seeing any damage to the pipes and fasteners themselves, you might need a new washer.

A washer is a ring-shaped piece of rubber that sits inside the screw fastenings of a pipe. It creates a seal that prevents water from leaking through the joint. These girls work hard and, over time, can wear out and need replacing. To change yours, first place your metal bucket (see page 41) under the pipes – there could be some really smelly water trapped in there so wear your long heavy-duty rubber gloves too. Unscrew the joints affected so you can lift out the bend. You'll see the black rubber rings, or washers, inside. Take these to a local DIY store to buy identical replacements. They usually come in multi-packs, so pop the spares in your emergency kit. Back home, pop them in place, tighten your fastenings and run your taps. There shouldn't be any leaks now. If there are, it's time to call a plumber.

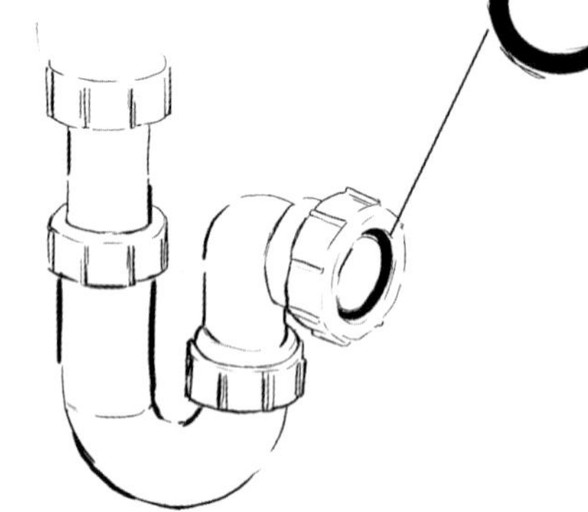

#SAFEISCHIC

Never unscrew anything under the sink without turning off the water at the mains. Your washing machine or another appliance could be connected to these pipes and if hot or dirty water hits you as you're repairing something down there, it can be dangerous as well as messy.

A dripping tap

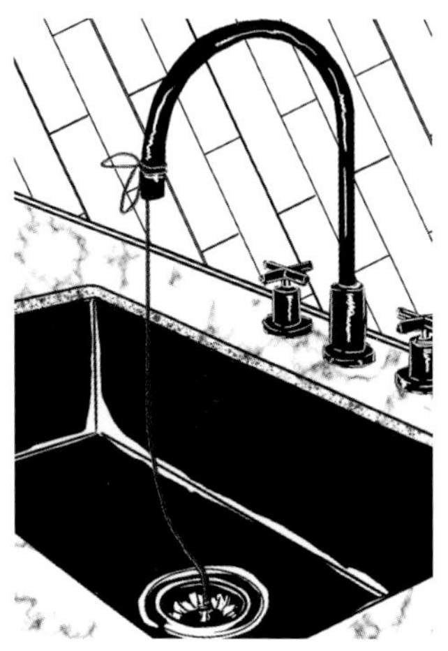

First off, this is doing the environment zero favours. It's wasting water, can stain your sink, will get worse over time, and finally, the noise! Water torture! If you have a tap that's just started dripping and is keeping you awake at night, tie a piece of twine from your emergency kit (see page 43) around the top of it. Let the other end of the twine sit inside the plughole. Instead of drip, drip, drip, the water will now flow down the string silently. This is just for emergencies, though, and not a long-term solution.

The drip will usually be caused by … drumroll, please … a worn-out washer. You'll also be relieved to hear that you don't actually need to buy a whole new tap.

You don't want any major dramas while you're fixing this, so turn off your water at the stopcock before you begin (pop back to page 16 if you're unsure how to do this), then run the tap until the water dries up completely.

If ever I'm taking something apart for the first time, I always make sure I'm aware of how it goes back together. I'll take a photograph, or draw or write in list form each step I take to disassemble the item, keeping a bowl next to me for parts. If there are several parts, you might need a few bowls – one for each stage of the process so you can keep them all separate. Losing screws is a total nightmare and putting something back together incorrectly is equally annoying.

Now, there are different types of taps, but most handles are secured in place with a cap fitted over the screw. This cap is the part that usually has 'hot' or 'cold' indicators on or around it. Here are two very common types but if yours looks different, you can easily find a manual online that will guide you through the removal process:

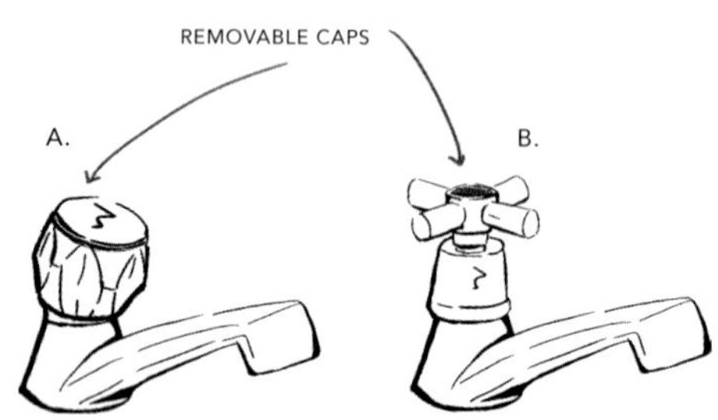

A: You can flick off the disc at the top to reveal a screw. Unscrew this and the handle will come off.

B: You can also remove the cap here, but these ones usually twist.

Most taps will have either these flick-off or twist-off caps. Over time they can become grimy and might be a bit stiff to remove because they're stuck on. If this is the case, you can scrape away any congealed matter and wash them down with some hot soapy water, which will lift any grease.

Once the tap handle is off, your valve should be exposed. If not, you might need to unscrew another part. This will usually be a decorative element that raises the handle further from the base, and is almost always found in tap type B. As this will be covering the valve that holds the washer, you'll need to remove this too.

Grab your adjustable wrench or spanner and twist anticlockwise until this part loosens enough for you to unscrew it fully with your fingers. There will probably be a little water so have a towel handy!

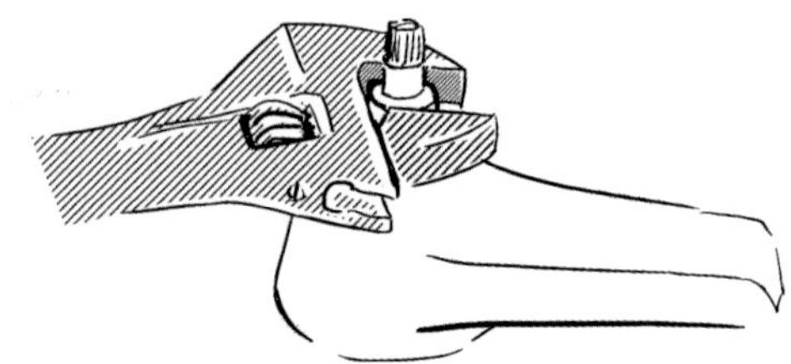

Out will come your valve, which looks like a steampunk lipstick or an earring you wear to Burning Man. At its base will be a black washer – this is who we need to replace. It will either peel off or, if there's a screw head visible at the centre of the washer, just unfasten this and it'll release it. Take her with you when you go shopping for a new one to make sure you get the correct size.

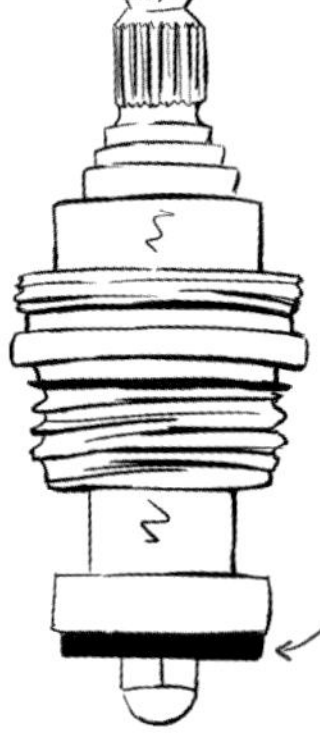

WASHER

Pop your new washer in place and put the tap back together carefully – just follow in reverse your list of steps taken, making sure you tighten all the parts well.

A blocked drain

A blocked kitchen sink is a total pain. It can be the result of many things – a build-up of grease and grime, food, and so on. More often than not, this blockage is located within the pipes under the sink and not further down, which means you can probably fix it yourself. Drain unblockers work well, but many plumbers warn me against using them as not all pipes can take the chemical corrosion. I also prefer to try the methods below first, before resorting to unblockers as they avoid the use of strong chemicals.

BLOCKAGE

Before you get started, don a pair of long rubber gloves. Oh, and I wouldn't be wearing my favourite crêpe-de-chine tee for this one. Also, if there are any large bits of food in the sink at this point, remove them now as they could create another blockage later.

Plunging

Grab the small plunger from your emergency kit (see page 44). Its circumference just needs to cover the drain.

Plungers pull air and water up then push it back down when you apply a downward force, which loosens any blockage. Before you begin, make sure to clog the overflow (the hole in the side of the sink – I usually stuff it with a rag) and, if it's a double sink, plug the other drain. For the most effective plunging action, you need things airtight.

Apply the plunger over the drain, making sure it creates a tight seal. Some people use petroleum jelly along the rim as an extra measure but that's up to you. When you push the stick of the plunger down, it will expel the air from the dome of the plunger down into the drain and pipe. As you release it, it will pull up water and air, then you can push back down again and so on. Do this about ten times but don't be too forceful – you don't want to damage your drain or sink.

As you've probably realized, the pull-up motion is doing more than the push-down one so next, for optimum pressure, pull the plunger off the drain in one swift motion. It will 'pop' and – hopefully – the blockage will be sent on its merry way. If this doesn't happen, go again.

#SAFEISCHIC

Never plunge a sink that has had chemicals poured down it recently. It's not safe to have drain unblockers come back up into the sink.

Get wired

If the above worked slightly and you now have slow-draining water (or if you don't have a plunger), a wire coat hanger is the ideal thing to break up the blockage and move it along. Simply unwind the neck of the hanger so that you can unfold it into one long, straight wire. Curl one end of it to fashion a hook. The key here isn't to use the coat hanger to push the blockage further down the pipe, you want to hook on to some of whatever's down there and pull it apart so it can flow down the pipe. You can also pick up really handy tools called drain snakes (online and in stores). They work in the same manner but are particularly good for bathroom drains as they easily remove hair build-up (gag).

Dismantle

This is a great solution if you know it's a stiff blockage or you think your pipes are laden with a build-up of grease. One joyful memory I have of doing this is after a football-loving tenant had moved out. It appeared that the kitchen sink was where they washed their boots. A lot. The muck and grass build-up was quite intense but this method cleared it quickly and easily. First of all, empty the sink of water as much as possible. You're going to be dismantling the pipes below so you want as little water coming down through them as possible. Give yourself plenty of space under the sink by removing products and shelves that could get in the way. Place your metal bucket directly under the pipes on top of an old large rag as this can get super messy!

Unscrew the U-bend, which is literally a U-shaped piece of pipe with a screw fastening at each end. When this comes off, a lot of dirty water and gunk might fall into the bucket. Be warned! Remove any visible blockage from the pipe ends or within the U-bend itself. If it's particularly gross inside, soak it in hot soapy water for a minute or two, clean it, then screw it back on tightly. Don't forget the #safeischic note on page 110: you do not want connected appliances on during this!

Vin-carb

Try this approach for slow-draining issues or when there's a bad smell coming from the drain. As you know, vinegar and bicarbonate of soda react fabulously when combined. They foam and bubble like mad and, if you add a kettle of hot water (which is a queen for removing most light blockages on its own) to the mix, imagine it flowing through your pipes. The mixture can neutralize most odours as it will loosen any gunk from your pipes and help wash it away.

So, pour a recently boiled kettle of water (hot, but not boiling) down the drain and give it a couple of minutes. Follow it with half a cup of bicarbonate of soda, then half a cup of distilled white vinegar. It will start to foam right away and you don't want it to come back up into the sink, so put in the plug or place an upside-down cup over the drain straight away. Boil the kettle again while the mix is fizzing through the pipes and finish off the job with a second kettle of hot – not boiling – water again.

If your sink is prone to blockages or you'd like to do some upkeep to ensure you don't get any, any time you find there's some water left over in your kettle when you're making a cup of tea, throw that water down the sink. A blast of hot water will keep the pipes clean and clear. We wash our dishes by hand less than ever, so our sinks have become more prone to build-up because of the lack of hot water passing down the drain on a regular basis. A monthly vin-carb would also be beneficial if your sink is particularly prone to build-up.

As with white goods, your kitchen sink and all her elements play a big part in the home, especially if they're connected to appliances. Making sure they can carry out their duties as smoothly and easily as possible will prevent any costly problems. It's important not to ignore slow-draining water, small leaks and little issues – especially now that you know how to fix them! – as they can build up into quite a messy task over time.

Leaking Showers

Speaking of leaks, a very common issue with showers is a leaking hose. It usually happens where the head screws into the hose or where the hose screws into the unit or tap. If you don't attend to it quickly, it can lead to a host of issues that you may not catch until it's too late. So let's look at how we solve it.

First things first, make sure all the fittings are nice and tight. They can loosen over time, especially if you often take the shower head off its hook. Tightening by hand will usually do the trick. If you still have a leak it's most likely caused by … yes, a worn-out washer. Over time they can wear out or become damaged, but they're incredibly easy to replace.

Shower hoses are usually a universal diameter at each end, but there are two variables to consider, one being the cone shape at each end. This will determine how the shower hose sits in the wall bracket and connects to the tap or shower unit. Usually these are pretty universal, and won't differ from brand to brand, but it's

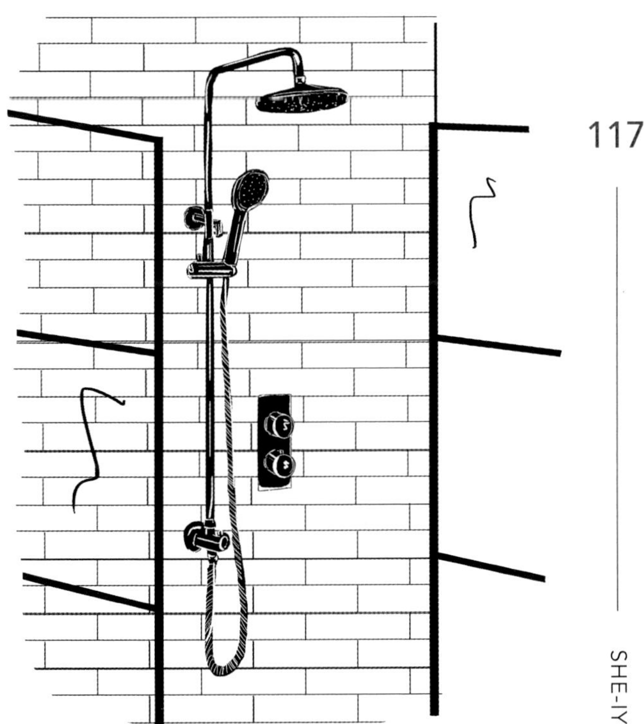

handy to compare your replacement to an image of your old one when shopping. If you're buying for an electric shower unit, buy a hose from the same manufacturer – it will always be its best match. The other variable is the hose length – make sure yours is the right size.

As the diameters of the hose ends are universal, it means you can pick up a pack of shower washers really cheaply and easily as one size fits all.

To replace this kind of washer you need first to remove the end of the hose that is leaking. This may still have some water in it so be warned: go slow. If it doesn't twist off easily, pop on a rubber glove to see if more grip helps. If not, you might need an adjustable wrench or spanner, but be careful as these can scrape off metallic coating on plastic fittings. Pop your rubber glove over it to be on the safe side and prevent marks.

Once it's off, you'll be able to see the old washer inside. Simply remove it and replace with a new one – make sure you push it right into place. Tighten everything back up and the leak should be sorted.

Changing Silicone

Re-siliconing the seal around a bath, shower tray or in the kitchen can update a space immediately. If done correctly it will also ensure you have zero water-damage problems in places you cannot see. But how do you know if yours needs to be changed? Well, it'll be starting to lift from its surface and may have some gaps, or it will be mouldy, which is a sign of weak spots in the sealant that are trapping moisture or the result of inadequate cleaning and ventilation. It's best to change the silicone if you notice any of these red flags. (A side note: gaps or cracks in your silicone will be letting water through and might be the result of an unstable basin or bath. Once you've removed the old stuff you'll need to see if your sink or bath needs to be secured further to prevent it rocking or any movement in the future causing the same problem.)

It's important to note that new silicone can't be applied over old silicone. This is a shortcut I've seen taken when someone has rushed a bit of DIY, but I've never seen it done successfully. The original silicone would have to have been extremely thin and in good condition, which would be a rare thing. To apply silicone effectively you need to create a waterproof seal – it has to touch all the right surfaces and not just sit on top of the old stuff. Here's a list of items you'll need to get started:

- Protective rubber gloves
- Something to remove the old silicone with: Stanley knife and scraper; silicone-removing tool; or silicone remover (see stage 2 on page 120 for more detail)
- Vacuum cleaner
- White spirit and old rag
- Silicone
- Stanley knife
- Silicone gun
- Sealant-setting tool

It's good to have an overview of this process before you begin, as it can help you make sense of the importance of each stage. Your aim should be to remove the old sealant entirely, then pump in some new silicone neatly. Finish it off by smoothing it correctly and leaving it to set for the right amount of time.

Stage 1: Buying silicone

Low-modulus silicone is flexible and great for use around baths, shower trays and sinks, as these items all move when filled with water or when we stand and sit in them. High-modulus silicone is more rigid and better for areas where there is little movement, such as kitchens. When choosing yours, make sure you consider what surfaces you're applying it to. There are also colours to choose from, so you need to decide which is best for the task in hand – I like to use clear sealant around glass, and white around baths. You can also buy anti-mould silicone, which is a fab choice for use in bathrooms.

Stage 2: Removing old silicone

This is probably the most important stage as it will affect how well your new silicone seals and thus how effective it'll be at preventing water from going where it shouldn't.

I'd advise wearing protective DIY gloves. You might need to go over the old silicone a few times to fully remove it, so put on some Dionne Warwick and clear your diary for the morning. There are several ways to do the job: three tools, three methods …

Stanley knife and scraper

This method involves cutting out the old silicone and scraping off what's left behind. Start by using the Stanley knife to slice along the top and bottom of the sealant, then pull it out. It can take a long time but stay focused and be super careful. Now, take the scraper that you can pick up at most hardware stores and run it over the remnants so that it all comes off. Be careful not to damage the surface of the bath or tiles.

Silicone-removing tool

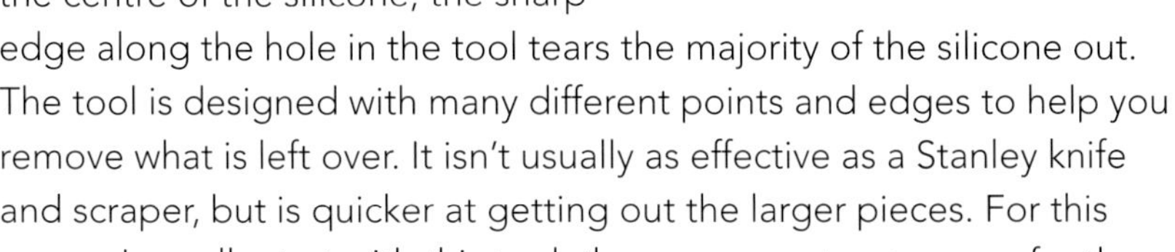

Here, as you drag the tool along the centre of the silicone, the sharp edge along the hole in the tool tears the majority of the silicone out. The tool is designed with many different points and edges to help you remove what is left over. It isn't usually as effective as a Stanley knife and scraper, but is quicker at getting out the larger pieces. For this reason I usually start with this tool, then move on to a scraper for the remnants, as in the first method.

Silicone remover

This is a chemical compound that essentially eats away at the silicone to help lift it from a surface. It sounds great as you simply apply, leave for a few hours and then come back to semi-dissolved sealant. I don't love using harsh chemicals if I can avoid them, so I tend to give the remover a miss and use tools. However, if it's a tricky area – around an old sink, perhaps – or you don't like the sound of the effort of tools, this can be fine. Although they say it will remove all silicone, you'll probably need a scraper to finish it off.

When removing the old silicone, make sure the plug hole is covered in your sink/bath/shower. You can then let all the old sealant fall inside for easy removal when you're done with this stage. After I've cleared these bits away, I'll hoover the gap where the silicone used to be to make sure no stray bits are left behind.

Finally, I'll go over the whole area with some white spirit on a rag. This will lift off the very last bits and won't leave a residue like some other products do. Before any new silicone can be applied, you need to make sure the surfaces it will be applied to are clean and dry, and free from dust or debris – otherwise it just won't stick and you'll be left with gaps you might not see but will worsen over time.

Stage 3: Setting up the silicone gun

Grab your tube of silicone and unscrew the nozzle – there should be a sealed tip underneath. Take the nozzle, go to the widest part of the gap you're filling and stick the tip of the nozzle in it. Mark about 6 mm further down from here with your knife – a little mark will do – this is where you should cut open the end of the nozzle. It means the opening from where the silicone will flow will be larger than the gap you're filling and there will be enough to adhere to the surfaces on either side. Slice the nozzle at a 45-degree angle, then cut the sealed tip of the silicone tube too. Make sure you don't cut off any of the screw threads as you need these to screw the nozzle back on to the tube.

Next thing to do is set up the silicone gun, which works like this: you pull the plunger back by the hook and move it forward by squeezing the handles. You'll need to pull it back to insert the silicone and push it forward to push the silicone out of the tube. You'll see that

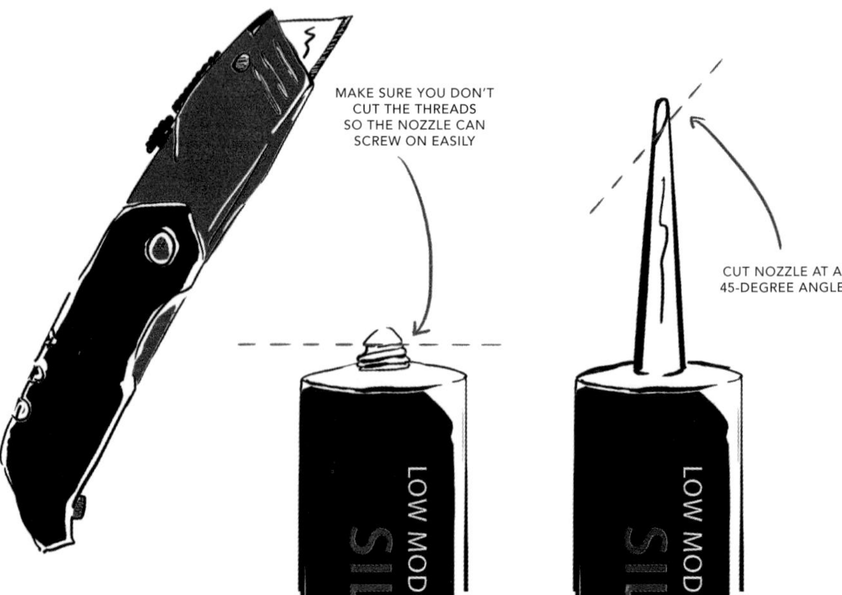
MAKE SURE YOU DON'T CUT THE THREADS SO THE NOZZLE CAN SCREW ON EASILY
CUT NOZZLE AT A 45-DEGREE ANGLE
LOW MOD
SIL
LOW MOD
SIL

#SAFEISCHIC

Always use Stanley knives correctly and carefully, cutting away from you. It's better to go slow and steady than nurse a sliced finger for weeks after.

the plunger has a disc at the top that is designed to sit at the base of the silicone tube. Each time you squeeze the handles, the disc pushes the base of the silicone tube further inside it, forcing the silicone out through the nozzle. After one squeeze, the plunger will continue to push the sealant out for a while and so, should you need to emergency stop, press the stop lever and pull the plunger back a bit. This will relieve the pressure in the tube and halt the flow of silicone.

To position the tube of silicone in the gun, draw the plunger back by the hook to pull it out of the main compartment and make room for the sealant. Place the tube inside the gun and squeeze the handles a few times to move the plunger down. Don't go too far just yet – the silicone will start coming out! You just want to make sure the tube is secured.

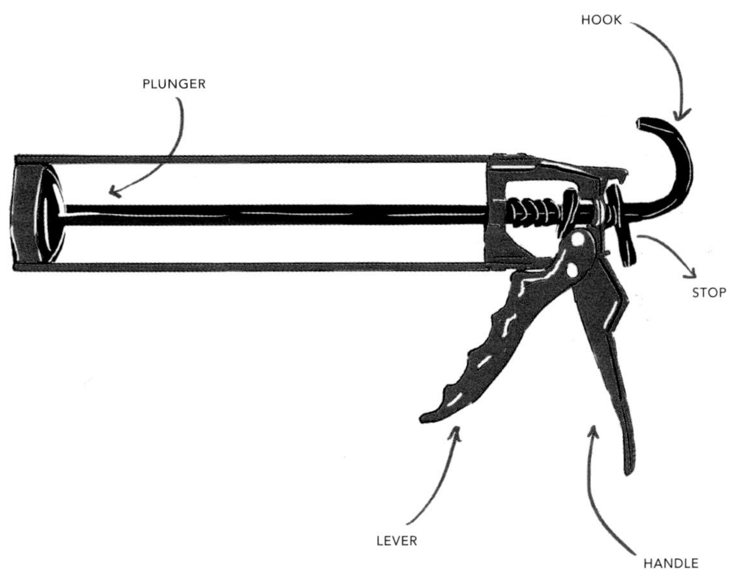

Step 4: Applying the silicone

Before you start, if you're re-siliconing along the bath, make sure you fill it first. It doesn't need to be hot, just an OK temperature for you to stand in. When you fill a bath and then sit in it, the weight lowers the bath ever so slightly. This is why you should use a low-modulus silicone for the job, as it has enough flexibility to accommodate some movement. It's also why you apply it when the gap is at its widest. If during the application you add the weight it's likely to endure during regular use, the silicone isn't going to snap over time.

Once you're standing in the bath (if that's the job you're doing), squeeze the handles of the gun to get the silicone flowing. Work slowly and carefully, letting the sealant flow in a strip (or 'bead') into the gap as you go. Keep steady and focused so the bead is smooth, even and tucked into the gap as well as a few millimetres above and below it. Don't forget your emergency stop if you need it. I also like to keep a rag handy for any spills.

Step 5: Setting the silicone

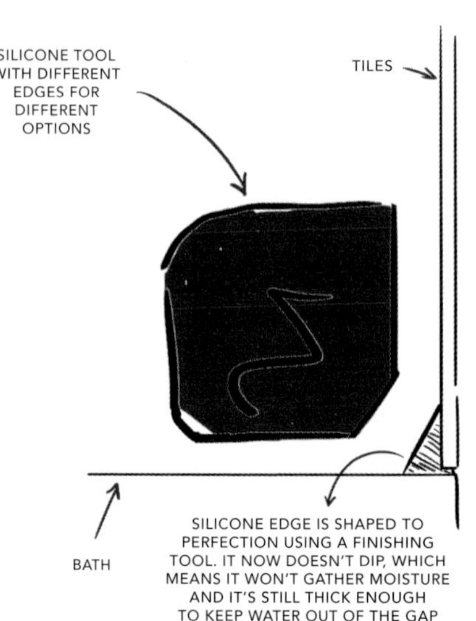
SILICONE TOOL WITH DIFFERENT EDGES FOR DIFFERENT OPTIONS
TILES
BATH
SILICONE EDGE IS SHAPED TO PERFECTION USING A FINISHING TOOL. IT NOW DOESN'T DIP, WHICH MEANS IT WON'T GATHER MOISTURE AND IT'S STILL THICK ENOUGH TO KEEP WATER OUT OF THE GAP BETWEEN THE TILES AND BATH.

There's so much mixed opinion out there when it comes to this stage. One piece of advice is to lick your finger and run it along the sealant to set it in place. Aside from feeling a bit off standing in a bath full of water rubbing my saliva on fresh silicone, there's another very important reason fingers and spit are best kept out of the equation. Both carry bacteria, which can cause mould to develop rapidly – you'll have essentially rubbed it into the silicone before it's even dried.

Another reason to keep your fingers to yourself is that they'll create a dip in the silicone. This can make the finished job look messy, wavy and dented. Water could also gather in it, which can lead to mould issues; its dipped nature can make cleaning more problematic than it needs to be; and uneven silicone is at risk of more wear and tear. For these reasons I like a more raised finish. It doesn't really look any different but it does help give the silicone a longer life and mould a shorter one!

To achieve this look, once you've pumped the silicone into place, use a sealant-setting tool to go over it while it's still wet. Pick the edge of the tool that suits the size of the bead of silicone to scrape away any excess, which will leave you with a perfect finish. It will be raised, look neat and will be even enough not to gather water.

Radiators

This section is for radiators connected to a central heating system and run by your boiler, and doesn't apply to electric heaters.

Have you noticed that your radiators are only getting warm up to a certain point? It can be quite frustrating when they're not working as effectively as they should, because the room won't heat up as quickly. This can lead to higher bills as you'll have to leave the heating on for longer to get the effect of a fully functioning radiator. It could also be a warning sign of a bigger issue and cause you problems if you leave it for too long.

Cold at the top when heating is on?

What does air do? She rises. If your radiator is cold at the top then this means that your central heating system has air in it and you need to bleed it to let the air out. This isn't as scary as it sounds if you know what you need to do and why you need to do it.

Gather your tools beforehand:

- Radiator key or flathead screwdriver
- Old rag
- Bucket

Before you begin, make sure your heating is turned off at the boiler and all your radiators have cooled down. It's bad for your heating system to be on while you bleed a radiator but, more importantly, it will keep you from being harmed by any hot water that might escape during the process.

You shouldn't need the bucket, but on the off chance you break something or turn the radiator pin so far that it comes out (and you need time to screw it back in), this will save your flooring.

If your home has more than one level, always bleed the radiators on the ground floor before moving upstairs.

Take a look at the wee square pin on the release valve at the top of your radiator, usually on the right-hand side. If the pin has a slit in it, this means you can use a flathead screwdriver to bleed it and may not actually need a radiator key. Radiator keys are super easy to buy from a local DIY store, though, or online. They're a universal size and I'd get a brass one – not only do they look chic, they won't break like the plastic ones do. The dent at the bottom is square in shape and designed to fit that pin on the release valve.

Hold your old rag under this valve before you begin, to catch any water that might come out of the radiator as you bleed it. Slot the key into place and twist it anticlockwise to open the valve. Be careful here. Turn it a small amount to start with – you don't need to open it fully, just maybe a quarter-turn so that the air can escape but not too much water will follow. You might hear the air hiss as it leaves the radiator then, when it's gone, the water will start to flow quickly. This will almost always happen sooner than you think and is why it's so important to do only a quarter-turn. As soon as you see water, close the valve immediately by turning the key in a clockwise direction.

Carry out the same steps for all affected radiators, then pop back over to your heating and switch it on – all should now be working fine.

Once you've bled your radiators, the pressure in your heating system will drop. It should be between 1 bar and 1.5 bar. If you have a modern boiler, it should reset the pressure automatically but if you need to top it up yourself, follow your boiler manual for guidelines on how to do this.

If you find you need to bleed your radiators more than once over the winter, you should book an appointment with a central heating engineer. Air is finding its way into your system somehow and you'll need to sort it as soon as possible before it becomes a costly issue.

Cold at the bottom when the heating is on?

If your radiators aren't warming up at the bottom, this could be a sign that there's a build-up of sludge inside. When metal, air and water meet, it can cause corrosion and result in this sludge forming. If your radiators have some cold spots when your heating is on, you'll need to book an engineer – it's not something I'd advise fixing yourself as it could involve flushing the whole system.

While radiators are a joy when they are working as they should, there's no point in living with one that is underperforming. You should always be aware of the health of your radiators, even if you're a tenant – it can be a costly lesson to ignore warning signs, and small issues with one radiator can lead to a bigger problem for the whole system, which means ££££. This leads us to another item in the home that is so vital and so easy to maintain but almost always forgotten about.

Cooker Hoods

So helpful yet so overlooked, the extractor fan in your kitchen works hard for her money. However, she's rarely properly maintained – perhaps because we don't know that much about her inner workings. That's why I've included her in this chapter as her upkeep is very important.

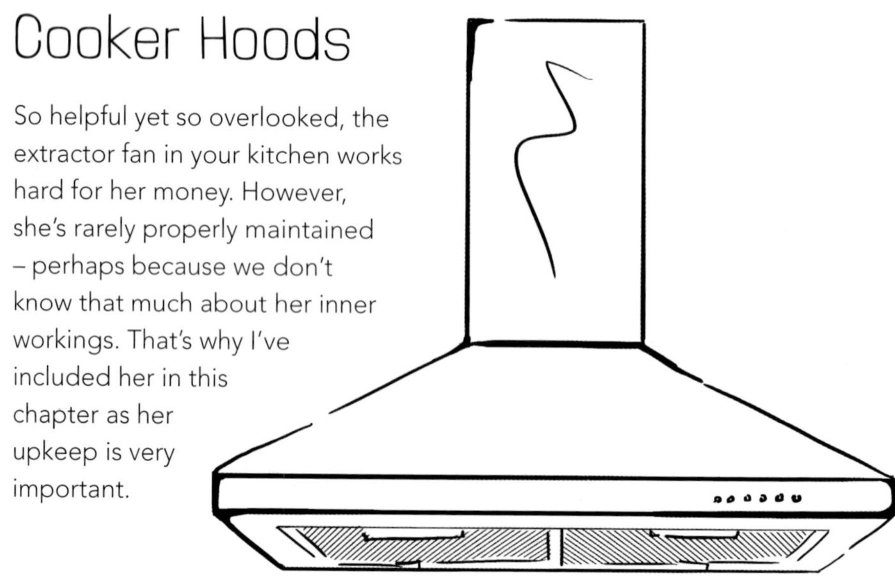

What does she do?

I'm sure you already know that she sucks in steam and odours, but did you know that she also takes care of airborne grease? Yep, that's a thing.

So, what kind of extractor do you have? I'm not talking about her style – whether she's integrated, visor or chimney. I'm talking about what she does with the air she draws in. She's going to be either a recirculation hood, which cleanses and filters the air as best she can before sending it back into the room, or a true extractor hood. These girls suck in the air and release it outside.

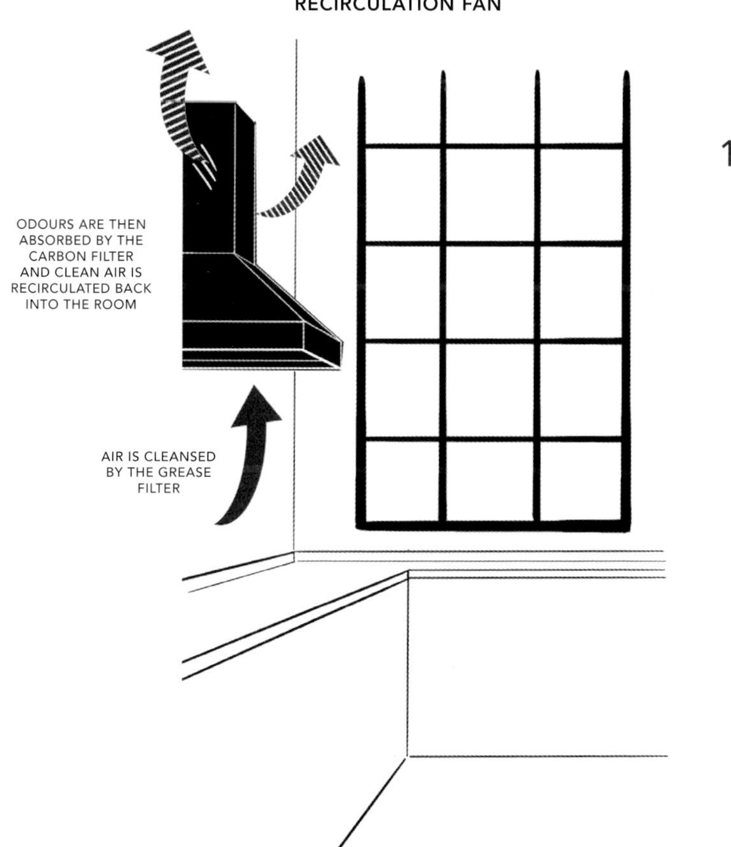
RECIRCULATION FAN
ODOURS ARE THEN ABSORBED BY THE CARBON FILTER AND CLEAN AIR IS RECIRCULATED BACK INTO THE ROOM
AIR IS CLEANSED BY THE GREASE FILTER

EXTRACTOR FAN

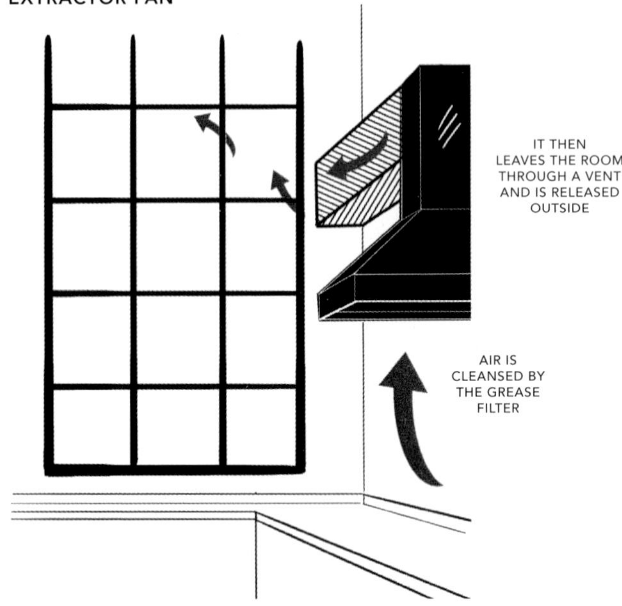
IT THEN
LEAVES THE ROOM
THROUGH A VENT
AND IS RELEASED
OUTSIDE
AIR IS
CLEANSED BY
THE GREASE
FILTER

Filters

What they do with the air is not the only difference between these two types of hood. While both have grease filters, recirculation hoods also have a charcoal or carbon filter to cleanse the air of any odours once it's passed through the grease filter. The air that enters the hood goes through the grease filter first, which traps the most awful bits so that they don't reach the rest of the machine. Think nightclub bouncer.

How to change a cooker-hood filter

Grease filters Let's start with these, as both types of cooker hood have them. They're the filter you can see if you look under the hood. The main reason you need to change them regularly is for safety. They can become a fire hazard, and the build-up of grease and odours can stop the fan from doing its job well.

What you cook – and how often – has a bearing on how frequently you should change your grease filter. Ideally it should be every 2–3 months, but if you never really fry food (or cook really infrequently) it will need changing less often. You will also probably notice your extractor fan is super loud when it needs to have its grease filter changed. Consult your manual to see what type of filter is in place – they can be metal, ceramic or fleece – and whether it's washable or needs to be replaced entirely. If you don't have your manual to hand, you should be able to find it online.

Your manual will also give you tailored instructions on how to carry out a filter clean for your model, as well as any no-nos, but here are a few general points.

- If your filter is washable, follow your manual's directions on how best to clean it and which products are safe to use. Some filters can even go in the dishwasher! I'd advise putting yours in on its own and making sure the spray arm can still rotate when it's in.
- If your filter is disposable, search for some eco-refills online. There are loads out there and they are a more conscious way to replace throw-away filters. They do the same job but will likely be chlorine-free, compostable and recyclable. They also tend to last longer as they're made of natural fibres. A win all round.

Carbon/charcoal filters Only recirculating cooker hoods will have these. Each model will use a different type of filter so be sure to buy the one that is designed for yours. Their main role is to take care of odours, so they will have a lot less grease on them. For this reason it's usually suggested that you change them every 8–10 months but check your manual for exact recommendations as models can differ. They are never washable as they literally absorb the odours and wear out.

Be aware of how to replace your filter and dispose of it safely. It can be more complicated to access than the grease filter but your manual will guide you through the process. Some brands now post video tutorials online, which can be a bit more fun and easier to follow.

How to change an extractor fan bulb

This is such an easy little job and won't take more than a couple of minutes! These bulbs are usually covered with a removable flap or cover that can get stained over time, so take the opportunity to clean this down when you change the bulb, as a build-up of grease can dull the light. The bulbs are usually screw-in ones and a universal size. If you think yours might not take the universal extractor size because of the hood's design, take your bulb to a DIY store or large supermarket to find a matching replacement.

Always make sure your hood is switched off before you change your filter or a bulb. When it comes to filters, make sure you have a new one to hand before you dispose of the old one – don't ever use your extractor fan with a filter missing.

Hanging Pictures

I speak more about how we can use walls cleverly in Chapter 6 as it's something that can really add to a space, so felt it was a must to include some handy guidelines and tips here on how to hang items.

Hanging anything on your walls can be a daunting prospect. One small error could have serious consequences: drilling into a live wire, knocking a big hole in some plasterboard, or hanging something unsafely thus risking injury later. To avoid all pitfalls, what's the best tool you can have? Knowledge! From getting to grips with what your wall is made of, to the weight of the frame you're hanging and the type of fittings it has will all lead to a successful hanging session.

#SAFEISCHIC

A plethora of cables and pipes that connect radiators, sockets and switches to their supply source are concealed behind your walls. They're usually neatly and logically placed to keep you and them safe, and some have protective casings. To avoid any risk of danger, you can easily pick up or borrow a handheld live-wire detector to locate these wires. Simply run the unit along the wall – a tell-tale beep will let you know which spots to avoid drilling into and which pose no risk.

Once you have your chosen item, let's start with where on your wall you want it to go. You'll know not to hang a piece of art in direct sunlight (to prevent fading), and to keep pictures hanging on their own – or those in the middle of a group – at eye level, but aesthetics isn't the most important thing to consider when it comes to the actual hanging. Knowing what kind of wall you have will help you choose what fixtures and fittings are needed to hang the item in the safest and most secure way. Most interior walls in flats and modern homes are hollow, and because of this, they're where the worst mistakes are made, so let's chat about them a little more.

Hollow walls

These walls are not as solid as brick, for example, and instead have strong vertical beams – studs – holding up sheets of plasterboard, drywall, and so on. From a hanging point of view, although not always possible, the ideal position for your piece will be over a stud and not on the plasterboard in between. The stud is the most solid part of a hollow wall and you can hang a variety of weights from it without the risk of the wall crumbling. If you hang from plasterboard alone, it's less likely to be able to hold something very heavy.

How will you know? (Sang à la Whitney Houston)

The old-school way to find out what lies beneath the plasterboard is to tap along the wall with your hand. You'll hear a hollow sound when you tap the plasterboard and then a dull sound when you knock on

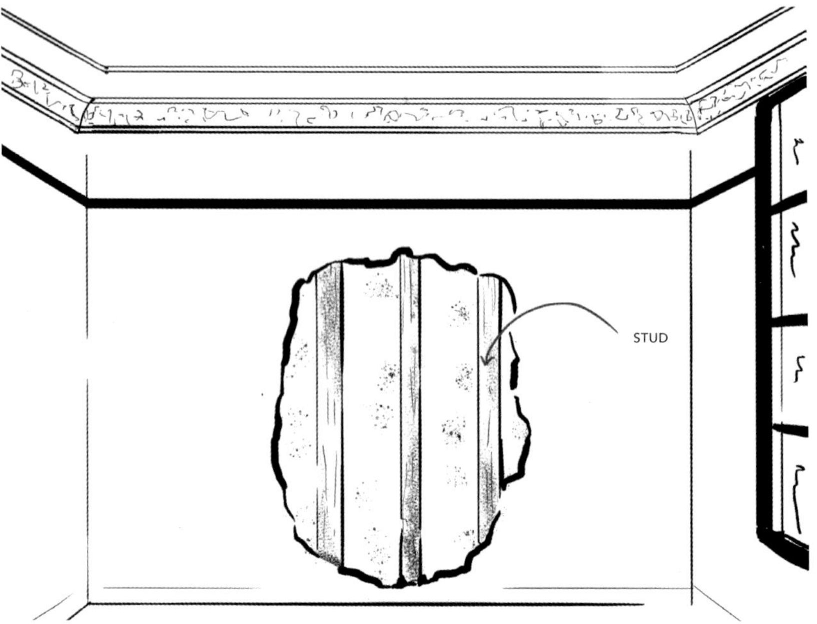

the stud. These days you can use a stud finder to be super sure. It's a wee hand-held electronic device that will let you know where the studs are when you run it along the wall. Even better, you can buy ones that find studs *and* live wires. Dream!

If the ideal hanging spot for your picture happens to be right on the plasterboard with no stud behind it, be mindful of the weight of the item you intend to hang there. If you were to simply hammer in a nail and pop a heavy mirror on it, chances are you'll pull that nail out of the wall along with some of the wall itself. You'll then have a damaged wall and mirror on your hands, which is not a look, let's be honest. To avoid this, the best thing to do is to work out the weight of what you are hanging, and then look up the hollow-wall options for that weight. To help you decide, below are some great, user-friendly options. Bear in mind that these can come in a variety of sizes that can hold different weights. Always overestimate the weight (I multiply by 1.5 to be on the safe side).

Lightweight frames on a hollow wall

The most common weight for a high-street frame is 1–3 kg. They're light because they're made from materials ideal for mass production and a low price point – lightweight wood or plastic edging, for example, and a pane made of plastic instead of glass.

A lightweight frame can be hung easily from plasterboard using a picture hook and a slim, angled nail. The position at which the nail sits in this style of hanger means it will essentially be able to hold more weight, as it's driven into the wall at an angle. It's also less likely to come back out of the wall in this position. This is handy to know if you're ever hanging something very lightweight – 1 kg, for example, and using a single nail. Drive your nail in at a 45-degree angle for optimum strength, instead of straight in.

Best of all with this type of hanger, the hole made is minimal and will barely be noticeable if you ever remove it. As I mentioned in

Chapter 1, if you have a white wall, running a little chalk over this hole will fill it. A final note on these hooks is that there are double-nail versions, which can be a great option if you wish to err on the side of caution (goddess move) as these can take more weight. The packaging will clearly state how much.

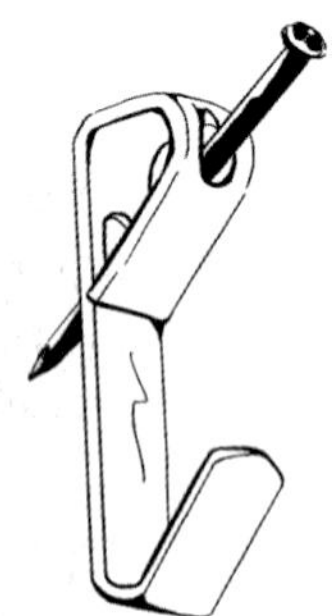

Solid walls These angled hooks can be a total pain to use on solid walls – the nail will be too long and thick and can make the wall crumble a little. I find the white round plastic hangers with a hook and three pin-like nails are amazing. Easy to use and remove, they leave very little marks.

Medium-weight frames on a hollow wall

While hollow walls are not designed for heavy weights to be hung from them by simply a nail or two, there are some wall fittings that will assist you in hanging heavier items.

First, a screw will always be more reliable than a nail as it's less likely to slide back out, but it will need to be anchored into a hollow wall. Anchors provide a protective layer around the screw which keeps it secure and the wall free from damage over time from the weight of the hanging piece.

The simplest anchor is a Rawlplug, which is cheap to buy and readily available. Just make sure you use a plasterboard Rawlplug and not one designed for use in a solid wall. Hollow wall plugs have little wings on them whereas solid wall plugs do not. You push a plasterboard Rawlplug into a pre-drilled hole before driving a screw into it. As this happens, the wings expand, anchoring the screw snugly into the wall.

To ensure that you get each part of this process correct you need to make sure your plug, screw and drill bit are all the correct sizes. It's essential that the plug isn't too thin for the hole in the wall, as it will come back out easily, and that the screw isn't too big for the plug as it can break it.

You'll be glad to know that you can buy perfectly matched plugs and screws in the one pack (hurrah!). There will be guidelines on the packet about which is the correct size drill bit to use, which removes a lot of guesswork! Once you've driven in the screw, there will be enough of it still sticking out for you to hang your piece from. Another note on these plugs is that their colours represent different sizes, but not all companies use the same colour-coding system so be sure to double check.

When inserting your Rawlplug into the wall, push it in gently – it should be a tight fit so tap it in at the end with a hammer to make sure it's flush with the wall and not sticking out. When inserting your screw, you might need a few light hammer taps to start it off, but be gentle – you don't want to damage the plug. I'd use some masking tape to mark on the screw the point at which you should stop screwing it in. Otherwise it can break through the plug.

Solid walls First, make sure you use the right plug for the type of solid wall. If you're using Rawlplugs in a solid wall and you're not well practised in using them, don't worry – just remember it can be easy to drill further into the wall than is required. To prevent this from happening, line the Rawlplug and drill bit alongside each other, grab a bit of masking tape and mark on the drill bit where the Rawlplug ends, leaving a few millimetres extra. Now you have an easy-to-see but easy-to-remove guide to where you should stop drilling.

Medium-weight or larger items on a hollow wall

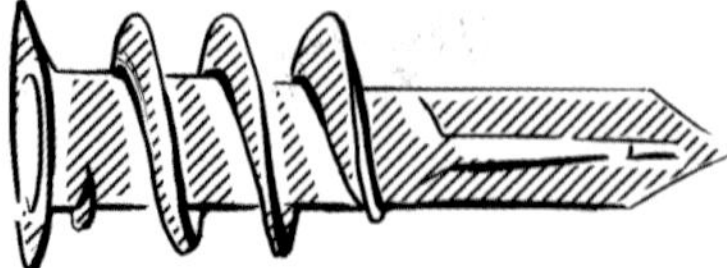

Spiral anchors are like the grown-up sister of the Rawlplug. They've lived abroad, kissed loads of boys and can handle a lot more. I prefer the metal variety over plastic or nylon as they are more durable. They can be screwed directly into the plasterboard with a regular or electric screwdriver. They create a sturdy home for your screw so that it will not be relying entirely on the support of the wall to stay in place. Instead, the screw's edges will be resting within the metal anchor. They come in a variety of sizes to support different weights, and some even come with picture-hanging hooks to use with them instead of screws.

Heavier items on hollow walls

We're talking about things such as large mirrors here, and you need to be incredibly careful. I would never hang something very heavy above a bed, for example, or at the top of a staircase – you never know what might cause these items to fall down over time.

Securing your chosen picture-hanging fitting into a stud will ensure the wall can take the weight of a heavier item. If there isn't one in a suitable place for your item to hang, the best thing is to note its weight and dimensions (if you bought it from a shop, chances are all these details will be in its product description online), then head to your local DIY store. Speak to someone there who will talk you through your options and give you the confidence and necessary guidance to do it yourself.

Solid walls If you have a solid wall, your options are great for heavier-weight items. However, the process might be more difficult. The challenge will be more about fitting the fixture rather than the hanger itself. Drilling into bricks and mortar, or making mistakes in wooden panelling or tiles, can be a total pain to fix. Be sure to research this fully but remember you can totally do it with the right tools, care and caution.

Preparing to hang your frame

If your frame is vintage or came without any fittings on the back with which to hang it up, here are my top tips for the options you have:

Saw tooth hangers

Ideal for lightweight canvases, these hangers are super easy to apply. You just fix them centrally to the back of the canvas frame at the top, with the nails provided. The canvas will then hang from a nail or hook on the wall. The packaging will tell you the maximum weight they can take – this can vary from 1 kg to 6 kg – and you can double them up for larger canvases.

Picture wire

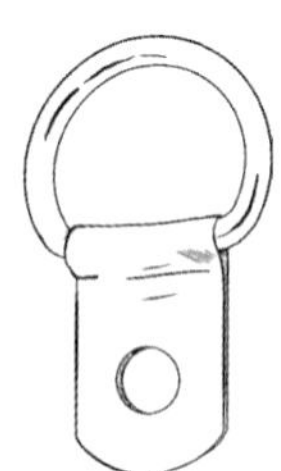

This is the preferred option of most professional framers – it stops the frame from warping like it does when you hang the picture from the board at the back – and is easy to do yourself. There are two common mistakes made when attaching hanging wire to a frame – the placement of the D-rings and securing the wire itself – but here is the best way to avoid both.

When placing your D-rings on the frame, the optimum position for them is one-third of the way down from the top. Any further and the frame will tilt forward.

Screw the D-rings into place. Many high-street frames have a lacquer coating that gives the appearance of real wood, but which can be hard to screw into at first. If your frame has such a coating, you can make things easier for yourself by using a bradawl (a long pointed tool for making holes in wood) to give your screw somewhere to start off. Just chip the lacquer with the end of the bradawl, or tap in the tip of a nail very gently, to make a hole for your screw to get going.

When tying on the picture wire, a common mistake is to wrap the wire haphazardly around itself. This can lead to a wonky frame that can't sit level; the wire is also likely to come loose over time. Here's how to do it correctly.

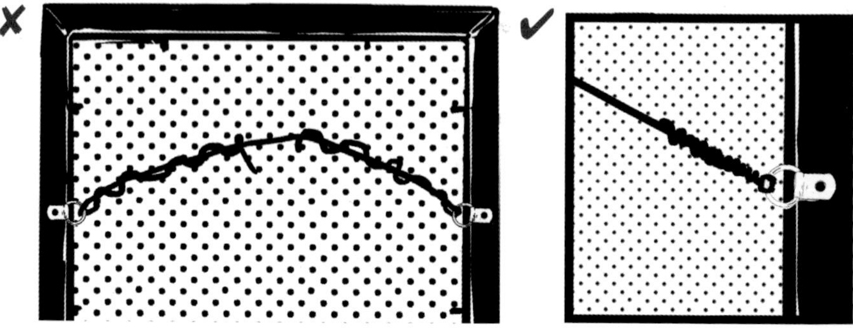

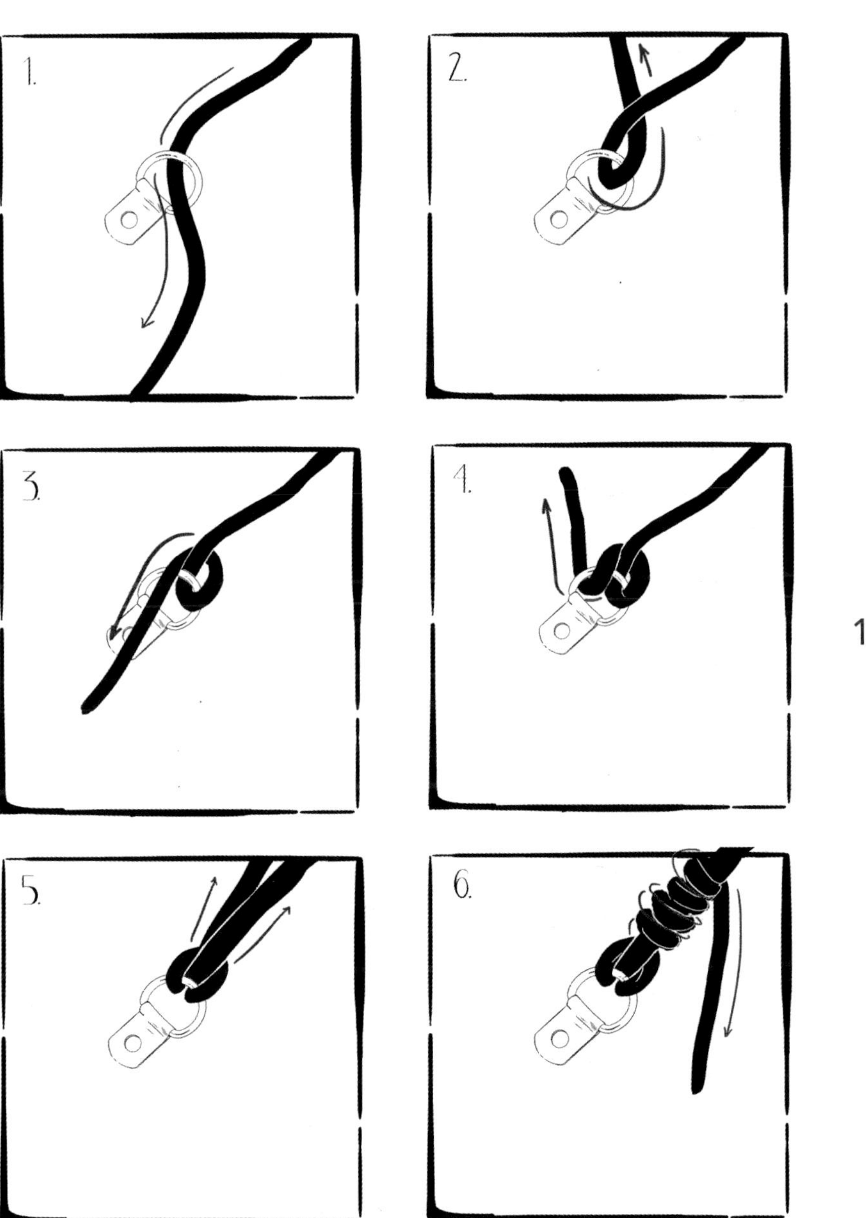
1.
2.
3.
4.
5.
6.

Hole-free hanging

If you're renting your property, or don't want to make holes in your walls, adhesive strips are a great way to hang framed pieces. However, although they get a lot of good press, there are some issues to be aware of when using them. I've often viewed properties for sale where strips have failed and the frame is now on the floor. This is likely the result of the adhesive not bonding well with either the frame or the wall. Make sure you check that the strips are the most suitable ones for what you're hanging and where you're hanging it. Most brands will have different options for indoor, outdoor, vinyl and more.

Always follow the pack's instructions to the letter – this includes the wall prep. Many people skip this step, thinking their walls can't be that dirty and it'll be grand to throw the strips straight on. Rest assured, if you light candles, open windows, cook and so on, you're guaranteed to have something sitting on the surface of your walls that could interfere with the strips sticking to them perfectly. For this reason always clean the wall as directed. Rubbing alcohol is usually recommended. Unlike some cleaning products, it doesn't leave behind any residue. Don't forget that rubbing alcohol can remove paint, though – use sparingly! On the subject of paint, don't apply these strips to freshly painted walls or wallpaper either.

Strips can also fail because the frame is too heavy for them. Don't underestimate the weight of your item – I always go with a stronger strip than I need, to be on the safe side. There is a wide range of them suited to a variety of different weights so choose carefully.

Sometimes the strips won't live up to expectations for reasons beyond your control. High humidity and temperatures can affect how well they bond to surfaces so make sure you're aware of the manufacturer's guidelines for their strips to work at their best.

As well as being really useful in rental properties these handy strips can be great if you want to experiment with a hanging pattern or particular location for an artwork, but I'd always err on the side of caution. Never use them to hang something over a bed or in an area that could risk harm to anyone below should they fail, and never use them for anything that is fragile or difficult to replace should it fall and get damaged.

Planning your frame placement

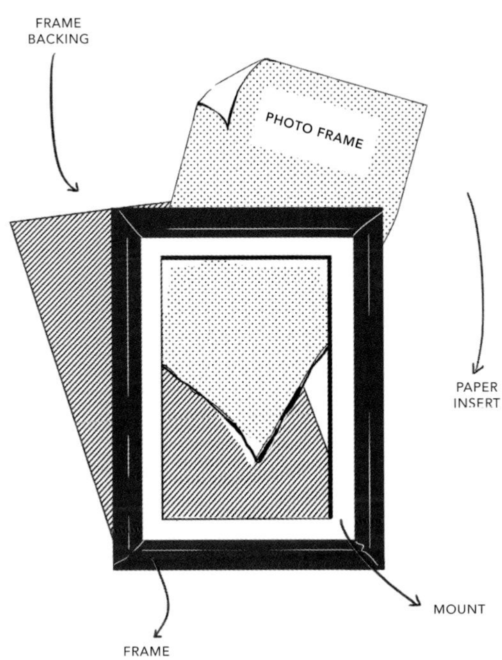

If you're planning a feature wall or hanging multiple frames in close proximity to each other, here's a tip to help you experiment with layouts without drilling multiple holes in your wall. Inside new picture frames you'll usually find a piece of display paper that you throw away before putting your own image inside. Hold on to it! It's almost the same size as the item you'll be hanging minus the thickness of the frame.

If the frame is very thin you might be able to skip the next part and do things by eye, but if it's a thick frame try this:

To increase the size of the paper to the same dimensions as the frame, grab some wide masking tape and apply a border on all four sides. You can buy super-wide masking tape in most DIY stores or, if you only have standard-size masking tape, you can overlap strips – the key here is to make it even wider and longer than the full size of your frame to begin with.

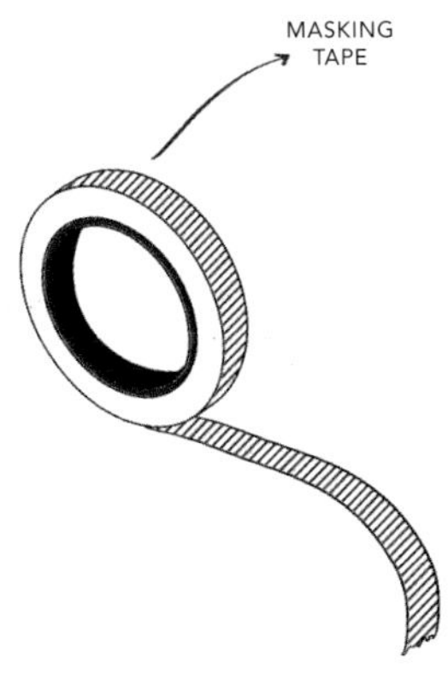

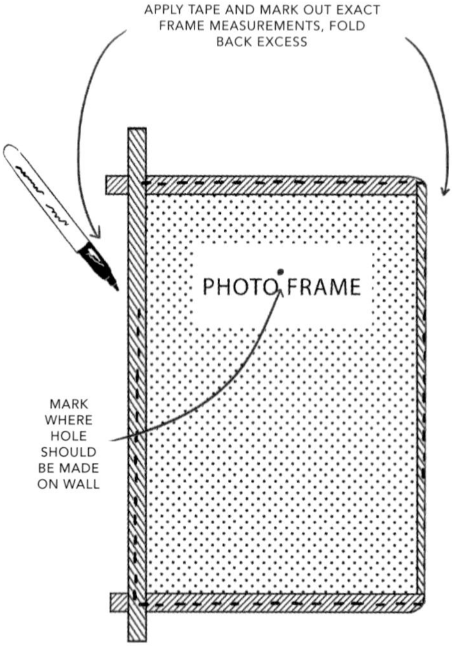

APPLY TAPE AND MARK OUT EXACT FRAME MEASUREMENTS, FOLD BACK EXCESS

PHOTO FRAME

MARK WHERE HOLE SHOULD BE MADE ON WALL

Place your frame over the paper and draw around it. Fold back any excess tape along these lines so that the paper-and-masking-tape 'frame' is now the same size as your actual frame. *Et voilà*, you have a dummy frame. If some sticky parts of tape are still exposed at the back, this is great as they will help you stick it to the wall later.

Next, mark on your dummy frame where the wire will sit on your chosen picture hanging fixture. If there's a hanger already attached to your frame, mark it in exactly the same place on the dummy frame.

TIP

A common mistake when nailing a picture hook to the wall is to drive the nail into the point where your pencil marking is. The pencil indicates the part of the hook where the *wire* will sit, not the *nail*. Some nails on picture-hanging hooks can sit up to 1 cm from the hook, so take this into account or you'll throw off your desired look.

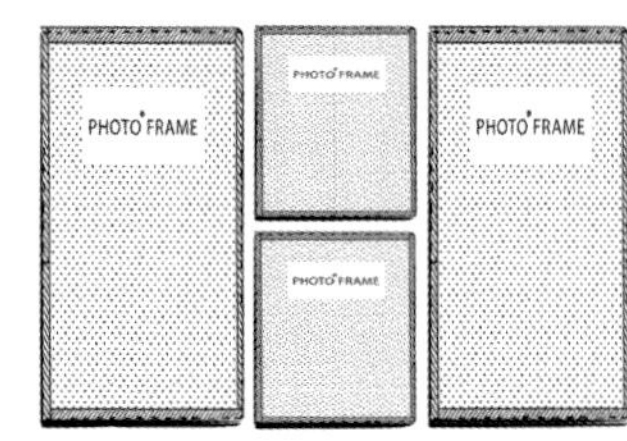

If you're trying to decide how to arrange multiple frames on your wall, make a dummy frame for each one and play around with their positioning on the wall. You'll be able to see if they sit well together and move them around until they're just perfect. When you're happy with your final positions, take a pencil and poke its tip through each dummy frame to mark the wall behind at the point at which the frame will meet its fixture. Once you take the paper away you will have the locations of the picture hangers marked for all your frames.

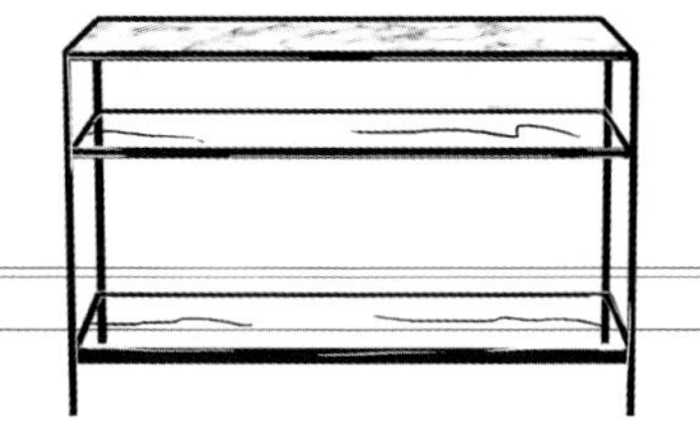

TIP

There are a few accessories on the market to help prolong the life of your frames. You can buy raised stickers called bumpers that you affix to each bottom corner of the frame. They're usually made of rubber, plastic or felt and lift the frame away from the wall the tiniest bit so that air can flow behind it. This stops moisture gathering at the back of the frame (hi, mould!). They also grip the wall so that once you set the frame's position it doesn't move. I always put these on first so that if you need to apply hangers such as D-rings or saw tooth hangers, you can see clearly which is the bottom of the frame and work away accordingly.

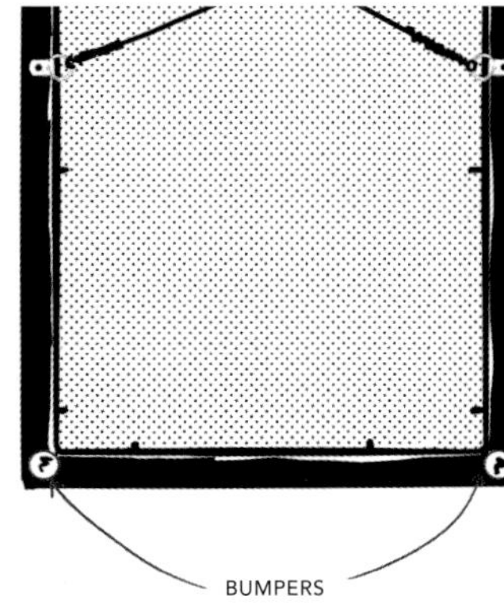

Replacing Lightbulbs

Although this seems like a simple task to many, it's still worth covering as not all lightbulbs are straightforward to change.

#SAFEISCHIC

Before you attempt to change any bulb, make sure the light is off. If you're not sure, turn off its circuit at your fuse box (see pages 18–20). Bulbs generate a lot of heat so make sure you leave enough time for the bulb to cool down before touching it – around 20 minutes should do the trick. To reach any bulbs up high, only ever stand on something secure to reach them, such as a step ladder. If your ceilings are particularly high and you have to stretch, have someone hold your ladder.

Know your bases

The first thing you'll need to do is remove the old bulb. Here are the standard bulb bases found around the home and how they can be removed:

Bayonets

A B22 is the most popular bayonet bulb and the 'regular' bulb that you will be most familiar with in the home. The number after the B relates to the diameter of the cap. Smaller versions will start with the letters SB but are rarely for domestic use. The bayonet's distinguishing feature is the two lugs that stick out of its base to hold it in place. Here you just need to hold the fitting with one hand, push the bulb *very* gently, twist it anticlockwise and pull it out.

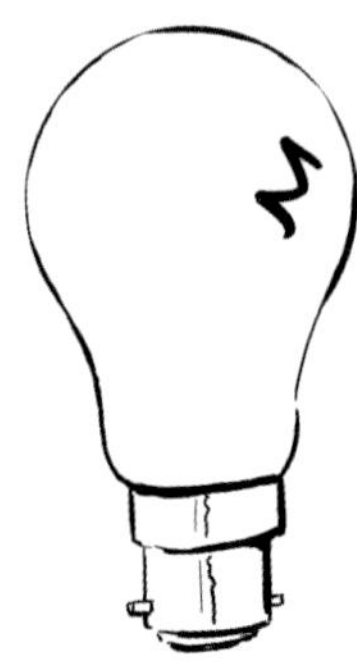

Edison/screw-ins

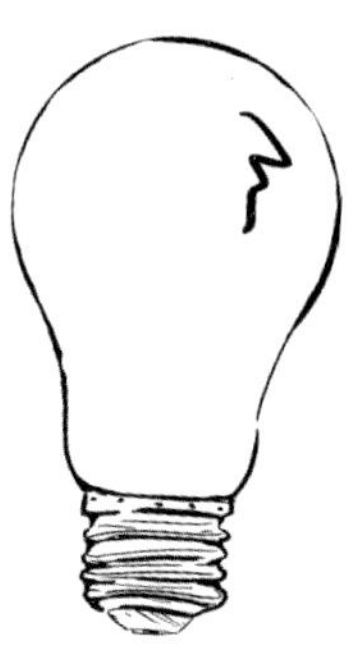

Edison (or E) bulbs have screw bases. (Yas! They are named after Thomas Edison.) E27 is the most popular type. Again, the numbers after the E relate to the diameter of the cap. Smaller versions used in lamps, chandeliers (oh, honey) and so on start with the prefix SE. Starting to see the pattern here? To remove them, unscrew them in an anticlockwise direction.

Spotlights and downlights

At work, 'a bulb has blown' is one repair request I receive a lot from tenants. Changing bulbs during the course of a tenancy isn't usually up to the landlord or part of the lease terms. It *is* something, however, that can be done to help out tenants and as a gesture of goodwill. I've realized this request comes from some tenants having no idea how to change ceiling bulbs and, in many cases, they will live without a working bulb for a lot of their tenancy. Today we learn!

Ceiling lights, other than the traditional pendant lights that take Edison and bayonet bulbs, can be a little scary, as they appear trickier to change than they are. The good news is that most of them will take the same two types of bulbs and it's just their casing design that sets them apart. This casing design is created to throw light in different ways so let's understand these a little more.

First up are the lights that are attached to the ceiling:

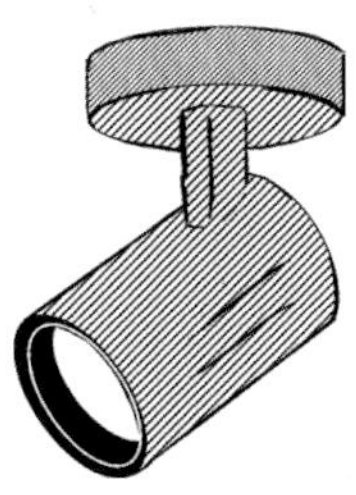

Spotlights are moveable lights, usually on a track or fitting where you can adjust the focus of a light's beam so that it shines on to something in particular. They're great for focusing on artwork or areas where more light is required for tasks, such as kitchen counter tops. They're also a great option if you have only one location for a light fitting but want to throw light in different directions, as their beam can be moved around.

Then there are lights with circular trims and a bulb inside, which fall under the blanket term of 'recessed lights', as they sit inside a hole in the ceiling.

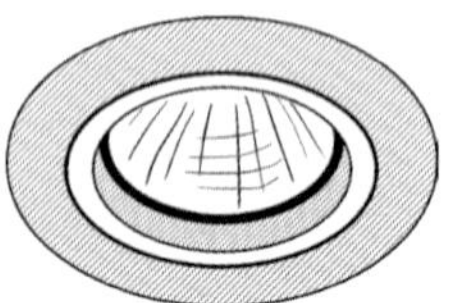

Downlights are the main type of recessed light we see in homes, and are in a fixed position in the ceiling, throwing light on what is directly below them. They're often mistakenly called spotlights, but now you know. They're super common in living rooms and kitchens as they cast a wide beam but have a minimal appearance.

Finally, there are adjustable downlights that you can push to angle the direction of their beam, but are still recessed – unlike spotlights.

As I mentioned, no matter what the fitting appearance, these lights all usually require one of two types of bulb: one you twist to lock into place, the other you push to lock. It's super easy to know which replacement bulb you need if you have the old one already in place. If you don't, don't worry – the fitting's bulb socket can help you figure out which type it requires. Here are the two bases for the two bulb styles.

The channels on this base show it's a twist-to-lock bulb.

These two holes indicate a bulb that has straight pins that will click into place.

Let's get to know these two bulb types a little better …

Twist-to-lock bulbs

The GU10 is the most common downlight and spotlight bulb. Its most distinguishing feature is its pins, which look like a pair of legs wearing a chunky Miu Miu-esque platform shoe and which help to secure the bulb in place once twisted into the base. (The '10' indicates the number of millimetres between the pins.)

You need to twist these bulbs anticlockwise to remove them and clockwise to lock them into the fitting.

Push-to-lock bulbs

Also known as MR16s, GU5.3s are often confused with G10s because they look the same when viewed from below. Their bases also have pins but they're straight and thinner than a GU10, with no Miu Mius.

A GU10 will happily work with the 120 volts supplied by the mains but a GU5.3 requires a lower voltage, which means it needs a transformer or LED driver to reduce the voltage going to it. This transformer part is hidden above your ceiling and is wired in between the bulb and the mains cable to reduce the voltage to the 12 volts it needs.

To remove and insert GU5.3s simply push them in and out like a button.

Recessed lighting

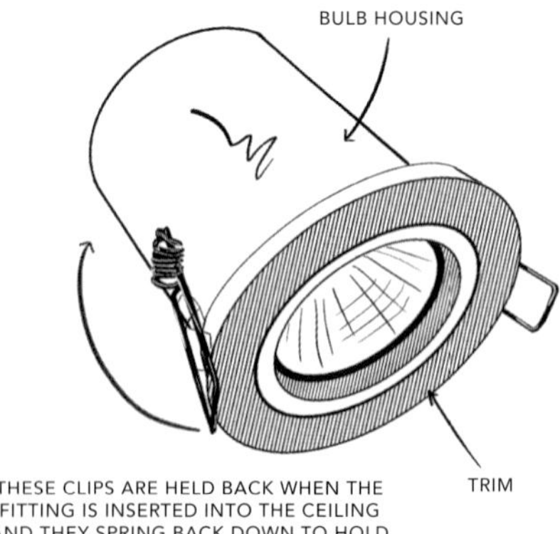
BULB HOUSING
TRIM
THESE CLIPS ARE HELD BACK WHEN THE FITTING IS INSERTED INTO THE CEILING AND THEY SPRING BACK DOWN TO HOLD THE FITTING IN PLACE

Bulbs in spotlights are pretty straightforward to change, as the bulb is usually exposed and easy to access. Recessed lights, on the other hand, can be confusing, so it's important to get to grips with the component parts of these fittings before trying to change a bulb. The main thing to understand is that the trim is our focus and not the bulb housing itself. Here are the differences between the two:

The trim

This is like a frame for the bulb and can be chosen to match the aesthetic of your room – you can even get one with a protective layer for above a shower. It's the only other part you see aside from the bulb when everything is in place. On some recessed lights you need to take part of the trim or trim wire off to gain access to the bulb.

Bulb housing and clips

You can't see these parts from the outside. The bulb housing protects and holds the bulb in place, and is then held inside the ceiling by the tension supplied by two spring-loaded clips. It's important to note that you won't be removing this casing or pulling the clips out of the ceiling just to change the bulb.

#SAFEISCHIC

The clips that hold the bulb housing in place are pretty dangerous as they spring down like a mouse trap. *Be careful* with these. Never pull the whole fitting out of the ceiling unless you know what you're doing and why. If you do, then hold the clips in place until you can slowly release them once the downlight is out. For the love of god, heed my warning on this.

It's important to note that not all trims are the same and most will cover the bulb slightly, so we need to know how to remove them to get to the bulb. Here are the most common trim styles and how they work:

Trim and wire clip

These clips are usually what hold the bulb in the correct place. Access to the bulb is easy once you remove the wire. To do this, pinch its two ends together and it will come out of the fitting. Your bulb will follow, attached to its socket, which will be wired into the ceiling. Hold on to the socket, twist the bulb anticlockwise or pull gently and it should then come out. Repeat in reverse to secure the replacement bulb.

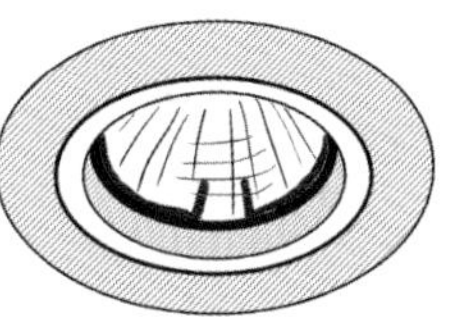

Twist trim fitting

There are usually two trims on this fitting: the outside one is like a regular trim and the other has grips. The latter is removable for access to the bulb. Place two fingers on two grips and turn in an anticlockwise direction – the trim will loosen and drop down with the bulb and socket still attached. Hold the socket and twist the bulb anticlockwise to remove it, or pull gently. The bulb is attached to the trim by a fastening like a hair clip, so simply slide the bulb to one side and it should come out of the setting. Slide the new one in and refit the trim.

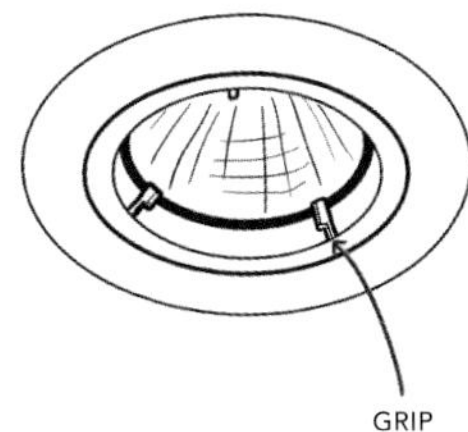

Single or double rim with no grips or wire

If you don't see a metal clip, or the grips that indicate a twistable rim, try pushing the bulb to see if it clicks out, or press two fingers against it gently and twist anticlockwise to see if this releases it. If this doesn't work or you can't get a good grip, you'll need a suction cup, which is really inexpensive and easy to buy online as well as in stores. When you push the suction cup against the bulb, it will grip it and allow you to twist or pull as needed. As we've already seen, it's difficult to tell whether your bulb is a MR16/GU5.3 or a GU10 when it's in the ceiling, as the bulbs look the same from below. This means you might not know whether to twist and pull (GU10) or just pull (MR16/GU5.3). Go for a gentle pull first – if it pops out then you know it's an MR16/GU5.3 as its prongs are straight. If that doesn't work, try a twist and pull.

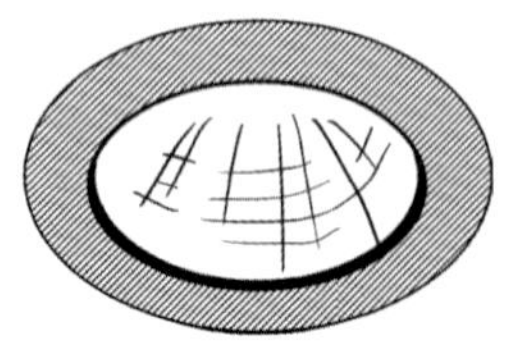

Tube lights

Tube lights, such as the G5, are now found mainly under kitchen cabinets to give more light to worktops. Here again, the number after the G represents the diameter between pins in millimetres.

These bulbs have two pins on either end and the bulb itself is super delicate. I find that holding it gently between two fingers and rolling it can unhook it from its position. Try turning it away from you first, as this is the most common fitting. I've also found that when I'm in a new property and it looks as if these bulbs have blown, I've twisted them slightly and they've started to work again – they were just in the wrong position. Try this before forking out for replacements.

Now that you know how to replace the most common types of bulbs, having got to know their bases and fittings, it's also important to learn about the bulbs themselves. There's a fabulous section on pages 181–9 that takes us through lightbulb shapes, colours and what the terminology on the box really means. Being armed with this information will help you choose the perfect lighting for your home.

Replacing Broken Window Handles

Over the years, prepping properties for tenants, one thing I picked up quickly was that I could save a lot of cash by learning how to replace broken UPVC window handles. UPVC is a type of plastic and accounts for the majority of modern double-glazed window frames. Over time their handles can break due to wear and tear but they're a DIY dream: all you need for the job is a replacement handle and a drill or screwdriver.

When you move in or out of a new property, the issue of lost window keys or broken window locks might come up. It poses a safety risk and many renters end up losing a chunk of their deposit when the handles then have to be replaced by a contractor. It's actually such a simple thing to fix yourself, so let's learn how!

First of all you need a new handle. It's important to find the right replacement as you won't usually be able to return your purchase once the packaging is open. There's also a safety issue if you install the wrong handle and it gets stuck. There are many different types of handle out there, so you need to know which parts of them have universal measurements and which will be specific to your window.

Identifying which replacement handle you need

The two main types of window handles you'll find in your home are espagnolette (always shortened to espag, thankfully) and cockspur.

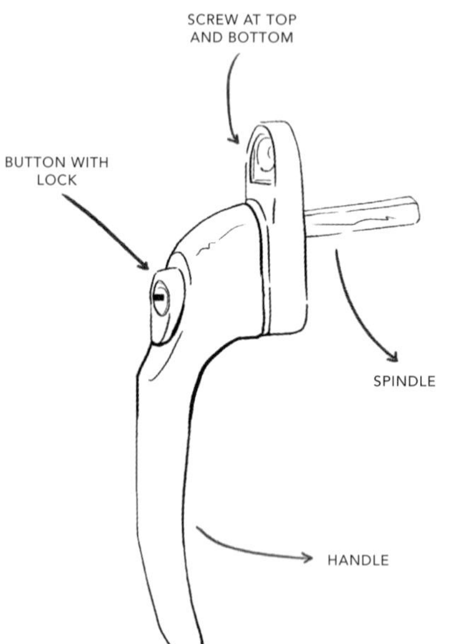

Espag handles have a long spindle that slots into a locking system which runs along the length of the window frame, securing it in more than one location. Cockspur handles, on the other hand, work independently of the window and lock it in just one place – at the handle.

Espag handles

There are two types of espag handles: cranked and inline.

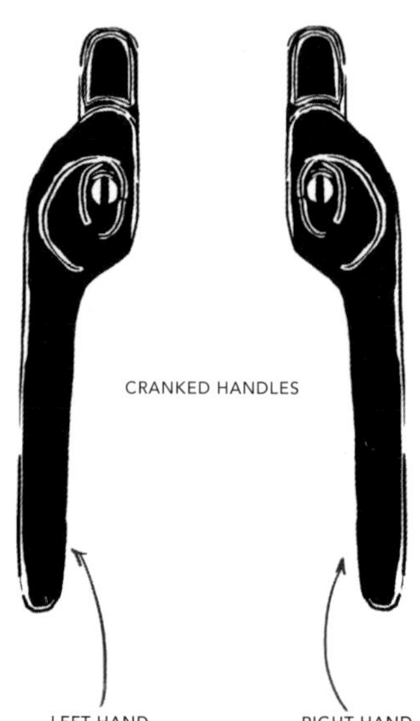

Crank it up

A cranked window handle is specifically designed either for a left- or right-hand opening window. You need to be super sure which one you have so that you buy the correct replacement.

Get in line

Inline handles are the universal handles of the espag world and can open left- and right-hand opening windows. When shopping for an espag window handle the spindle measurement is very important. Many people will bring the broken handle to the DIY store not realizing that it's the spindle that determines the size you buy.

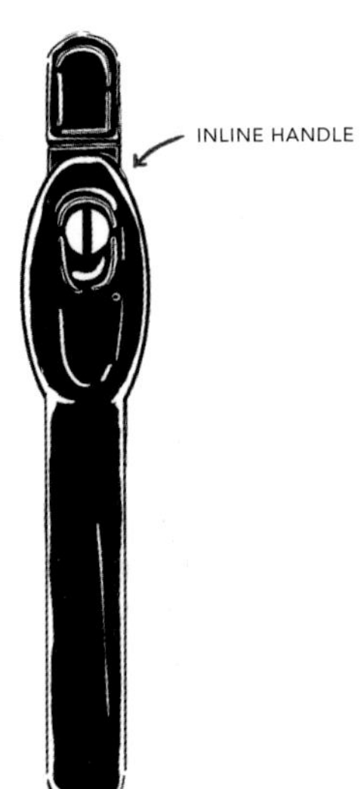
INLINE HANDLE

Cockspur handles

This girl differs from the other two as she doesn't have a spindle. Instead, this wee triangle protruding from her handle is what fastens the window shut. Once she's slid into place the window cannot be opened.

As mentioned before, it's always best to remove your handle entirely and take to a store in order to buy the correct replacement. However, if you're buying online you need to know the stack measurement. Here's how to take it.

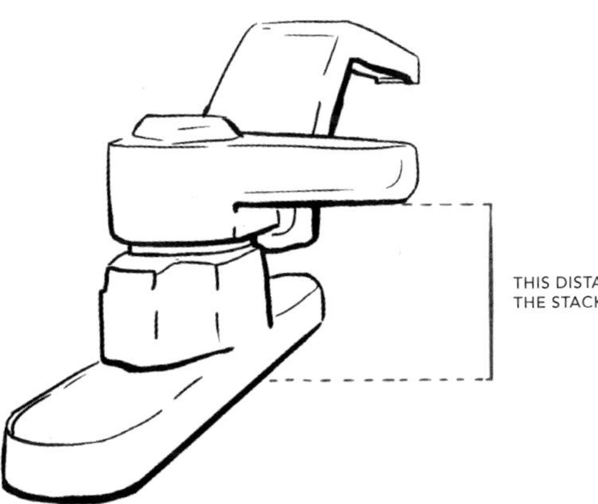
THIS DISTANCE TELLS YOU
THE STACK MEASUREMENT

Changing the handle

If you're unsure where to start, take a closer look at the hardware currently in situ. There will probably be some branding on it that will help you determine the manufacturer. If you have no joy, look for little stickers on the window as these might hold a clue. You can then do an online search for the name of the manufacturer followed by the window handle model, and you'll find some options for price comparison (remember always to check delivery costs first to see if the cheapest really is the cheapest overall!).

If clues continue to elude you, experience has taught me that you probably just need a universal, basic handle, which will be easy to find. Most DIY stores, even small ones, stock them.

The first step when changing a handle is to remove the old one. On older or more basic windows, the screws that hold the handles in place are usually exposed and therefore easy to locate and remove.

Some more aesthetically pleasing handles have a plate or cover that hides the fittings. You usually only have to twist it to the side to expose the screws.

Once you've removed the handle, screw in the new one and test that it is fully functional.

Told you it was easy!

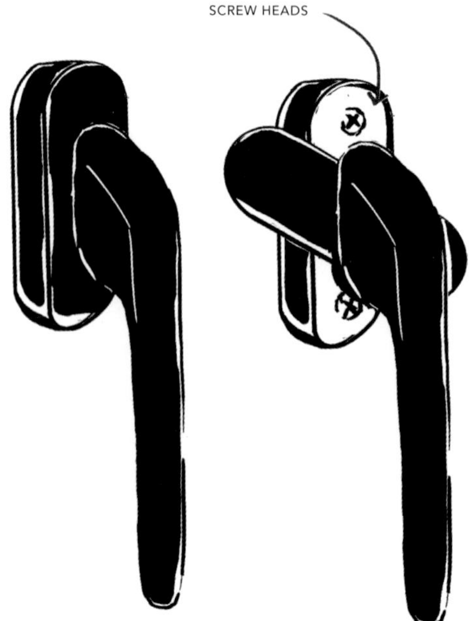

Now that you're armed with a little knowledge in how to fix those little niggles we often turn a blind eye to, it's time to immerse yourself in the joy that is adapting your home to suit your life, and how you can help it help you feel more relaxed, fulfilled and at one with your space. I hope the next chapter will fill you with a passion for creating a home that works for you and ensures the tasks you do often are smooth and enjoyable to perform. You're about to begin my favourite chapter so please, get comfortable (lipstick/wine/vitamin-packed juice optional) and let's get ready to consider the art of décor and zoning (*shriekkkkk!*).

6. DÉCOR GALORE

I'm super passionate about zoning. Perhaps it comes from living and working in so many small spaces in London, where rooms need to serve multiple purposes but not feel cramped. Perhaps it comes from seeing how people's needs, including my own, have changed over time. Many of us require a workspace at home these days, as well as somewhere to work out, and we're more aware of the benefits of a calm space with minimal clutter. Our lives are busier, our roles have evolved and our need for order in the domestic sphere is greater than ever. Or perhaps I'm addicted to the buzz I get from the wonderful difference zoning can make to a room as well as our routines.

Helping Your Home Work for You

I believe that you should always feel like your home, your space, your sanctuary is working for you and not against you. That it should suit your needs no matter its size. That it should readily provide the surfaces you need when you need them, the right lighting for different moods or tasks, and adequate and easy-to-use storage. It should offer you comfort, and above all, enhance how you live.

In order to do this, you need to assess the needs you have that you want your home to fulfil. This in turn will help you figure out your zones. Every home and every person will be different in terms of their 'must-have' areas, but the key is knowing what they are. This will help you decide what zones you need and how to edit each one so that it serves its purpose effortlessly and continuously.

One thing I feel strongly about is that when you're frustrated by a space, you're less likely to treat it well. You don't see its value, you resent it and, instead, you think about the next space you may have.

However, when you invest your time and focus on setting up your home to work to its full potential, you in turn feel more responsible for helping to keep it working that way. When you enjoy your space and use every part of it well, it will encourage you to repair, maintain and look after it.

Managing Space

They say if you can't manage €100 well, you won't be able to manage €1 million well. I think the same goes for space. People often think they need a bigger house, a conversion, another room to help them live well. If you're feeling similarly frustrated, you must first put on a coat of red lipstick and something that makes you feel fabulous, take a seat and assess your current space with a positive mindset. We often think we need more room when instead we need to cleverly tszuj what we already have to make it work for us.

If you learn to align your home with how you like to live and want to live, not only will you be more content in the present, but when you do get that bigger space in the future, it will work even better for you and not just be about being able to house more stuff. Setting up your home to help you live well will also encourage great habits. 'I want to eat better, I want to do more yoga, I want to be earlier for work' – all of these things can be more achievable if your home is ready to help you do them.

Zoning is also fabulous for renters. Although there are more of us than ever before, we truly are the forgotten ones when it comes to interiors advice. Cleverly organizing the space we have, however, gives us an opportunity to feel ownership over what we're paying for. I think the days when renters would live meekly within a landlord's walls, begrudging the décor, are over, because it's not just about what a space looks like – you can easily make some changes to appreciate the space you rent when you see it suiting your life. (That said, I will always begrudge a magnolia wall.)

How to Zone?

We're now more aware than ever about the importance of decluttering our spaces and how to reduce the amount of stuff we own by recycling or donating things we no longer need. I don't have to tell you how to go about doing this – some amazing women have paved the way and continue to show us the best ways to store, clean and downsize. Instead, I'm going to focus on the art of zoning and getting the best use out of your space.

The great thing about zoning is that you can start with what you have – you don't necessarily need to buy anything new. It's all about allocating a use to a space and providing that space with everything it needs to carry out its purpose. You don't need to be moving into a new place or own where you live to start zoning, as it needs minimal work. Giving your home – or a room – some careful consideration can be so much fun and the benefits you reap from it can be instant.

What zones do I need?

Just because you've seen a wonderful mud room or walk-in wardrobe online doesn't mean you need one. Usually living rooms, dining areas, bedrooms and workspaces are the zones that will be used most. Around these core zones you can add some more lifestyle elements, such as a clutter-free space for yoga, perhaps. Maybe your thing is drawing, practising darts, tap-dancing, making margaritas … and so on.

Remember, a zone can be any size, it just needs to enhance the way you live so you can concentrate on being fabulous. It can be a counter space in your kitchen that you arrange to make cooking a breeze and a task you enjoy. Or a dressing table with your favourite skincare products laid out in order so that you can follow your routine with ease. It can be a bedside space where everything required is within arm's reach, or it can be an entire living area zoned to perfection for your evening needs.

Everyone will need different zones and some are far more obvious than others, such as those where you sleep or cook. However, there are two less obvious ones I'd love you to consider as you draw up a mental list.

Switching on

What helps you at the start of your day? What ten minutes or so do you use to switch on? Is it breakfast, a workout, catching up on social media, reading the news, or dressing to suit your mood while taking in a podcast? Whatever it is, your home should have a dedicated zone that helps you to switch on easily. Take a moment to think about what your ideal switch-on would be each day. Next, compare it to what you currently do each morning.

Think about how you can enhance your morning ritual with some order and to bring it closer to your ideal switch-on, the one that you know would lead to a better day. Consider what should be within easy reach. If it's a coffee and an online scroll, for instance, there should be somewhere you can seamlessly make the perfect cup then sit down comfortably. You have enough going on – your switch-on shouldn't be something that's a struggle, spent searching for what you need, sitting uncomfortably or feeling out of control. Mornings can be hard enough as it is!

Switching off – finding your goddess zone

Is there a space you associate with winding down? One that helps you switch off?

I'm talking about during stressful times and moments when you need some Zen, as well as relaxing at the end of a long day. It's super important to feel that your home has somewhere – a goddess space – where you can decompress and calm your mind.

There's always been huge focus on getting motivated and getting charged – a get-up-and-get-'em approach to life has always been seen as something we should aspire to having. Instead, I think what's even more important and powerful, and needs to come first, is the opposite. What will actually help you to set and achieve your goals, and lead you to be more Zen in general, is learning how to switch off properly, rest your mind and give yourself a break. My mother always says answers never come to a busy mind … and she's never wrong.

When creating a zone that helps you to switch off, it doesn't need to be a large area or one that has a single use. It could be somewhere you use differently during the day, but with a few moves it instantly becomes a space just for you – your goddess zone. It could be an area of the floor in your living room where you can roll out a yoga mat, for example, or an armchair to read in.

To boost the calm atmosphere of your goddess zone, you can add and remove as you see fit, until you feel it provides what you need. A lamp with a soft warm light will give the perfect glow for a Zen moment or if you use your switch-off for reading or drawing. Clearing any clutter near by can help make the area even more enjoyable and stress-free. There are things that will enhance a goddess zone, such as candles and comfortable soft furnishings, and things that will hamper it, such as piles of paperwork or post which can remind you that you have a to-do list.

My goddess zone is an armchair in my living room. It's not one that faces the TV or one I sit in a lot during the day, but I've come to

associate it with being my goddess zone. This means that when I sit in it, I do so with the purpose of calming my mind without even realizing it any more. I've gradually placed things that make me feel calm and happy near by and I keep it clutter-free. By creating this small space I now find it easier to switch my mind to a Zen setting, even during hectic times.

What, where

Once you've decided what zones you would like to feature in your home, you can start to map out where they will be and how they should be arranged. Begin with the biggest zones, such as where you will dine, sleep and hang out, for example. These will involve the largest pieces of furniture and so need more consideration.

Unless you need to make use of a large open floor area on a daily basis, a common mistake when organizing a room is to line the walls with furniture. You're then left with a big space in the middle that isn't used to its full potential. Poorly positioned furniture can also mean you're left sitting facing the kitchen once you've finished dinner and are trying to enjoy the rest of your evening, which can prevent you from truly winding down. The same goes for when your workspace is in the same area you use to switch off – try to face these zones away from each other so you are not reminded of any to-dos.

Noting non-negotiables

The first things to figure out when considering placement in a new space are the non-negotiables. There will always be places where furniture cannot go or has to go. When you're planning a space it's a good idea to open all the doors, cupboards and windows so you can see where certain items of furniture would hamper them from functioning.

One non-negotiable in the living room, for example, will be the location of the TV outlet. If I'm letting a furnished property, I'll never know whether a future tenant will want a TV or not, but it's always safer to put in a simple unit next to that outlet point, then work outwards and arrange other furniture around it. Even if a TV is never used there, that unit can still be a great display area and focal point for the living-room zone. Sockets can also dictate where a bed is placed and where appliances will go.

Once I have my non-negs noted, I can start to think about which zones can go around them. The dining area will usually be near the kitchen, for ease. An armchair might be near a plug socket so it can have a reading lamp near by. Perhaps you'd like a unit by a window for plants and so on.

Setting some boundaries

We know a zone is an area with items specifically placed in it to help that space serve its purpose, but how else do we define a zone other than by its contents? When I'm creating my zones, I like to start with what I call zone boundaries. These are not physical walls, instead they are things that create visual boundaries so we sense when we're entering a new zone. This is especially useful in a single room that serves multiple purposes – now very common in apartments, where there will be one room that will be a kitchen/living/dining area.

Over the page is an example of one room zoned to have four uses. Note the items used to close off areas subtly from others and also to enhance the zone itself.

I always find it easiest to start with the placement of the sofa in the living room. It's usually the largest item of furniture and where it goes will normally depend on the non-neg position of the TV outlet. The back of a couch can easily serve as a low wall and a fabulous zone boundary. Try pulling the sofa away from the wall – if that's where you

have it – and seeing if it can work with its back to the zones where you 'work', such as the kitchen. Not only will it create a zone boundary, facing away from the other areas of the room will help you to relax more when sitting.

Another great way to divide a room is to place a sideboard or shelving unit along the back of the couch. This gives you another boundary, but one where you can also store and display items. With these, use a bit of cop on and the anchors provided, and don't stack the heaviest items on top if the unit is tall. You want to avoid any topples.

As well as large items of furniture, rugs are also a brilliant way to define zones in a multi-use room. A flat-weave one is fab to place under the table and chairs – it sets the dining area apart from the kitchen or anything else it shares the space with, establishing it as a separate zone. The reason these rugs work well here is because they don't have a pile, which means food and spills are less likely to be absorbed, and most of these kinds of rugs can be laundered. An added bonus is that they're much cheaper than pile rugs and are available in larger sizes. Just remember to secure them well with a rug grip so they don't pose a trip or slip hazard.

Speaking of dining spaces, small ones in a multi-purpose room work really well with either an extendable or circular table. I love a circular table in particular as it feels as if all of those dining are in a little bubble, facing into the centre. You can add more chairs easily and there is no 'head' of the table or anyone having to sit at a corner. They're also nicer to sit at solo or in a pair as they don't feel like they 'need' to be filled as rectangular tables can do.

Kitchen zoning

A small note here on kitchen zoning as it will be a zone everyone will have to consider. Often kitchen counters can be cluttered with things that are common kitchen items and supposed to 'go' there. If you haven't put sugar in your tea since the nineties, why have an empty sugar tin on your counter? Stop and think about what you need and will use in *your* zone. Storage permitting, I'd only place small appliances that you use on a daily basis on the counter – your kettle or coffee machine, for example – and store everything else away. Next, zone the counter tops, placing the items for that zone above and below the work surface.

The best way to begin zoning your kitchen is to think about what tasks you do most or want to enjoy doing more. For example, the act of making hot drinks seamlessly involves little more than placing your cups, teas and coffees in the cupboard above the kettle. Apply this thinking to whatever way you use your kitchen. If you're a regular ramen girl, keep large bowls, chopsticks, noodles and herbs in the one zone. It will not only help you prepare food more safely as you won't be leaning over lit stoves, or reaching back and forth for utensils, it can also cut down on the time you spend doing the job. In my opinion, a task done with ease becomes a task to please.

How you store and organize items within your cupboards is your business – advice and trends change constantly. I'm less about it all looking perfect and more about it working well for the individual. For example, if you regularly use taller bottles, such as those which oils often come in, it's pointless storing them at the back of the cupboard and knocking over other items every time you reach for them. Instead, I'd suggest arranging items in descending order of size from left to right, instead of from the back to the front. This way everything is still clearly visible and less likely to knock over other things on the way out.

If you like to use baskets to group items together, go for ones with large gaps in them. You can still see what's inside them so you'll be reminded to use up what's in there. They're also harder for pests such as food moths to hide in than solid, bucket-like baskets. Low-rise baskets are also best as they stop us piling more recently purchased food on top and forgetting about the items at the bottom.

Kitchen display

Transferring all your food and snacks from their packaging and into glass jars and containers is a huge trend right now, but here's my advice. First of all, the packaging your food comes in has been designed to keep it as fresh as possible for as long as possible. If you like to have glass jars on display to store something bought in an airtight container, make sure your new glass container is airtight too. If an item's packaging had holes in it to breathe, or it can't handle sunlight, be aware of this when transferring it to a new home.

Always cut the best-before date off the box or packet and tape it to the bottom of the jar – it'll be easier to remove than a label. You'll then know when that item is past its best. I get that rows of glass jars filled with pretty snacks look great in celebrity kitchens, but the reality can be a lot of rotting food and biscuits that go stale.

We're now able to do product refills at stores to cut down on packaging, which is fabulous – we can choose to store our food in a more environmentally friendly way. Again, just remember to be aware of what needs to be kept airtight and so on, so that your food lasts longer.

Enhancing a Zone

Once your boundaries and main items of furniture are in place, there are some really easy-to-follow ways to enhance a zone. Here are some of my favourites …

She's up the walls

In a small room, or one with multiple large zones, the walls are your best friend. Here, you can easily bring your own taste to a room or vibe to a zone as there's more space for you to add to the walls, compared to the floor. If you can't go out, go up! Look at the use of frames below; it draws the eye up so you feel like the room is bigger than it is.

Hanging pictures can be an inexpensive way to add so much to a space. If you're renting and don't want to – or can't – nail or screw anything into the walls, check out my picture-hanging guide on pages 132–45. Adhesive strips are a great temporary solution and, if used correctly, can really help you add your own style by hanging a variety of items or frames. Remember, the contents and the frames themselves needn't break the bank, and you can also swap out the contents as you wish to give a whole new look to the space.

Plant power

Fabulous! Especially when you're renting! Plants are a wonderful addition to any home, for the joy they bring to the eye and their air-purifying abilities. They can help define boundaries and indicate the start of a zone as well as providing colour and a softness that furniture can't offer. Best of all, they can easily move with you to your next home.

Lights out

Lamps can be a great way to set the focus on one zone. During the day, their height can provide a boundary and in the evening, if your space is multi-purpose, you can switch off the kitchen lights and those in your work space, and just highlight the living room for a calm setting while the rest of the room is in darkness. Same goes for the dining area. If you can install an overhead light, or there is one already in place, this is fab, especially if it can be moved up and down so that the light can be cast over the whole table top. If you're renting, this might not be possible so a large arched floor lamp here can be a great choice. Remember to consider your table size when selecting your lamp and shade as you want the light cast over the entire table and not have some areas left in the dark.

Light and zoning go hand in hand, and later in this chapter I'll get into warm and cool lights, and how they can enhance a space further (see page 181), but here's a quick tip:

In a large room, one easy and cheap way to separate a kitchen from the living-room space is by using a cool light in the kitchen and warm lights in the living area. Even when all the lights are on, it still gives a feeling of two different spaces with two different functions.

Making up

Here's an important zone I'd like to take a moment to talk about. If you have a skincare routine (OMG, if you don't, start today) or a make-up moment in your day, you should have a zone to do it in. Somewhere you can easily access everything you need while you apply and dry. Taking time to care for your skin is a self-care moment. It should be enjoyed as much as possible, and be something to look forward to, even if it's just a couple of minutes before bed. You don't need a full-on dressing table set-up, but good lighting, a mirror and a wipe-clean surface (I wouldn't use anything antique or velour for tasks involving creams, lipsticks, mousses and so on – it will be a nightmare long term) are key.

As an aside, the other thing to be aware of is when your beauty products go out of date. I cannot stress this point enough. With such huge growth in the cosmetics industry, consuming and owning the same number of products as a professional make-up artist is now seen as completely normal because these products are now so easily accessible – and rather enjoyable. But collecting anything means you need to allocate a zone to store it in, so a plethora of cosmetics, whether we use them or not, needs dedicated storage.

Cosmetics are now being bought like clothing, meaning our bathrooms or dressing tables have become like wardrobes. They're piled high with bottles, compacts, highlighters and various other must-have items, meaning most dressing tables will also house a lot of products that are literally going stale. Unlike clothes, beauty products aren't designed to be stored for years and taken out for different occasions; they're formulated to be used frequently, and therefore used up before they go off. Any stored products will be getting closer and closer to a use-by date, dates that were put in place by European law to stop us from coming to harm by using a product that is past its best.

So how can we tell if something has gone off? All cosmetics are now required to have clear labelling that lets us know how long we can use the product for. Labelling for use-by dates on cosmetics is broken into two categories: those that need to be used within 30 months of manufacture and those that can last longer than 30 months. Each has a different symbol:

The first is the PAO (period after opening). The 'm' stands for months – fun fact: 'm' stands for months in many European languages, not just English. The number represents the number of months after opening that the product is designed to last for.

The BBE symbol indicates 'best before end'. This date is determined by when the product was manufactured and isn't influenced by when you first break the seal.

It might seem like a lot to think that a large percentage of your make-up could already be past its best, but here's a brilliant upside to culling your old products. A lot of brands will recycle your empties for you and reward you with free products or discounts for returning the empties! Have a look online to see who has such schemes before you dump anything – you could actually end up with a smaller, fresher selection and also be helping the environment.

Throwing shade (and light)

So let's talk more about using light to enhance our zones. The right choice of lighting can help us with tasks, set a great atmosphere and, if used correctly, can make a space feel bigger. It can transform how we feel in, and how we use, a space. For anyone who thinks otherwise, imagine your entire home has only harsh strip lighting throughout. How would you feel after a week spent living in it?

Lamps

When choosing lampshades there are some old-school rules about sizing – the main one being that your shade width should be double your base width. These days, most lamps and shades are sold as one, so it doesn't take too much consideration. However, if I'm buying them separately, or an unfavourable shade comes with a great base and I want to choose an alternative, I like to stick to making sure that the shade doesn't leave the bulb fitting exposed and that it doesn't overload the base, which could cause it to topple. After all, #safeischic.

When it comes to lamp designs, colours, textures and so on, for every rule you'll read there will be an absolute goddess breaking it beautifully, by ignoring rules and trusting her own style and taste. When choosing a 'look', go for something that you like – something that makes you think *yasss* whenever you see it. If you want an outrageous lamp to take centre stage, old heritage vibes, or something that blends in with your décor, just go for it. I love anything that looks as if it belonged in a Cleopatra-themed brothel, and I am yet to care if a visitor doesn't like it. If you stay with what is true to you, your whole home's vibe will come together perfectly. If you don't, you'll have odd corners and accessories that take away from the elements you love, stopping a true flow.

Here are some other things to consider when selecting a lamp.

Light and space If you have a small living room, tall lamps are brilliant for lengthening the room by brightening dark corners. Not only do they throw light around like a dream, their bases usually require very little room on the floor and the space they take up (from the elbow up) is rarely needed by anything else.

The illustration on the previous page shows how using just the central light on a small space can make it feel smaller as it's only highlighting the central floor.

If we pop a tall lamp in the far corner, however, our eye is drawn further back. This corner is now highlighted, giving a greater sense of space. It isn't interfering with the furniture already in place either, and now creates a new reading/Zenning/goddess zone (see opposite).

All shade Lampshades are designed to stop the glare of a bare lightbulb affecting our eyes, and have evolved over time to enhance a room's décor and cast light in a favourable way. There's so much I could say here but I'll keep it simple. How your shade will work for you is pretty much down to its shape and its transparency.

If it's light in colour and made of a translucent material that lets the light pour out, this will give the room a soft atmosphere and a glow, as well as brightening it overall. These types of shade tend to give off a calming vibe and can add a cosy feeling to a space, especially if the shade is dark in colour. If it's made of a more opaque material, has a denser weave or has a blackout backing, the light will be more directional – whatever is placed above or below will be highlighted.

The shape of a lampshade can also be something to consider as it can make such a great difference. Shades can be a great way to highlight the surface below them, such as a dining table, or for when reading. To do this, they need to have a larger opening at their base than at their top so the light is concentrated. downwards. An empire shade, for example.

If you're going to be working at a desk, something like a banker's lamp is ideal. Its

adjustable shade will help you see what you're working on, and because there's no opening at the top, there will be less glare in your eyes. In fact, green was chosen as the colour for the shade of this style of lamp because at the time it was believed to prevent eye damage.

Choose a tall lamp with a drum or cylinder shade if you want the focus of the light to fall above and below the lamp. These shades have wide bottoms and tops, so the light pours out of both openings. They're a fab choice if you have a bedside table with a framed picture above it. The shade will cast light on the table top for practical reasons and on the wall for aesthetic reasons. They're also great if you want to highlight a corner of a room.

Under-cabinet lights

Another non-permanent but super-effective lighting option is under-cabinet lights. They're widely available and provide an additional source of light to help with kitchen tasks as well as adding atmosphere in the evening when you don't want the overhead lights on. They don't always need to be wired to the mains and there are options that can be stuck on with adhesive strips or screwed into place, and powered by batteries, which is a brilliant way to add some highlights to a rented space or for anywhere you'd rather not have lights wired in. I also love them for under shelving – simply sticking them on immediately gives a more considered look.

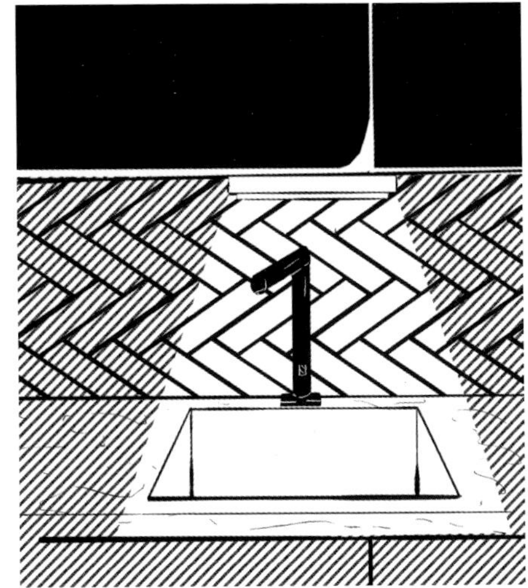

Warm and cool lighting

Lightbulbs can come in warm or cool tones. Warm tones such as yellows give out a relaxed glow and are best in living areas, bedrooms and anywhere you want to unwind. Cooler tones, such as blues, are a more 'clean' light and can make you feel more alert, which can be great for areas where you need to perform tasks or take care. They're a good choice for kitchens and can also add brightness to bathrooms. Bear these tones in mind when choosing bulbs for your fittings – you don't want a cool light overhead when you're switching off, before you sleep, or in a lamp where you relax.

Bulbs

If you get it wrong with bulbs, it can be an expensive mistake to rectify, but get it right and it can be so glorious. The key here is to know what you're buying. We've already covered how to choose the right bulb base for your fitting on pages 146–9 but we're yet to cover the bulb itself and what she's all about.

Remember when I spoke about the annual running costs of appliances in Chapter 1, and how some cheaper models can actually end up costing you more in the long run? You need to consider the bigger picture when you shop for bulbs, too. There are three main types – LED, CFL and incandescent/halogen. The price difference between them can be pretty dramatic, but the main rule of thumb is that the more expensive bulbs – LEDs – are more energy-efficient and will actually cost you less over time. They'll also serve you for longer.

LED LED stands for 'light-emitting diode' and these girls are premium. I'd highly recommend them because they can last for over twenty years with normal use. Their low-energy consumption doesn't mean they're any less bright and they don't contain mercury (like CFLs do – see below), so there's less danger to you should one break.

The high cost of LED technology was a huge turn-off for people in the past but costs are reducing over time. Now they're more cost-efficient, especially when you consider their long lifespan and low running costs.

TIP

People are used to buying bulbs based on watts and not lumens. It used to be that the more power used, the brighter the light – if you wanted a bright light you bought a high-wattage bulb. However, LEDs don't need more power to increase their brightness and use considerably less than standard bulbs. So, when it comes to LEDs, most packaging will say something like 9w = 60w. This means that a 9w LED bulb will do the job of a 60w incandescent bulb. This is great for your pocket as your bills will be lower, but it also means there will be less chance of an LED bulb being too much for your lamp base.

CFL Formally known as the compact fluorescent lamp, these bulbs are less expensive and also do a good job. They don't use as much energy as halogen bulbs (see below), but aren't as efficient as LEDs. They work by using electricity to make the gas inside them glow.

While they're cheaper than LEDs, they have some downsides: after they're turned on, they take time to reach their full brightness. This means I would never use one in a space where I need instant brightness for safety – so, a stairway, hall or bathroom. Also, they contain the smallest amount of mercury, so breakages can be dangerous and you need to dispose of these girls in the correct way (a quick online search will tell you where in your area you can take yours). This is another reason why LEDs are my favourite.

Incandescent

These girls are retired. They worked by heating up a filament inside and that heat created light. They had their advantages but were super draining when it came to energy usage and didn't last long, so they're now no longer produced.

Halogen

This is still a type of incandescent bulb, but one that is said to be up to 40 per cent more efficient. You'll recognize them as they look like 'traditional' bulbs – clear with a filament inside. It's tempting to go for them because they're a lot cheaper to buy, but they're still more expensive to run than LEDs or CFLs. Trust me, they'll cost you more in the long term, so it would be a false economy. They also have to be handled very carefully and don't last for long.

To summarize, you don't have to rush out and buy LED bulbs to replace what you have now, just keep the above advice in mind when your next one goes. If you feel your bulbs aren't giving you what they should and you want to swap them out, we'll now move on to what you should look for on the bulb packaging, from its colour to its lifespan.

It's a good idea to buy bulbs one at a time instead of replacing them all at once. What works in the kitchen might not feel great in the bedroom, and so on. It's best to try out a bulb in one area to see how you like its colour and effect before you multi-buy. This approach can help you decide if there's anything you'd change about that bulb if it were to be bought again for a different space – a slow-lighting CFL, for example, or a cool glow.

Reading (the box) is fundamental

The best thing about shopping for bulbs is that all the info you need to help you make the right decision is readily available on every box – you just need to know what it all means. Thankfully, this wealth of detail is pretty uncomplicated. Let's start with the EU energy label. I love an energy label, as you know. Anything that arms the buyer with information and helps them to make a more conscious decision is fabulous, in my opinion. All bulbs sold within the EU must have the following information on their energy label.

Energy efficiency

Like home appliances, all bulbs are awarded a rating for how efficient they are. This runs from A++ to G, A++ being the most supreme, fabulous and energy-efficient, and G being the least. This is always the main part of the label and the largest letter you will see. LEDs will almost always be an A+ or A++ whereas halogens can be as low as a D.

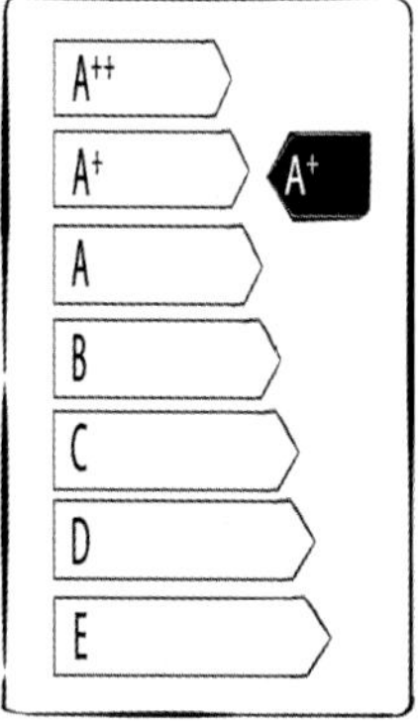

Lumens

The brightness of a bulb is given in lumens (lm). The higher the lumen rating, the brighter the light, but this doesn't necessarily mean it's going to use more energy. LED bulbs can shine much brighter using far less energy than other types of bulb and will also last for longer.

Wattage

Watts (W) tell you how much power a light needs to run when it's on and were the old-school way of knowing how bright an incandescent bulb would be. The more watts it needed, the brighter it could shine. Now, we can have brighter bulbs that require much less power, so pay more attention to the lumen rating for an indication of the bulb's brightness.

There will be two wattage figures stated on a bulb's packaging. One will be the annual wattage (kWh/annum) used to run the lamp – 1,000 hours is considered the average use for a bulb per year – and the other will be the wattage used for the bulb when it's on (W).

Watts are also important, as some lamps and light fittings can't take a bulb that needs a higher wattage to run normally. The maximum number of watts that a fitting can take will be stated on its label, usually near to where you pop the bulb in – the metal fitting on a lamp, for instance. It's very dangerous to exceed the wattage stated, so be sure to be aware of the fitting's limit and abide by this.

Lifetime

How long will the bulb last? This is always stated on an EU-approved box. Usually it's around 25,000+ hours for an LED, which is a long time indeed, whereas CFLs fall around the 8,000-hours mark. It's usually longer than the box indicates as that figure is based on averages.

As well as the manufacturer and model code, there are some other really handy bits of information on a bulb's packaging to make sure you don't arrive home and are disappointed in your choice.

CRI

CRI 90

Often a bit of info that is overlooked, this stands for Colour Rendering Index (measured in Ra). It's literally how the light reveals colours and how it makes them appear when they're in natural light. Think of it like an Instagram filter. The wrong bulb can wash out colours and make them appear different to how they would in natural daylight. This can cause you to strain your eyes when you're reading, for example, or change the tones of your décor, and so on.

The maximum and best CRI rating is 100. Incandescent and halogen bulbs were almost always 100. LED technology is slowly developing to reach this figure too, but for now the highest LEDs are in the nineties. Anything under 60 is classed as terrible and you should aim to purchase a bulb that is 85 plus. If you can, get something that's over 90.

Colour

Enter Kelvin (K). Kelvin is the unit of measurement for the temperature of light – whether it's warm or cool, essentially. The higher the Kelvin, the cooler/bluer the light. A good rule of thumb is as follows:

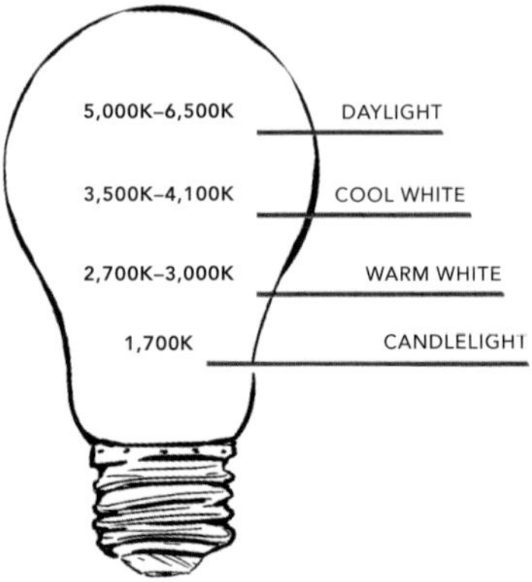

5,000K–6,500K DAYLIGHT
3,500K–4,100K COOL WHITE
2,700K–3,000K WARM WHITE
1,700K CANDLELIGHT

- 1,700K is like candlelight – this will give you an idea of why bulbs with this rating aren't as readily available.
- 2,700–3,000K can be called warm white. It's the kind of glow that old incandescent bulbs would give you, and what is most commonly used in living areas, bedrooms and so on. Most bulbs available in local supermarkets will be within this range.
- 3,000K+ is where we start getting into the cooler tones.
- 3,500–4,100K is cool white and I wouldn't go any higher than this in living spaces, personally.
- 5,000–6,500K is like daylight, and anything above 4,600K is only recommended for areas where you need some seriously cool light. This kind is more suited to commercial or display areas where really intense lighting is needed.

In a bedroom or lounge, a warm light is usually the best choice as it helps us to switch off, relax and creates an intimate atmosphere. A cooler light might be better for where you eat breakfast, if you want to be more alert in the morning. Bathrooms are a totally personal choice – a warm light will basically make you look better in the mirror, but a cool light will make the surfaces look cleaner. My personal choice would be cool ceiling light and a warm over-mirror light. The same goes for under-cabinet lights in the kitchen – a cooler light will help you with focused chopping and cooking, as it's perfect for keeping you alert during tasks and ensuring you can see clearly.

The bulb packaging will also tell you how many times the light can be turned on and off before it burns out, if it's dimmable, and how long it takes to reach a certain brightness. You'll also find the dimensions of the bulb so that you don't end up with

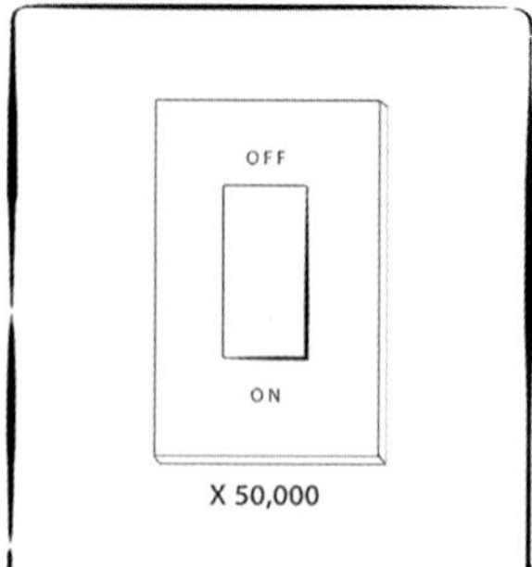

its top poking out of the lampshade or a screw-in that's too big for your fitting.

Now that you're armed with the basics, it's time to look into bulb shapes.

Shape

If a bulb blows and you've been happy with its performance thus far, I'd simply take it with you when shopping for a replacement so that you get like for like. If you're starting from scratch, here are the most common shapes and what they are good for. Remember, the 'beam spread' can usually be found on most packaging and will tell you, in degrees, how far the light will spread if uninterrupted.

Arbitrary bulbs The regular shape of bulb we often see. The reason the shape of this bulb is still going since Edison first invented them is because it works in almost every space and does its job so well. It comes in a range of bases and sizes, and is pretty fail-safe.

Globe and golf-ball bulbs These are larger than arbitrary bulbs and rounder, hence their name. They've become super popular in the interiors world in recent times as exposed bulbs are such a big trend. Exposed bulbs can distract the eye, however, so I love the ones that look as though they've been dipped in gold. This takes the edge off the light and diffuses the glow in a softer way.

Mini globe bulbs, often called golf-ball bulbs, can look better in lamps where the bulb is visible from above, and are perfect for low-rise shades where a regular bulb would peek out at the top.

Candle and flame bulbs These are usually used in decorative lighting as they're exposed and look prettier. It also helps that they are taller and slimmer and can fit into smaller candelabras, for example. Some even come with a really exaggerated tip, and have a flicker effect to resemble a real candle. If that's what you're into, knock yourself out.

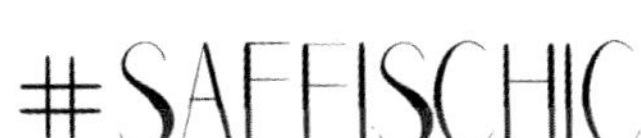

Before you swap out a lightbulb, be sure to read pages 146–53 where I explain how to remove and replace them safely.

Colour Me Fabulous

We've spoken about content, placement and lighting so far – next, we need to talk about colour and how to add it to our zones.

The colour that we choose to use in our home is such a personal thing, and something that we can use to establish the way we perceive a space or operate in it. Some colours give us focus while others make us hungry; some make us feel safe and others overwhelmed. We hear so much about not using dark colours in small spaces, only using brights as accent colours, and so on. Forget it all: if you want a space to be somewhere you feel wonderful, you need to decorate it accordingly. As I've mentioned already, for every interiors rule you hear, there is someone out there breaking it and creating a breathtaking space full of no-nos that make us feel yes-yes.

When deciding on colours for your home, here are some things to give you food for thought. Think of them as some light takeaways, if you're not sure where to begin.

Mood

If you're trying to decide on wall colour for a space, you need to first consider mood. Take a step back and think for a moment about what that zone is used for. What's its function? What mood works best alongside it?

For example: if you want the atmosphere in your kitchen to lift you each morning when you enter it, then go for lighter, brighter tones. If you'd like your living room to feel cocooned and cosy, use deep tones and consider painting the ceiling the same colour. I love a dark-ceiling-and-dark-wall combo – I mean, what's there to hate about all-over navy? Bliss!

Problem-solving with colour

Colour is such a powerful tool and can help you make a small space work to its full potential, particularly if the illusion of space is super important for you. You can also use it to play with light or help to distract from anything you may want to take the focus away from.

All white, all right

All-over white can really enhance a room – it can make the ceilings appear higher, the walls wider, and give a feeling of a much airier space. If you have particularly low ceilings and want to give an illusion of height, paint the skirting and ceiling the same shade of white as the walls. The cut-off points will be less obvious, giving the walls a much taller appearance.

Colour blocking

If you want to make the most of natural light, clever colour blocking can help you play with the available light and bounce it into dimmer areas. Painting the wall that gets the most light a cool white, for example, will mean the light is then bounced on to other darker walls. Colour blocking is also great for a room of multiple uses where there is no one true function and mood. Colour can help you define the different zones a little and ensure one has a definite mood to it. There's nothing to stop you from using more than one colour to make different areas pop, or to create a visual boundary. It doesn't have to be too regimented either – diagonal colour blocking can add a playful element to an office/living space, for example.

Complementing and distracting

Using the right shades can also help simmer down colours you hate. If you can't stand the flooring or tiles in a particular space, a great colour used on the walls can draw the eye away from it/them.

Equally, paint is such an easy way to update a room that's looking a bit dated. If your bathroom suite has seen better days, a fresh coat of white to the walls, skirting and any other paintable surfaces can instantly make it look like a cleaner and more sanitary space.

The psychology of colour

There's a Pantone brown that's been called the ugliest shade in the world. Apparently, it's used on cigarette packets to deter people from picking them up! Colour can have a huge impact on how we perceive a space and how we feel in it, so it's important to be aware of the effect some common colours have.

Red

Red stimulates a mild adrenaline response, which quickens the heart rate a little. As it's one of nature's warning signs, perhaps it's ingrained in our behaviour to associate it with having to be alert and aware, rather than calm and relaxed. It's said to be linked to feelings of worry and stress, and is essentially distracting.

There are even studies that have found that people who sleep in red rooms are less productive and get a worse night's sleep – perhaps because they're unconsciously on high alert from the physical response the colour can provoke in us. However, it does stimulate appetite, so can work well in a dining room or a kitchen. It's a rich and warm colour that can set a great vibe, so long as it's not covering an entire bedroom. Unless racy is what you're aiming for …

Grey

Right now, many people are keen to grey their house all over because of the masses of grey-home inspiration being consumed daily on social media. Before we dedicate a whole house to a particular colour, we need to be aware of trends that might date a property. It's easier and more effective in the long run to paint walls white and then add your chosen colour with accessories such as cushions, curtains and rugs. If you do want grey walls, consider your space. Warm and cool greys do different things. Consider a few different – *cough* – shades of grey before settling on one.

Yellow

Some studies show that houses with kitchens painted bright yellow achieve lower sale prices in comparison with their non-yellow-kitchen counterparts. It's a colour that can make people feel slightly off and overwhelmed if sat surrounded by it for long periods, but can create a cheery entrance hall, for example. Because it's a bright and positive colour with such a modern vibe, yellow can work really well on a feature wall, woodwork or fireplaces, or for accessories. It doesn't have to be on every wall to be your accent shade. Rooms that have more muted walls and furniture with yellow pops here and there can look very considered. You also don't have to use bright yellow – mustard accessories are a great way to add a more plush tone to a space.

Blue and green

These hues work well in any room you sit in for long periods of time. We've spoken about how colours found in nature can stir emotions in us – red, in particular, we associate with danger. Think for a moment about blue and green. They are two colours we are constantly surrounded by – blue skies, bodies of water, green grass, trees, and so on. Our minds can function without disruption in rooms painted in these colours as we're so used to their presence. A room in green or blue instils concentration and calm in us.

Blue is great for a study, home office or anywhere you need to concentrate. Green can have the same effect – the added bonus is that it can also help us feel at ease. Deeper tones can sometimes create a downbeat mood, which is great for rooms where you don't spend a lot of time, but want to feel switched-off and relaxed. However, choose bright and light shades to enhance the mood if you're considering these tones for a living room that is used on a daily basis.

Pink

Pink can have such an effect on one's mood. Did you ever hear of Drunk-tank Pink? It's a shade of pink that has been used to paint the inside of prison cells in the hope that it calms the inmates inside. It has been the subject of many studies and results have always shown an improvement in subjects' behaviour. It's claimed that looking at the colour also lowers testosterone, which has led some football teams to paint their opposition's locker rooms this particular shade. The hope is that it will have an effect on the visiting team's pre-match hype and lead to a victory for the home team.

However, it's worth noting that pink bedrooms appear to be another under-performer in studies related to property sales; it's also not advisable to paint a room entirely bright pink. After long periods the colour can overwhelm and has been said to induce feelings of nausea.

Neutrals

When you want the focus in a room to be something other than the walls, neutrals are a sound choice as they don't fight with other colours or objects for your attention. Most art galleries and showrooms use the 'white is right' rule when displaying pieces. Neutrals are also brilliant if you want a look that will help sell your home, or simply last for years, as they can't be pinpointed to a certain year or trend. (I promise you, grey is going to be the perm of the interiors world.)

If you live for brights but are a renter, there are so many ways to introduce vibrant colours into your home without painting walls. Rugs, curtains, ornaments and art will all give pops of colour and personality to a space.

The main advice I'd give when decorating is to consider how colours make *you* feel. Mix them up, play with shades and tone. Your home should make you feel good, and colour is a great way to help you achieve this.

Testing colours

When testing colours, don't start swatching until all your lighting is in place. It can change the room dramatically and potentially alter the shade of the colour you have in mind. Then make sure to test multiple swatches on *every* wall on which colour will be painted. Natural light in the room will vary throughout the day and change how the shade appears.

Pay particular attention to how the colour is affected by the light at the times you use the room the most – for example, mornings and evenings for the bedroom. What you might think is a gorgeous shade on the tin can look far less appealing on different walls when shadows and items near by come into play. Remember too that paint dries to a different shade than when it is wet, so don't be too freaked out when you first start painting. Walk away and come back when it's fully dry before you start to consider how it looks. Also remember that if you're going to need two coats for the final job, make sure you do two coats when you swatch.

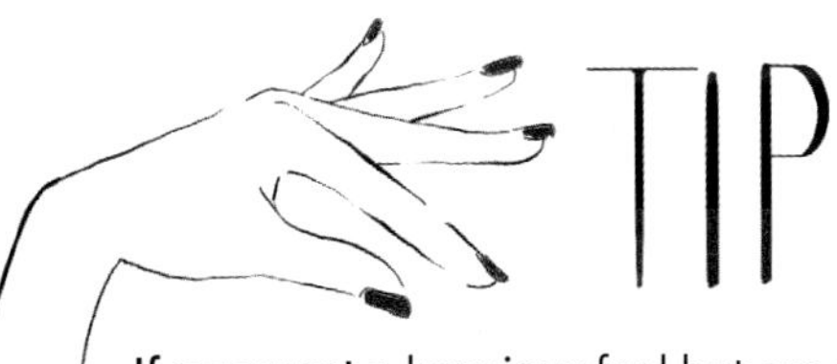

If you want a luxurious feel but are on a budget, turn to luxury brands for inspiration. You can browse high-end paint manufacturers to see what's currently hot in the luxury paint world, then take the colour card to your local paint store and colour match. A lot of high-end paints are expensive because of their consistency and quality, so your finish won't be the same, but it's great to be inspired.

Smart Styling for Rental Properties

The above can be fabulous food for thought if you own a property or are about to change the look of your home, but if you rent, chances are the choices of colour, fixtures and furniture will be out of your control. The same goes for if you don't have the budget or time to redecorate. This is why I feel it's important to run through the most common décor issues I encounter and how to turn them around easily without having to spend a lot of money or time.

Before I begin, I want to start with a note to landlords – to save the renters of the future from having to deal with poor furniture choices. If you're about to choose something new for your rental or are redecorating, here are some things to consider.

When you're creating a space on what I am assuming is a smart budget, you need to keep your strategy going all the way through to your décor. Keep any trend-based items and colour choices to accessories and lower-priced furnishings. Long-term, high-priced items need careful consideration and some bigger-picture thinking.

A couch, for example, should always be in a commercial colour such as charcoal or navy. This means that tenant after tenant it can be easily added to by you, or can be dressed easily to the tenants' taste by them. Light-coloured sofas will need a heavy cleaning between tenancies and give you one big headache, trust me. Dark colours, especially those with a twist or a fleck to the fabric, will hide stains, and wear and tear, much better.

With beds, follow the 'buy cheap, buy twice' rule. It's cheaper in the long run to buy a more durable, comfortable mattress than lots of cheap ones. Tenants will never stay long term in a property with a bad bed. If it's mattress staining you're worried about, then buy a mattress protector to ensure it's as good as new after each tenancy.

When it comes to the styling of the property, don't get too into trends. Nods to them are fine but overdoing it will pose two problems:

- You cut out anyone who doesn't share your taste. It's vital to keep your property looking appealing to as many prospective tenants in your target market as possible. This means keeping things low key with a comfortable, commercial edge.
- Each time the property comes up for renewal you'll need to give it a total overhaul to bring it up to date, as a dated décor can affect its market price. Just having to change some cushion covers or a pair of curtains instead is a much smarter option. It's also extremely sound to decorate with good commercial basics so a tenant can add their own style easily. If you want to dress the property for marketing, but don't want to pay for or deal with a lot of accessories or soft furnishings in the lease, consider putting in some of your own pieces for photos and viewings, such as bedding, ornaments, books, then remove them for the tenancy itself. If you still decide to put in a cheap black fake leather couch and red rug after all this advice … Girl … *shakes head*

Now, back to tenants. I've got some advice when it comes to styling your space. There's no point feeling like 'it's not mine'. It's your home while you're paying for it. Even if some of the furnishings aren't to your taste, there are clever and easy ways to make an already furnished property work with your style.

As there's almost always a crap couch in rentals, it's a good place to start. What *can* you do to update one you don't live for?

While throws can instantly fix a couch that is worn-out, there are other ways to work with one you hate. You need either to enhance or distract. Many a time I've been left with a sofa that I can't stand or understand. The first thing I do is some online research into that particular style of couch, with the aim of enhancing its true aesthetic. Having worked in fashion, I know one thing for sure: most things – clothing or interiors – originate from a trend. What was once a high-end and well-executed idea washes down to a not-so-well-executed high-street version and finally ends up in rental accommodation.

When I need inspiration for dinner and have a mix of ingredients in the fridge, I type them into Google and recipes will appear with images of deliciously styled dishes using these ingredients. It's the perfect inspiration to help me turn what I have into something amazing. Typing 'tan leather couch' into something like Pinterest will yield the same kind of results décor-wise. You'll see the original trend from which your battered couch derived and how it was meant to be styled. The images that pop up can be a fantastic way to see what colours complement and enhance the look, and how people with great taste have styled their sofas. Have a go at this approach before you cast a throw over your rental couch as they can look sloppy. You might find that you're missing out on some inspired styling tricks and creative approaches.

If you still want to use a throw, try to keep it clean and off the floor as it can end up taking over the room. Taking a layered approach, such as a faux sheepskin over a knit, can look great instead and much more intentional. It says more hygge than hidden, yet still covers the sins.

The simple addition of some cushions to distract from the couch is also great, especially if it is worn or stained. Team them

with a throw that doesn't take over, just covers the parts you hate, and it will look like you've styled it to perfection. Your cushions don't have to all match, and I think a mix of textures always looks great. Go for an overall look rather than one colour.

You can only do so much, so remember, if your couch is in particularly bad disrepair, ask your landlord if they plan to replace it. If they plan to later and are fine with what happens to the one in place, or they don't mind you doing some alterations in general to what is there, ask if you can make the changes below. Quite often a landlord won't really care about a knackered old couch and it will be cheaper for them to let you transform it than buy a new one right away.

If the cushions are sagging, you can look into replacing them altogether, but this can take money and time. This issue often crops up for me at the end of tenancies and one option is to unzip and literally fluff the insides of the cushions with your hand so that the filler is spread more evenly – much like when you shake out a duvet. If you're lucky, this can be an instant fix, but if things are still looking a little lacklustre, you can buy the same kind of filler that is in the existing cushions and top it up yourself. It's usually polyester filler and quite inexpensive. If there's no zip on the cushion inner, you can unpick the seam and sew it up by hand when you're done.

If your landlord says you can remove the back cushions from your sofa for good, you can buy large individual cushions to sit in their place instead. This can really give your couch a new lease of life and is a great way to inject some personal style.

If your sofa is sagging in the middle because it's worn out, a common fix is to buy a specially designed layer that sits between the seat cushions and the base of the couch and will bring some much-needed firmness. Sometimes plywood is recommended but this can be a little too rigid. The inserts to go for are thin sheets within fabric, which fold out and give enough stability without feeling like you're sitting on a wall. They are usually inexpensive but can make a huge difference to your comfort levels as well as the visual appeal of your sofa.

Flooring

If you absolutely abhor your floor, there are some easy fixes. As I mentioned earlier in this chapter, flat-weave rugs are far cheaper than those with a deep pile and come in a range of sizes. They're great for hiding old flooring or a carpet that you either hate or is in a bad state, especially if you rent and can't make any drastic changes.

If you have real wood floorboards and want to update them (and your tenancy allows it or you own your home), these can be painted. I love the richness dark floorboards can add to a space, but also how fresh a whitewashed look can make a room feel. Just make sure you use the correct paint for the job and do your research on what prep needs to be carried out beforehand for your particular floor – does it need to be sanded first, for example. Don't forget to start at the corner furthest away from your door or you may paint yourself in!

I've arrived at a new property before that I'm planning to rent out and thought the carpets were too bad to achieve the optimum rental price, but a professional clean literally transformed them. You can always send images to prospective cleaning companies to see if they think the stains will lift, as some may not. Also remember when getting quotes that they will usually be for a whole property so get all your carpets done at once.

When it comes to zoning and adapting your home to suit you and your lifestyle, remember that it doesn't have to cost a fortune. It also doesn't have to be done to an entire property – you can apply it to a room you rent in a shared property too. Start with the things you do on a day-to-day basis and apply the zoning method to these tasks. If we make the tasks we perform every day more seamless and enjoyable, the knock-on effects will be endless.

You don't need to make drastic changes to enhance your home, you just need to take some time to think about how you want it to make you feel and go from there. If we all started by working with what we have first, I think we would appreciate our homes and ourselves a lot more. We don't always need bigger and better; little changes can reap huge rewards. Which leads us on to another topic where a small tweak can make a big difference …

Are you ready to help your home help the world?

7. SHE'S AN ECO GIRL

We're all aware of how we should generally reduce our consumption, recycle, and be more environmentally aware. Let's face it, we've made a mess of the planet and if we don't start making more changes the repercussions will be catastrophic.

Change starts in the home and there are so many small steps we can take that will make a big difference. I'm going to take you through some amazing ways to reduce energy, water and paper consumption within the home with little effort.

Mindful Usage

The very first step in consuming less is mindful usage of our utilities. This can be as simple as turning off the tap while you brush your teeth or not leaving lights on when you're not in the room. From energy consumption to embracing the paperless revolution, here are more little things to consider.

Waste less water

The easiest way to reduce your water consumption is to take a shorter shower. If you're a condition, exfoliate, win-a-fake-debate-in-the-shower kind of gal, then there are other ways to minimize your water usage while still keeping your routine.

Water-efficient shower heads that reduce water flow are easy to find online and are available for purchase in many DIY stores. They're a great idea, but can cause a reduction in water pressure. If this is a deal-breaker for you, there are also heads available that maintain a good pressure but pump air at the same time, so overall less water is used.

Dripping taps, shower heads and leaking pipes are all sources of wasted water and should be fixed ASAP. Most leaking fixtures are easy to repair yourself and are usually the result of a worn-out washer. See pages 111–13 for more advice on how to replace one.

Go paperless

Ever since I went paperless I've been reaping the benefits. Moving house didn't require as much mail redirection. I have to open and file less post and it's helping work towards a happier planet. With just a few online clicks you can switch all your communication preferences from utility providers, banks, and so on. You'll receive your statements and all other communications online. I feel safer knowing my personal information isn't at risk of being intercepted for the purposes of fraud, and relieved I don't have to file it away safely. I also like not having to spend time shredding. Should I ever need statements, I can access them online easily and print or screenshot only what I need.

Another great way to reduce paper coming into the home is to put a 'no junk mail' sticker on your letterbox. This should keep circulars and hand-delivered junk mail to a minimum. You can also adopt an 'unsubscribe' approach, as you would with junk email – contact individual senders of mail you don't want to receive and ask to be taken off their mailing list. Check your postal service for details on how to stop any of their own circulars being sent to you and most importantly, go online and make sure your details are taken off the open register – this is how most companies find you.

Finally, do you receive mail for someone who no longer lives at your property? This can be a huge source of waste as the post isn't even getting to the right person and it's your responsibility to dispose of it. Each postal service has different rules, so check online and find out what steps you need to take to stop letters arriving for the person(s) who lived there before you. If you're a landlord, find out what the guidelines are and advise current tenants on how they can prevent the previous occupants' post from stacking up.

Heating your home wisely

Before we go any further, I need you to know I'm not someone who is always warm and grand in cold weather. I am not. I feel cold just thinking about winter and hate being chilly in my own home. My tips on heating your home mindfully are less 'put on a jumper!' and more geared towards a gal enjoying her space during winter without incurring high bills and power usage.

I know you're reading this with one eye closed for fear I'm going to tell you never to turn on your heating. I'm not – it's all about approaching this cleverly. Timers are a must. They'll allow you to create a warm bubble to wake up to every morning and walk into every evening during those cold months, so that you're less likely to blast the system mindlessly at full heat for a prolonged period. If you set your heating to come on before you rise and before you arrive home from work, you can guarantee your usage will reduce dramatically. Your rooms will have had time to warm up without any heat escaping from doors opening, and you'll get to enjoy the glory of it all. Next time you turn the heating on, note how long it takes for your place to warm up and cool down – this will help you pick the times to set the timer.

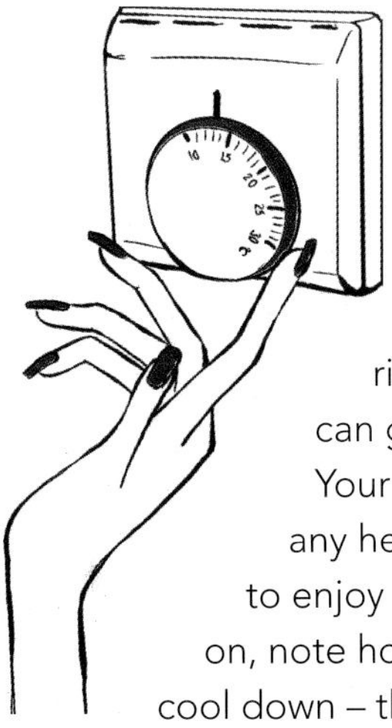

In the winter evenings, mine is set to come back on after dinner (the heat given off by the cooker and moving around while cooking makes me barely notice it's off). This way, the flat heats back up again when I'm hanging out before heading to bed, as there are fewer open doors so the heat is kept in.

Most people have the temperature of their hot water and central heating set higher than they need it. It was probably raised one winter evening when it was particularly cold and never reduced again. Check the advice in your boiler manual and try reducing it by 1 degree, which can make a great difference annually to your energy bills.

We've spoken about zones from an aesthetic point of view in the previous chapter, so now let's talk about temperature zones. There's no point heating every room in your home to the same temperature.

If you have central heating, you'll mostly likely have thermostatic radiator valves, which help you control the temperature of the radiator. Most people will set theirs to max in every room and not give it a second thought. You might want rooms such as the bathroom or living room to be warmer than others, but you might prefer your bedroom to feel a little cooler at the end of the day so that it's easier to sleep. You might also find that rooms you don't sit in a lot or use as often – a spare bedroom or utility room, for example – don't need to be heated to the same temperature as your living room.

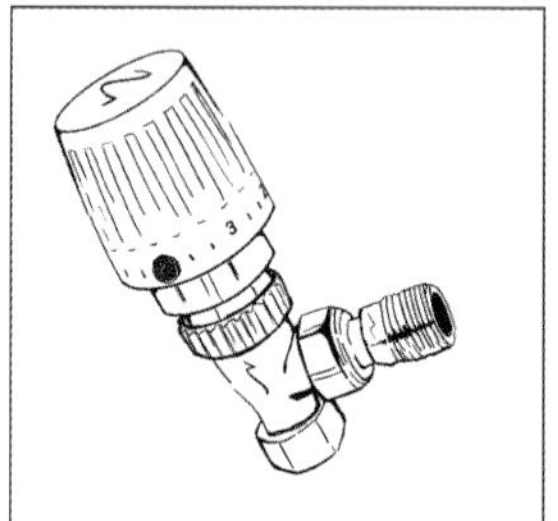

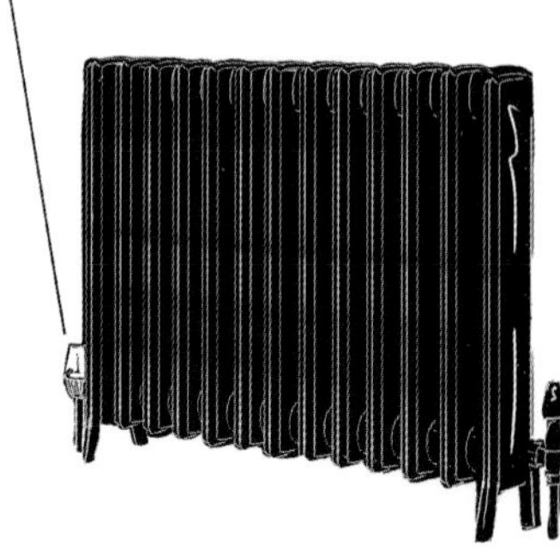

Assess which rooms you'd like hotter and which could be cooler, and adjust your radiator valves accordingly. Doing so can reduce your bills and still keep you feeling comfortable. When you do heat rooms to different temperatures, though, it's important to remember to keep the doors to those rooms closed. At the risk of sounding like your mum, you really will let the heat out …

Off-peak energy use

If everyone in a neighbourhood set their appliances to run during off-peak hours, the demand for energy during peak times would be greatly reduced. This would benefit us environmentally for a host of reasons, such as lower costs for consumers. The need for more generators to be built in order to accommodate growing peak usage would also reduce. Speak to your utility providers to see if they offer cheaper tariffs for off-peak energy use. This way you can set your washing machine or dishwasher on a delay timer to run when it's cheaper to use.

Washing appliances

Speaking of your washing machine and dishwasher, use the eco-wash setting as much as possible to reduce your water usage and energy bills. Just remember, you'll still need to run hotter washes occasionally to keep your machine healthy, so do this when you're doing a monthly vinegar clean (see pages 100–1) or when you're washing workwear or anything heavily stained.

Both these appliances do their best work with a full load, so ensuring you run them in this way every time can minimize your water consumption. It also means you'll do fewer washing cycles. Bear this in mind before you whack on a half-load.

Eco-friendly cleaning products

Everything you use to clean – your house, your clothes, your dishes – will be flushed back into the environment eventually so choose your products wisely. Harsh chemicals can be bad for your health and hands too, so it's worth switching to eco-friendly products next time you run out of your current supply. I also live for lemon, vinegar and bicarbonate of soda – they're the ultimate natural cleaning products and, when combined, can do some amazing things. Flick back to pages 53–7 in Chapter 3 and page 116 in Chapter 5 if you need reminding of their stain-removal and cleaning power.

Power down

Switching off unused appliances at the wall makes a huge difference to your energy consumption. It's age-old advice but rarely heeded. This tiny change will not only reduce your bills, it will also help you to reduce the amount of electricity your home is consuming overall.

It's also worth shopping around to see if you can find a green energy provider. These companies are amazing, and one thing I've noticed since I switched across to one is that their ethics run right through the business. Their communications are generally paperless, their community of suppliers and employees is fairly paid, and they're usually active supporters of other ethical and local businesses.

Savvy insulation

If you have draughts in your home, there are many simple tips to minimize them and keep heat in. You're paying for all that warmth, so you should ensure it stays inside.

For under-door draughts, foam draught excluders that wrap around the top and bottom of doors are available, or you can easily fashion one that sits at the bottom of the door, trapping any cool air coming in.

If you have draughty windows, the easiest way to prevent the cold from seeping in is by shutting your curtains once the sun has gone down. This will keep the warm air in and block any draughts from single glazing. If single glazing is your problem and you don't – or can't – upgrade to double glazing, you can also buy a plastic film online that will insulate your window panes. Once taped into place, a wall of trapped air between the film and the glass is created, producing the effect of double glazing and thus ensuring a warmer home. It's super easy to apply and can provide a removable alternative to double glazing – perfect for renters!

Old floorboards can mean cold air comes up from below, so rugs can be a great way to keep your room cosy. They prevent draughts from seeping through cracks and can stop heat from escaping too. They're also warmer underfoot than a bare floor.

Lightbulbs

You'll have read about the ins and out of bulbs on pages 181–9, but the bottom line is that LED lights use the least amount of energy and last the longest. Getting to know which products use less power and require less of your cash is a great way to reduce overall costs in the home.

My final word on being mindful about your energy consumption is that you can be conscious about how much you're using without compromising on style or the enjoyment of your space. As consumers, we're constantly being given access to new ways to reduce and reuse while still maintaining a level of style and comfort in our homes. It's all about a considered approach. You don't have to live off the grid to make a difference for the generations to come – you can start right now at no cost.

8. UNINVITED GUESTS

Moths, mice and mould – three things every person dreads invading their space. Tell-tale signs of each can bring worry and a feeling of powerlessness, which is never good to experience in your own home. The world brings enough stress and surprises – we don't want more of the same in our domestic sphere.

Because these issues are so serious, I wanted a dedicated chapter to cover all three in depth so that you'll be armed with the knowledge to spot signs of them easily and prevent them from growing into larger problems. While early detection and preventative measures are ideal, don't worry – we'll also cover some handy how-tos if they've already taken hold in the home. Mouldy bathroom, anyone?

Moths

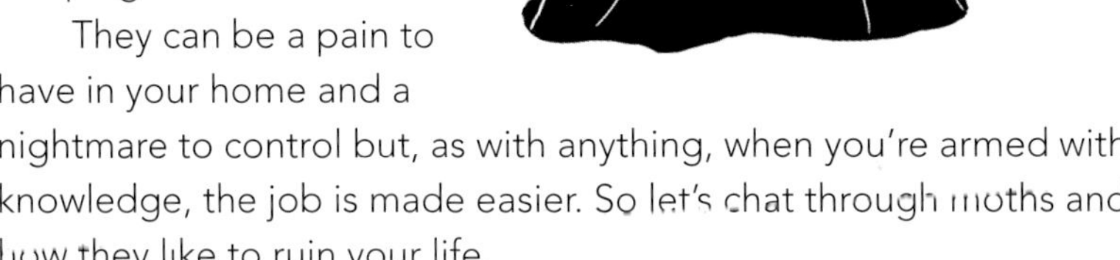

Even writing about this sends me into a blind panic. These girls have a taste only for your finest things and will stop at nothing to get to them. They love natural (read expensive and chic) fibres and their calling card is the holes they leave in your clothing. I'm weeping.

They can be a pain to have in your home and a nightmare to control but, as with anything, when you're armed with knowledge, the job is made easier. So let's chat through moths and how they like to ruin your life.

Who are they?

It's been well documented that moth numbers have almost doubled in recent years and aren't likely to slow down. This is due mainly to climate change, which has given them a much longer breeding period. In the past, the cold months would kill them off. With that in mind, it's key to understand more about them and how they operate in order to deal with them effectively.

How do they operate?

You may not know this, but it's not the adult moths that are ruining your Prada. Those girls don't even have mouths (I'm not kidding). It's their larvae that live for devouring your cashmere. The female moth will suss out your threads and drop as few as 50 eggs (which is the norm) or up to 1,000 (internal shriek) on to whatever garment she thinks is the best feeding ground for her larvae.

The moth hole you find in your prized oversized, drop-shoulder cashmere sweater is where the teeny eggs have been laid, hatched and the larvae have then nibbled the fabric. It's not where the adult moth has landed and dined.

The larvae don't usually bother with cheap, man-made fibres. They turn their noses up at polyester or a fast-fashion playsuit (very rightly so IMHO). Instead, they'll head straight for your hand-printed silk shirts, linen maxi dresses and soft cashmere cropped sweaters. They love it all.

- Silk
- Fur
- Wool
- Cashmere

Cotton and linen aren't as popular but are still a target, especially if mixed with another natural fibre.

The reason moth larvae live for these fabrics (literally) is that they contain a protein called keratin. It's also why they love natural fibres that have been in close contact with the body and picked up sweat, oils, and even hair, as these all contain proteins too.

These girls like their privacy and won't hang out in the open. It's why they love to settle in wardrobes and other dark areas where they won't be disturbed. The larvae will thrive on clothes that aren't moved or used often, so don't usually like or survive on items that are worn a lot. It's why they always seem to attack your more special pieces.

There are, in fact, three main types of moth larvae that will ruin your clothes:

- *Larvae of the brown house moth* – more into fibres from animals, such as fur and feathers, and materials such as leather.
- *Larvae of the common clothes moth* – will leave irregular-shaped holes in fabric.
- *Larvae of the case-bearing moth* – will leave more regular-shaped holes in fabric.

How can I tell if I have clothes moths?

You may have spotted some adult moths flying around. It's said that the males fly high and fertilized females fly low. Either way, if you've seen them you know you have them, but how do you know if they are clothes moths?

- Check the folds, gathers and pockets of your clothes as moths love dark, undisturbed places. Remember to pay particular attention to those made from natural fibres as these are their favourites. You might find some dead moths, or some might take flight when you shake out the fabric (shudder).
- Look for little holes in your clothing.
- Little white cocoons on garments will look almost like a thin thread. They're super hard to see but a sign of a moth presence. Larvae can be the size of a pin head, so are even harder to find, but are still visible to the naked eye.
- Set up a moth trap. The number of moths you trap over a few days will indicate if you have a moth presence and, should you have many, how great the issue is (more on these on page 220).

Treating an infestation

So, it's confirmed: you have clothes moths. What do you need to do with affected clothing? Get rid of any larvae that may still be on the fabric as soon as possible. Here are three different paths to take:

Heat

Heat can kill off the larvae right away. As a result, it's often recommended that all freshly laundered garments should be ironed before they're hung up or put away in drawers. I also make sure I treat every piece of vintage clothing I buy before it's added to my wardrobe. I'll use a moth-killing spray, iron the piece, or wash it on a high temp – it all depends on what the fabric can take.

One thing to note here is that while lower-temperature washes are amazing for the environment, a 30-degree wash won't necessarily kill the organic matter on clothes that larvae love or any larvae laid on them. For this reason it's best to do one wash of any potentially affected clothing on a hot wash if the fabric can take it. Some clothing labels will advise dry cleaning. However, if high-temp washes or dry cleaning would damage the garment, I've also heard that tumble-drying, the heat from hair dryers and placing garments in the sun can also kill the larvae. Again, be sure your fabric can take these approaches before you try them out.

Freezing

I'm sure you've heard someone say that you should put clothes with evidence of moth damage into the freezer. This can actually be a good course of action for any garments that can't take extreme heat. Freezing works because the larvae can't thrive in sub-zero temperatures, but be careful how you freeze.

Don't simply put the garments straight into the freezer. They need to be placed in a sealed bag to prevent frost damage. You also need to leave them in the freezer for at least a week so that the cold well and truly does its job. When you take the garments out, make sure you give them some time to come up to room temperature before you remove them from the bag because the fibres could still be super fragile.

Cleaning

While your clothes are being treated, it's important to treat where they live. Clean out your wardrobe, drawers or storage box thoroughly by vacuuming it first, then giving it a wipe down. Vinegar is actually a great candidate for this job, so mix a 50:50 ratio of distilled white vinegar and water in a spray bottle for a great natural cleaning product. Not only will it repel moths, it will also kill larvae. Make sure you pay particular attention to wardrobe or drawer corners and any other areas where they might be hiding.

Prevention is better than cure

Contrary to popular belief, I think mothballs are awful – they can be bad for both you and your pets. I personally don't like them and believe there are better and less toxic ways to deter moths.

Great housekeeping

This is the best and cheapest way to prevent moths. Regular vacuuming and cleaning can help remove any matter in your home that is attractive to moths or that their larvae may feed on. They love dust and pet hair as well as clothes. Make sure you vacuum inside any storage as well as in any corners and areas where moths may hide.

Savvy storage

Wash any soiled or worn clothes before storing them – moths actually prefer dirty clothes and will seek them out. So before you put away items at the end of a season, wash on a high heat (if the care label allows it) to clean the fabric and kill any larvae, then store in a sealed bag or container. A wash in excess of 60 degrees Celsius will be effective in killing any larvae, as will dry cleaning.

Repellents

Moths' super power is their sense of smell. They depend on it for so much – to find food and lovers – which is why it's a great thing to use against them!

Cedar Moths can't stand cedar wood. Like, they absolutely hate it. So hanging precious garments on cedar hangers can deter them from settling anywhere near those pieces. It's worth remembering that the scent can fade as the wood ages, so they won't be as effective at repelling moths after a while. You can treat the hangers with cedar oil after a few years, but be careful not to get the oil anywhere near your garments. There are other cedar products online – pouches and cubes which you place or hang near your clothes as per the manufacturer's guidelines.

Lavender Gorgeous, calming and a natural repellent! Place dried flowers in a wee cloth bag and hang it from your clothes rail or place in drawers. Let the scent fill the space to deter moths. In fact, moths hate a host of herbs and spices so get to know what they are (cloves, rosemary and thyme are a few options), choose the ones you like the smell of most and make your own mix to place in sachets.

Natural sprays You don't want to use any chemical moth repellents that will harm you or your pets. Thankfully you don't have to as there are so many natural sprays on the market now that you can apply directly to clothing. Have a look at what's available and select one that suits your needs.

Dehumidify your home Moths thrive in a humid environment so reducing the humidity in your gaff can make it less attractive to moths. Dehumidifying units or simply airing the property well and frequently can both help.

Monitor the mating cycle You can also buy moth traps with a glue sheet inside that will help you to trap male moths. But how do they work? Remember how moths use their super sense of smell to find a mate? These glue traps actually emit a scent that imitates the pheromone released by female moths, so male moths come flocking to the sheet and get trapped.

Make sure you're in the know when it comes to the type of moth you're dealing with as different species of female emit different pheromones, so you'll need a matching trap. If you're not sure, there are traps out there that can catch multiple moth species.

By catching the males you are interrupting the mating cycle, but that won't do anything about any fertilized females already in your home. It can, however, be a good way to see if you have a problem and breaking up the mating cycle will ensure there are fewer moths down the line.

MOTH TRAP

Mice

I'll keep this brief as I think a professional is always better at dealing with this problem. If you have a very low presence, however, there are things you can do yourself.

Who are they?

Mice are everywhere and there's little we can do about them outside the home, but as they can spread disease once inside, it's important to make sure you do all you can to prevent them from entering your living space.

The house mouse usually sets up shop out of sight but can be heard and sometimes seen. Their super powers are their sense of hearing and ability to fit through small spaces. They mainly come out at night and can be a total nightmare in the home. Let's get to know their habits a bit more in order to prevent or deal with their presence.

How can I tell if I have mice?

- You may hear them
- You may just see one running by
- They may have left droppings
- Food packaging has rips and tears in it from nibbling

Treating an infestation

If you know you have mice, you need to set up some traps. These can be humane and don't have to harm the creature. Once the mouse is caught, you can release it outside. Remember that the cartoon cheese we are all familiar with is a myth; mice prefer sweet foodstuffs such as peanut butter.

Some people will advise that you put down poison but I personally don't think that's the best way to manage things. There's nothing stopping a mouse that has just ingested poison from wandering into a wall cavity, then you'll have a bigger problem on your hands. It's also not the most humane way to deal with the issue.

Once you've seen signs of a mouse and set up traps, make sure you do a deep clean of your home. This will remove anything that is a risk to you, such as droppings, and will also remove anything that might be luring the mouse. Make sure you wear gloves and take any necessary precautions, such as disposing of any droppings carefully. Pay extra attention in the kitchen. A 50:50 mix of distilled white vinegar and water can be great to use here as it will kill bacteria on surfaces. Make sure there are no tempting food sources for mice lying around and that any dry goods are stored in sealed containers. If there's nothing to eat and no way to get at any food in storage, they'll go elsewhere.

Prevention

Prevention is key when it comes to keeping mice out of the home. By taking some simple measures you can ensure that you aren't encouraging them to nest in yours. These steps don't need to be harmful to the mouse or affect your day-to-day living, they're just a few tips to deter mice from thinking yours is the perfect spot to stay in.

Block all access

Identify how the mice might be getting into your home. As they can squeeze through the smallest of gaps, it's best to block any openings and holes – the most common usually being around pipes and fittings such as radiators. It's warm and dark back there and the mice can usually pass through unnoticed. Wire wool and tin foil are great materials to fill these spaces with as they can't be bitten through. If you have any larger unnecessary holes, repair these as soon as you can.

Repellents

There are many non-toxic scents that we like and mice hate, such as peppermint oil. These odours won't kill them or keep them away for ever but will repel them for long enough to give you time to set up some more long-term preventative measures. You'll be able to find these products online without any trouble and use them to target the areas in your home where you think the mice are entering.

Great housekeeping

Again, this is a cheap and easy way to prevent mice from wanting to hang at your gaff. Make sure food is impossible to get at by storing it well, and ensure your kitchen bin lid seals completely when closed. Keep floors well swept (clean the dustpan after use) and wipe down all surfaces after preparing or eating food. Outdoor bins should also be kept away from entrances to your property.

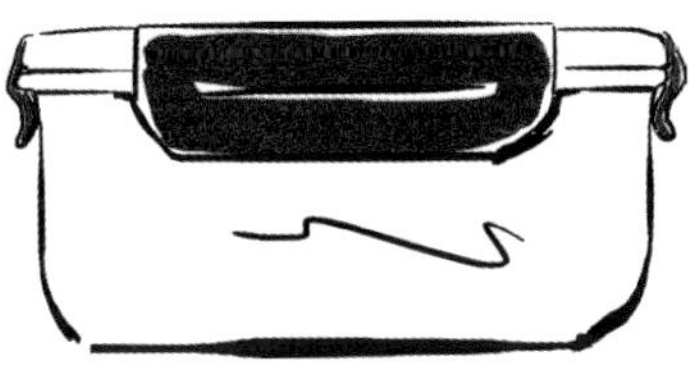

When to call a professional

If your infestation extends to a mouse or two, it can be a case of simply trapping and relocating them. However, if you feel you have a bigger problem on your hands, it's best to call in the professionals. The sooner they can come and assess the issue the better, as mice can breed quite quickly. A pest control team will have knowledge and equipment that will eradicate the problem as swiftly as possible.

Remember, mice are everywhere – especially in big cities – so don't beat yourself up if it happens to you, just act promptly and cleverly.

Mould

As with mice, if this is a big issue in your home, it's best dealt with by a professional as mould can be harmful, especially if you suffer from asthma or allergies. However, there are ways for you to treat small areas and prevent it from coming back.

What is it?

Outside of the home, mould exists everywhere. It's a naturally occurring fungus that is needed for the world to work as it should. Don't be too mad at yourself or your landlord if you find it in your property. Unless there's an underlying issue in your building causing excess moisture, it's usually the result of people creating an environment in which mould spores can thrive. To stop this from happening, we need first to understand how mould works.

Mould spores can't be seen with the naked eye but are all around us. How they go from being invisible and airborne to unsightly mould patches is mainly the result of moisture. When spores settle on surfaces in damp and wet environments they thrive, as they have all they need to grow. Once the cause of excess moisture in that area is found and controlled, the mould won't be able to take hold.

Mould on ceilings and walls

As well as thriving in poorly ventilated, damp areas, mould also appears in areas with little or no natural light. This is why it's super common to find it in windowless bathrooms and en suites. One of the main contributing factors is hot steam hitting cooler surfaces – the ceiling, for example – and condensing on them. This moisture doesn't get a chance to evaporate quickly enough and remains on the surfaces for long enough for mould to form. There are still ways to keep mould at bay in these rooms, however, even if the spores do settle. I'll cover bathroom mould separately on pages 230–1 as it's such a common problem.

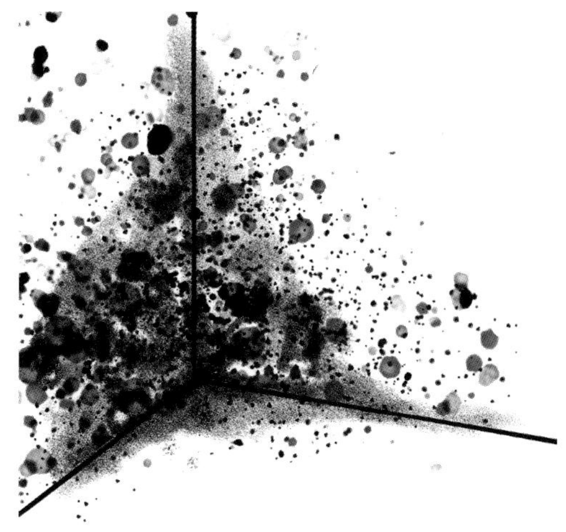

If you have mould patches on non-bathroom walls, or if you find it in some random places that make no sense, there may be a few reasons for this:

- There could be a leak in an adjacent property. I've experienced this situation before and each time the neighbour had no idea they had a problem. Damp can be a scary issue to arrive at anyone's door so I'd avoid going round to check with a neighbour all guns blazing. A quick 'I've noticed some damp on our side and want to be sure your property is OK as we think you may have a leak' is far better than 'You're damaging my property.' Trust me, you'll both need to work together to resolve things, so it's best to treat your neighbours as you would like to be treated if it was your property with the leak.
- If you find mould on an internal wall that isn't shared with a neighbour, suss out what's on the other side. It could be caused by a leaking sink, perhaps, or a damaged internal pipe. If it's an external wall, pop outside and check what's attached to or above it. The culprit could be a leaking outdoor pipe or rainwater dripping from a blocked gutter.

Getting rid of mould

Should you currently have a small mould issue in your home, there are quick and easy ways to remove it and make good the area. Here are my top tips.

#SAFEISCHIC

Before we begin, this is one of my most serious safety notes in the book. Do not tackle mould without kitting yourself out with the correct safety equipment. You're about to risk setting mould spores floating through the air so you need to wear:

- Protective glasses
- A mask (if you inhale these spores they can go deep into your lungs and cause serious illness)
- Gloves (rubber or DIY gloves are fine here but be sure to wash them thoroughly afterwards)
- Old clothes (spores will stick to whatever you're wearing so you want to be able to strip off your cleaning outfit once you're done and put it straight into a hot wash – using vinegar at the rinse stage – to kill them)

You will need:

- Mould remover
- A cloth (microfibre is great as it's quite thick, but whatever you have to hand is fine). Never use a brush to remove mould (imagine how much this would flick the spores at you and around the room).
- Distilled white vinegar
- Mould-repellent paint

You also need to prepare the room:

- Close the door so that spores can't travel into other areas of your home.
- Open any windows and turn on the extractor fan to make sure the spores don't just circulate around the room.
- Remove as many items and soft furnishings as possible from the room, and cover anything that must stay. This will prevent the spores settling anywhere else.

It's up to you whether you choose to use a natural or heavy-duty mould remover, but be aware that there are many cleaning chemicals that you should never mix. Read any instruction labels carefully if you decide to use multiple products.

Once you've chosen your remover and are kitted out in your safety gear, apply the treatment as per the manufacturer's guidelines and wipe away the mould with a cloth. Always dispose of any cloths used or clean them thoroughly on your washing machine's highest heat setting after soaking in distilled white vinegar and water – a 30:70 ratio is fine.

Make sure the area you've cleaned is ventilated enough to dry, so don't rehang any curtains or move any furniture back into the room yet. I'd wait a couple of days – you want to be sure the treatment has worked as well as be confident the area is fully dry. Wash or wipe down anything that may have come into contact with spores.

The next step is to apply a mould-repellent paint. There are many different brands available so take a look online or in a local DIY shop to find out which one is best for you and your budget. Apply to the cleaned area and it will work its magic over time to fight against mould and keep it at bay.

Checking for and minimizing excess moisture

Generally speaking, if you can keep humidity levels low in your home you are at less risk of mould developing. You can check them easily with a piece of kit called a hygrometer, which can be found in most DIY stores. Check the product's packaging for details of where it should be hung – it will give you an accurate reading when placed in the right spot. Humidity should be around 55 per cent in the summer months and 45 per cent in winter to avoid damp and mould, so if you find your readings are higher, make sure to follow the advice below. As I've mentioned, you can never guarantee a mould-free home, but these steps will help to minimize those moisture levels.

- A dehumidifier is a great way to suck moisture from the air inside your home and can have a really positive effect on your living overall – the air quality will be better and the reduction in moisture levels means your home will have fewer dust mites.

Bear in mind this isn't a long-term solution, though, as these appliances are designed for removing moisture following floods and large leaks. More effective long-term solutions are extractor fans and vents that can draw the moisture out of a property entirely.

- Ventilate your property as often as possible. Even if you just open a couple of windows and all the internal doors to let the place breathe for a few hours on a Sunday – that's fine during the winter but do it as much as possible during the summer.
- If you have a ventilation system throughout your apartment, make sure that it's always on when windows and doors are closed. It's also helpful to remember to turn it off when they're open. If you don't have a ventilation system, open windows where and when possible but don't leave them open when it's raining as your home will fill with damp air.
- Make sure all existing vents are working properly. Never block them with furniture, and open window ones where possible to allow moist air to leave your property. You can also twist circular vents anticlockwise to make sure that they are open fully, which is handy in a bathroom.
- Open doors and windows to rooms where heat and steam accumulate, such as bathrooms and kitchens, during and after use to make sure they are aired out and any surfaces have the opportunity to dry off. Shutting the bathroom door and turning off the fan as soon as you've finished your shower is not the way to go. Remember to test your extractor fan with a length of tissue paper, as per the instructions on pages 6–7.
- Make the most of extractors – they are designed specifically to pull moisture-rich air from your rooms so mould and damp can't set up camp. Always use your cooker hood when cooking,

especially when boiling and steaming food. Even a little move, such as using lids when boiling something on the hob, can reduce the steam and moisture in the air. Make sure its filter is cleaned regularly so that it functions as well as possible.

- If you dry clothes within the home, open a nearby window – or dry them under or near an air vent – so the damp air is encouraged to leave the property.
- Wipe away any condensation as soon as it appears on windows and sills so that there's no time to create a home for mould to thrive.

Bathroom mould

This is such a common problem and can look so awful that it needs its own section here. If you're sure that your extractor fan is working and there is no rising damp or sign of a leak, then you can help by ensuring you make the following changes to your routine:

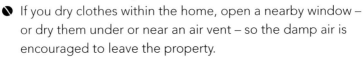

- Extractor fans should be on during *and after* showering, until all condensation from mirrors and glass has evaporated. If your bathroom has a window, leaving it open while you shower will always help. However, if you can't – for privacy reasons or because it's cold – remember to open it afterwards.
- Mould grows on silicone seals if moisture is allowed to sit on them for long periods. To make sure yours stays mould-free, don't store any products on the sealed edges of the bath, shower tray, or on your sink. Doing so will trap water after you've taken a shower or run a tap, creating little pools of moisture that will very quickly lead to mould.

- Bath mats and shower curtains need adequate time and space to dry thoroughly. Ensure you pull your curtain flat after showering, with the ends inside the bath or shower tray so that residual water can drip down the drain and not on to the floor. Always hang your bath mat somewhere to dry. By making sure both these items can dry easily and quickly, you'll drastically reduce the length of time that there's a lot of moisture in the air.
- If your shower area or sink has a lot of water on it after use, wipe it down. There's no point ignoring the issue, as it will lead to further problems, such as a mould issue you cannot control without professional help or having to replace plasterboard.
- Cleaning your bathroom regularly and keeping it clutter-free will ensure a happier, mould-free space. Do a weekly cleaning blitz, using hot water and either a bathroom cleaner or a natural cleaner with vinegar, which will kill mould spores and stop mould developing. Mould loves soap scum – it's almost like a food source. Leaving this residue on surfaces will only worsen your mould problem.

Uninvited guests are terrifying at the best of times, but those that don't leave at the end of a soirée, such as pests and mould, can be a nightmare. If you do begin to find evidence of some in your home, don't be so afraid of them that you turn a Chanel liquid-lined blind eye – investigate right away. A small, manageable problem dealt with correctly will not only remove the uninvited guest, it will also mean you'll have preventative measures in place to stop them from coming back. If you ignore it, you'll have a bigger problem on your hands.

If you've moved into a property with issues, don't be shy in asking for help. Start by taking pictures and requesting quotes online. It's one small step that will put you back in control. As soon as you start speaking to professionals you'll see how easy it will be to fix and you'll feel more reassured, I promise.

9. A SAFE HOME

A safe home is a happy home, and there are many measures you can take to ensure you feel secure in yours. In this chapter I'll run through the different types of safety alarms and intruder deterrents to give you peace of mind in your sanctuary, and give some childproofing tips should you have little people in your life to consider. Some are must-haves, others are food for thought, and some are small tasks for rainy days.

Remember, there are no heroes when it comes to home safety, just chic, safe gals who don't put themselves or their home at risk.

Fire Safety Alarms

When it comes to fire safety, prevention is key. Keeping fire risks to a minimum is usually common sense: knowing how to safely use anything that involves a naked flame, for example; not using any unsafe equipment; and always knowing when to call a professional for help or to carry out a repair.

If you're not sure about something or want to know more about prevention in the home, government advice and information on fire safety is readily available. Government websites will include some really good tips about how to handle situations where fire is involved. I'd advise reading up on this info and ensuring everyone in your home knows what actions to take in case of an emergency.

Online you can find the legal fire safety requirements for landlords and tenants in your city or country. If you're a tenant or you have tenants, make sure you know what should be provided in your property to keep you/them safe. Once you know these legal requirements have been met, you can then take any additional measures yourself, as needed. I always find my estate agent can help outline these requirements and point me in the right direction of contractors who can provide the relevant certification and so on. If you have an agent overseeing a tenancy for you, ask them, or ask to be put in touch with the company's property management team who will be very well-versed in what's required.

It's important to be fire-prevention savvy but it's equally important to have the right alarms in place to alert you should something happen. Early detection is key when it comes to fires – here's what you should have in place as an absolute minimum …

Smoke and heat alarms

Not everyone is aware of how many smoke alarms they need in their property or where they should be placed. Professional advice is that you should have a minimum of one smoke alarm on each floor of your home, positioned in the hallway(s)/landing(s) of each storey, and, for even faster fire detection, in any room where a fire can start. This means rooms containing electrical equipment, even if it's just a phone charging. They shouldn't be fitted in a bathroom, kitchen or any room where there is a lot of smoke or steam generally – these need heat alarms (see more on heat alarms below).

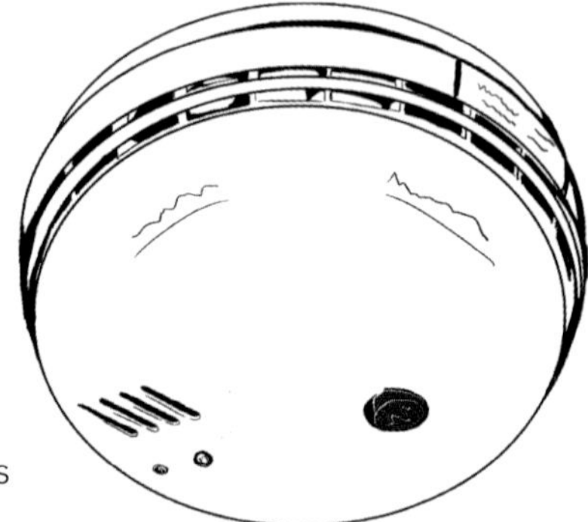

Some alarms, battery-operated and wired, can be linked together so that when one goes off on the ground level of a three-storey house, those on the upper floors will go off too. Most fires happen when we are sleeping, so this is a super-safe option to give you more time to react.

Heat alarms are ideal for rooms such as the kitchen or the bathroom. They are designed to detect a higher-than-normal temperature rather than smoke, so they won't go off if you burn your toast. They might sound more complicated, but they can be bought and installed just as easily as smoke alarms, and are also inexpensive.

Purchase

As with anything: buy cheap, buy twice. This goes for the alarm itself and the batteries too. When it comes to alarms, you can choose battery-operated or wired. If you choose an alarm that is wired up to mains power, you will need an electrician to install it. Never do it yourself.

All alarms should meet an EU safety standard in order to be sold, so make sure yours has the right safety labelling. It will look like this:

THIS EU SYMBOL STANDS FOR 'CONFORMITÉ EUROPÉENNE'

#SAFEISCHIC

If anyone in your home is hearing-impaired, or there might be a delay for any reason in them hearing the alarm or reacting to a fire, make sure there is a plan in place to help them.

Installation

Read your alarm's manual from cover to cover – it will help you choose where to place the alarm in your chosen room(s). They should almost always be fitted at ceiling height. The manual will also tell you the most effective ways to attach them.

Neither smoke nor heat alarms should be placed too near cookers – the steam and smoke given off while food is cooking can cause many false alarms. Not only can this wear out the battery, it could also result in you (or your tenants) removing the batteries for some peace when cooking and forgetting to put them back in. This is a huge issue with badly placed alarms and another reason why heat alarms are actually better in the kitchen.

Maintenance

Test your batteries and the health of your alarm every week. When the low-battery alert starts beeping, replace the batteries straight away, or the alarm itself, if necessary. Many alarm manuals state how long the unit should work well for – usually up to ten years. You can write down the date you bought it to help you remember. Most new alarms will have this information already written on the casing or they'll have a blank label for you to fill in. Some alarms have ten-year batteries so you replace the unit and batteries in one go. Wired alarms also need to be replaced every ten years by an electrician.

If you move into a property and have no idea how old the alarm is, you will most likely find a sticker on the side of the unit with a date written on it. Some are inside the casing, so take your alarm off its mount and have a look inside. It'll tell you either the year it was made or the year it needs to be changed. If there is no date, it's most likely over ten years old. Better to be safe than sorry here, and replace it.

To make sure your alarm is working to its full potential, vacuum it to remove any clogged dust. This should be done every 3–5 months to prevent it having any issues with detecting a fire.

If your alarm goes off and it's a false alarm – if something has burnt while cooking, for example – don't remove the batteries to silence it. Instead, fan the vents and air out the room. Some newer alarms have a function to allow you to silence it until the smoke clears.

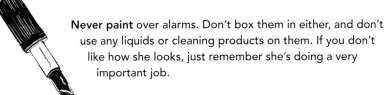

Never paint over alarms. Don't box them in either, and don't use any liquids or cleaning products on them. If you don't like how she looks, just remember she's doing a very important job.

Carbon monoxide alarms

Carbon monoxide is known as the 'silent killer'. If you have gas supplied to your home, you need to have a carbon monoxide alarm. No excuses. Carbon monoxide is odourless, tasteless and undetectable by us, so we need alarms in place to ensure we're made aware if there's ever a threat. It's a highly poisonous gas and exposure to it can lead to death. This sounds pretty terrifying, but it's important to know the risks so you take the alarm requirement seriously.

Purchase

Buying a carbon monoxide detector is easy, inexpensive and they are widely available online and in DIY stores. Remember to read up on the lifespan of your unit and pop a sticker on the back stating when it should be changed if there's not already a date filled in. Not all alarms will warn you when they are past their best so it is important to be on top of this.

Installation

Every room that has a fuel-burning appliance in it should have a carbon monoxide alarm monitoring it. This usually means living areas, kitchens or the room your boiler is in. Make sure you can hear the alarm from anywhere in the property when it goes off. It should also be loud enough to wake you from your sleep. If you find you can't hear it well, place additional alarms in your hallway or link them up to all sound when one goes off.

Make sure you don't place your alarm above an air vent or window – the airflow may compromise the unit's detection of carbon monoxide. Your manual will advise you where best to place your alarm and you should follow these details carefully – they are not like smoke alarms.

While we're on the topic of gas, you should have a gas safety inspection carried out for your home each year, to obtain a gas safety certificate. Landlords must legally supply these certs. Gas safety appointments include some additional measures to a normal boiler service, but you can book the same engineer to do them both in one go. The engineer must be gas registered to confirm your home is safe and they are the only people who can issue these certs.

Intruder Deterrents

The best place to start when reducing security risks from the outside is to think like an intruder. How would you access your home if you were a burglar? Consider the weak points of entry and address those first. Remove any wheelie bins from under windows and secure them where they can't be used to give a step up. Don't advertise your expensive possessions to the outside world either. Computers and electronic equipment left right inside a window can lure opportunistic thieves.

Locks

If there's a particularly weak point of entry to your home, such as a utility room at the back of the house, consider fitting a lock on this room's internal door which can be used when you're out. If someone manages to gain access to this room from the outside, the lock could help prevent them from getting into the rest of your property.

Let's talk more about locks. They're something that people can often let slide but they're the first port of call when it comes to securing your home. Especially a flat.

If you have a weak lock in your home – one that is damaged or not doing a great deal to keep intruders out – or one that isn't in use because the key has gone astray, consider this your nudge to get it sorted. A door is most secure when it's locked in more than just one place, for many reasons. Not all front doors have multi-lock systems around the door, securing it to the frame – these are usually found in newer doors and developments. However, you can add additional locks such as deadbolts should you wish to ensure your door locks in more than one place. This is not only a deterrent but also means that your door will be held closed in another position should one lock be compromised.

Finding a locksmith

Getting the locks changed or upgraded on a property is incredibly stress-free and easy. It's a simple appointment and one that won't cost as much as you imagine. Always use someone who is certified and checks out. You don't want to put you or your property at risk.

When getting a quote I always take pictures of the front and back of the door in question as well as supplying the door width. Some locks will lock into your door frame at just one point – the lock – whereas others may have a multi-locking system, so it's important to show these details to ensure the quote is accurate. If you'd like your new lock to be a particular colour or material – brass or chrome, for example – it's important to specify that at this stage as it can affect the price. If the locksmith knows all these details beforehand, there won't be any surprises on the day and you can rest assured that all the work will be carried out in the one appointment.

Before I book a locksmith, I'll shop around and get three quotes. I'll always let businesses know I'm doing this as it usually leads to a discount, or they might highlight where they differ from their competitors in terms of quality and service. This is really useful information to have as it may mean the lowest quote is actually not the best.

Shopping for a lock

If you decide to fit a lock yourself or are purchasing it for your contractor to install, never buy one that doesn't meet EU standards. You should also make sure you go to a certified locksmith or a reputable DIY store that stocks certified brands. You can easily verify their credentials online now and can also check that they have the most up-to-date knowledge and will help you choose what is right for your property. From the type of door you have to the level of security you need, there are so many things to consider.

Whenever you replace a lock, remember to check your home insurance requirements. You need to make sure you are fulfilling your side of the policy so a claim isn't deemed void. Some locks won't meet the standard required in your policy so always check.

Consider purchasing a lock that has a key registration service, which means no one can copy your key without your knowledge. This is super handy if you rent out your property, especially on a temporary basis. In order to copy a registered key you have to take a form of certification with you. This usually consists of the paperwork for the lock along with your ID. This means you can rest easy should you have to let your keys out of your sight for any reason. This may go without saying, but *never* put the address for the keys on the keyring. I tend to see it a lot when keys are given back to me after tenancies end but also when I buy properties and it's such a security risk.

There are now also 'smart' door locks on the market, which combine standard locks with technology. There are codes, fingerprint scanners and apps available – all options that make it more difficult for a lock to be picked.

Deterrents

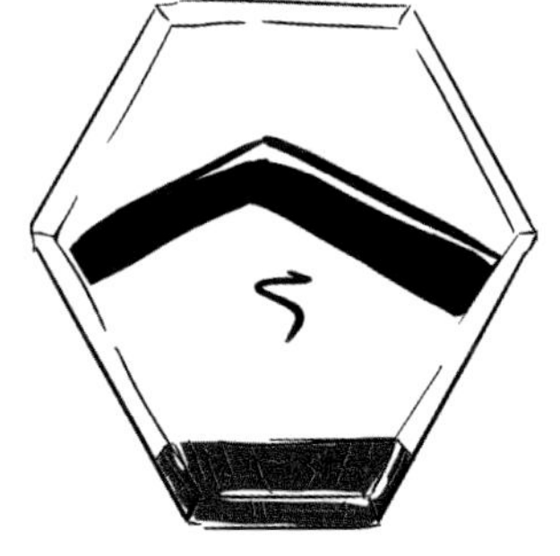

There's not much you can do to stop intruders entirely once they've decided to break into your home, but there is a lot you can do to put thieves off targeting your nest in the first place, as a lot of surveys show. The main thing you can do is to put deterrents in place which delay their entry and draw attention to them. Below are just a few options to consider.

Intruder alarm

I'm not saying that an alarm sounding is going to physically stop anyone from entering your property, but the presence of one can put off a potential intruder. The key to putting intruders off is to have numerous deterrents that make your property unappealing to them. It's the attention an alarm draws more than anything else. Remember, most insurance companies won't accept an alarm on your policy unless it's been installed by a professional.

Outdoor lighting

Sensor lights at the entrance to your property – or any other outdoor area – that are switched on at night can be a great asset. They prevent your front or back door from becoming somewhere a potential

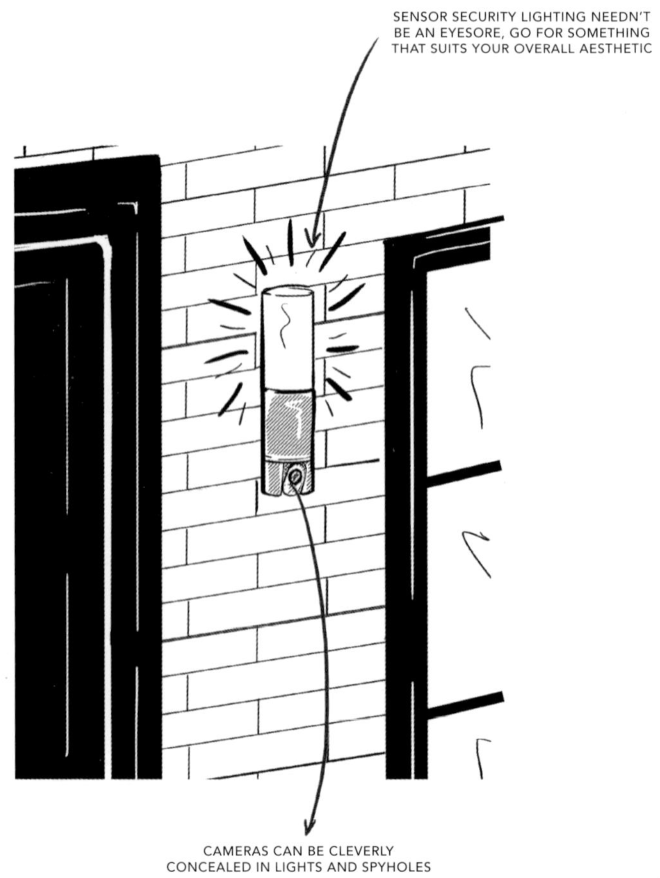
SENSOR SECURITY LIGHTING NEEDN'T BE AN EYESORE, GO FOR SOMETHING THAT SUITS YOUR OVERALL AESTHETIC
CAMERAS CAN BE CLEVERLY CONCEALED IN LIGHTS AND SPYHOLES

intruder can take time to tamper with your locks unnoticed. Instead, the sudden light can attract attention and scare them off. These lights also highlight areas for security cameras and allow you to see what has set them off – be it a false alarm, such as a fox, or an actual burglar. In addition to being a useful security measure, they're also handy for when you yourself are approaching the property at night – you'll avoid tripping and they'll help you get inside safely.

Security cameras

Cameras are one of the biggest turn-offs for would-be intruders as their footage can be used as evidence. Even if you live in an apartment, you can still have a camera installed. There are so many different models on the market now – wired, battery-operated, connected to your phone, linked to a security company, and so on – that there's sure to be one to suit your needs. They don't have to be unsightly and can even be installed in your spy hole, or as part of a light fitting.

Signs

Some old-school deterrents are measures that make someone think twice, especially an opportunistic thief. When someone is considering breaking into a property, it's all about being able to get in and get out quickly, so many homeowners will put up 'beware of the dog' signs or a notice that reads 'this property is under 24-hour surveillance', even if that's not the case. If you do use fake security company signs, any professional burglar will know these signs well and be able to spot a fake so it could put you more at risk, therefore choose wisely, research well and don't rely on these measures on their own. Signs should be more top-up measures than deterrents in themselves; something to be used to add an extra layer of 'not my gaff, hun'.

Fencing

Erecting a fence around your property is a great idea. You don't need planning permission if you keep it below a certain height and this is usually greater than is possible for someone to climb over easily. Check your local authority's website to see what the height restriction is, as it varies from country to country.

A trellis can be a great way to add some extra height to an existing low wall or fence. Again, check with your local authority for

restrictions. It will still allow light through and won't look awful, but will make the fence less easy to scale. You can add some gorgeous (very thorny) flowers or paint and it'll look less like a security measure and more like tasteful decoration.

Hedges

More natural and prettier deterrents can be large or prickly hedges. These can give you privacy and also prevent unwanted access to your property.

Window bars

Not all window bars have to be ugly. With a little research you'll be able to find bars that suit the character of your property and your weak-spot windows or doors. Even if an intruder smashes a window to gain access, the bars will prevent them from climbing through.

Lighting timers

If you're heading away on holiday, lighting timers are really useful when it comes to making it appear that someone is still home. The one piece of advice I'd give here is to buy the ones that allow you to set your lights to come on at different times each day for a period of your choosing. Some timers even have a random setting so it's not obvious to anyone looking in from the outside that you're not at home. If you set the lights to come on at the same time each day it can be a bit obvious that you're not there, so it's great to have a function that makes things look a bit more natural.

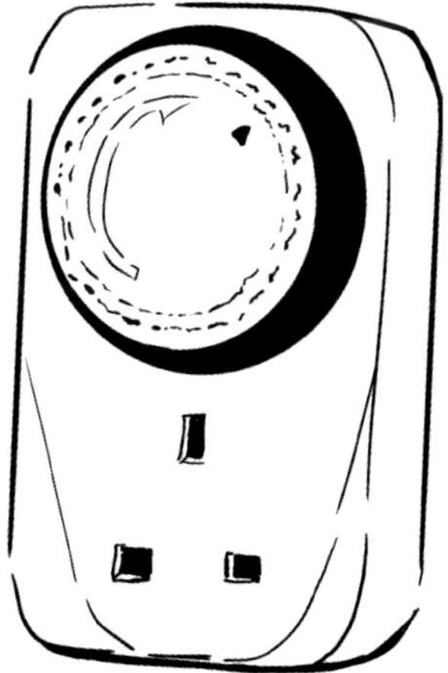

Childproofing

I'm not a baby expert, but how you do anything is how you do everything, so I've compiled some handy tips and advice for beginning to make a home more child-friendly. What follows are simple measures I'd put in place if I had a baby or toddler coming to stay, and where I'd start if I had a baby at home. It's not only about putting Versace plates out of reach, it's also about preventing accidents and providing a safe environment for a child to enjoy himself or herself, and to explore their surroundings without coming to any harm.

When it comes to childproofing your home, there is a mountain of information and advice out there, and it's hard to know where to start. I'd begin by assessing each room individually.

Kitchen

The kitchen is where many hours can be spent with children but also where many hazards lurk. Here are some easy ways to prevent accidents without compromising the use or look of your kitchen too much. While style is something I love to experiment with in my home, nothing is more goddessy than a safe space. While childproof locks might not look great, the peace of mind they bring and the safety of any children outweigh everything else, so just go for it. It won't be for ever.

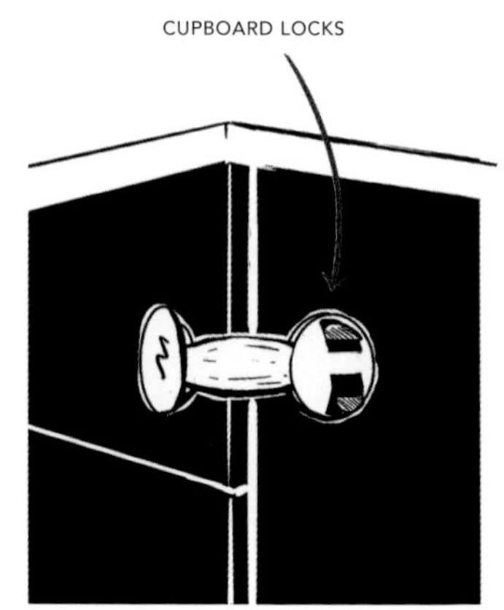

Cupboard locks

These are cheap to buy, easy to install and easy to use. Simply attach them to all cupboard doors that are within reach of little hands. They'll keep cupboard contents safely away from children but are easy to open for adults.

Decoy cupboard

A decoy cupboard is always handy. You can fill it with kitchen items that are OK for a child to play with and will keep them distracted from the more risky contents of other cupboards. Choose one that is easily accessible, away from appliances, and which doesn't slam shut or have anything inside that is at risk of falling or being pulled down.

Safe storage

Dishwasher tablets and washing capsules look like a whole lot of fun to children, so make sure these are stored up high and out of reach. I'd always recommend putting a child lock on the cupboard under the sink as it can house some risky items.

Bathroom

Many statistics highlight the fact that most accidents happen due to lapses in supervision. No one can have their eyes on everything all the time, so it's important to reduce risks where we can. In the bathroom, water – especially hot water – sharp objects, and hard and slippery surfaces are the main dangers. Here are some ways to help make bath time easier.

Mats

Anti-slip mats are great as they protect your child from losing their footing and they'll also help you if you're holding them in the shower or the bath.

Tap protectors

These are great and can come in some really fun shapes, which means they double up as a distraction for your child as well as preventing them from being able to turn on or touch a hot tap. They're usually made of rubber and are fixed over the metal spout, so won't pose any danger should your child knock against them or play with them. (I particularity enjoy the hippos that spurt water out their nostrils.)

Lid locks

These are great to make sure a child cannot lift open a toilet seat lid.

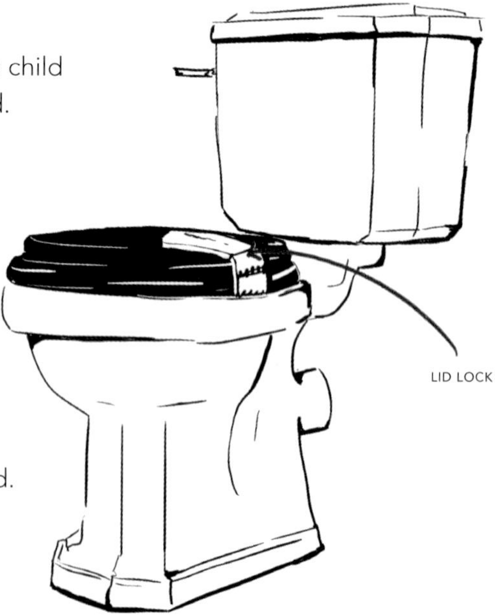

Bath caddies

To avoid those moments when you have to turn away from a child you're bathing to reach for something, and therefore minimize any risks at bath time, I'd have a handy caddy next to the tub, containing everything you need. Your sponges, towel, shampoo and baby wash are all within easy reach, and the caddy can be moved as one with you, so you won't have to turn your back.

LID LOCK

General

Throughout the home, risks include trip hazards, sharp corners and items within reach that are harmful to children. Like children, not every home is the same and each will have different needs. It's impossible to remove every single danger and hazard, and some accidents are just unpreventable. Here are some handy tips to consider and start you off when assessing your space. Don't panic, you've got this.

- Always ensure all pull cords on blinds are secure and out of reach. Your blinds should come with instructions on exactly where and how to secure the cords, but if this is missing consult the manufacturer's website.
- Eliminate trip hazards throughout your home, for both you and your baby. Assess all areas and deal with them ASAP. Make sure rug corners are secure and there are no raised floorboard edges. (On the subject of flooring, if you know some of your boards are exceptionally loud or creaky, and you need to avoid them while the baby is sleeping, tape an X over the points that cause the noise so you and guests can avoid them easily.)
- To prevent little fingers from getting trapped in doors, you can either buy specific products that stop the doors from slamming or purchase a length of foam tubing to fit around the edges.
- Safety gates are a great way to block off an entire part of a home. They can be secured to most doorways and walls quite easily, once you've bought the correct size. To do so, measure the width of the space carefully and make sure you note any obstructions that could prevent you from attaching the gate successfully, such as hinges. Be sure to place a gate at both the top and the bottom of

staircases to make life a little easier – remember to take into account a height measurement here too, as you'll need to attach the top of the gate to something.

- If you have a fireplace, always make sure you have a fireguard in position, and one that can't be pulled down.
- Don't forget to install a safety latch on all bins, especially the bathroom one, which is usually much smaller than the kitchen bin and will sometimes have razor blades and other dangerous items inside. When there are kids in the home, I wouldn't recommend having any open-top bins. It's safest to have ones that can lock or have a lid lock applied.
- It is vital to secure all your free-standing furniture. As babies learn to walk, they'll use furniture to pull themselves up. They will also climb up and into drawers, and reach for shelves as they grow. This means any items of furniture that have the potential to topple can pose huge safety risks. Free-standing flat-pack items of furniture now come with brackets to help you attach them to the wall or floor when needed. If you don't have any brackets, you can buy them online and in DIY stores. There's a great variety of options available to ensure the least amount of damage to your walls and the piece of furniture.
- Sharp edges. Go around each room to see which sharp edges and corners your child could come into contact with. There are so many options out there for covering them, you'll be spoiled for choice. They don't have to look awful and, as your child grows, many are easy to remove and fit on to the next place they're needed.
- Get to know which plants can be dangerous for babies if ingested and give them away to someone.

We've covered the basics of adapting your home to make it more secure and to reduce risks. I hope it's given you some food for thought and made you consider some ways in which you can make your property less vulnerable. Don't forget this is something that's important to keep on top of, and with security and alarm technology constantly evolving, it can be helpful to look into what's out there that could make safety even more accessible for you. It can seem a little overwhelming at first but you need to remember, the safest girls really are the chicest, in every part of life.

10. BACK TO BASICS

It's fabulous when everything in the home is working as it should, but the world needn't stop if the fridge or toilet does. Water outages happen, fridges break down, washing machine deliveries get delayed. That's life. This chapter outlines some tips on how to carry on should something fail. It will ensure that life can continue even if you find yourself without some necessities, and how to go back to basics should you need to.

Fridge Failures

Don't fret if your fridge breaks down and you're waiting for a repair/replacement – or if you just need to live without one for a while. There are ways to get by and also to deal with any contents in need of short-term accommodation.

What to do with your refrigerated food

When it comes to it, you'll find that many items don't actually need to be stored in your fridge, they just need to be kept out of direct sunlight and in a cool dry place. Once a fridge is turned off/breaks down, it will stay cool (if the door isn't opened!) for about 4 hours. If there's a short-term power outage, simply avoid opening the fridge for as long as you can so you keep what's inside fresh for as long as possible.

If you're going to find yourself without a fridge for a longer period of time, you can immediately transfer your fruit and vegetables to a more suitable setting (just remember to keep those that emit ethylene away from the more sensitive ones – see pages 85–9 for details on where you can store fruit and veg outside of the fridge). The same goes for jams and marmalade – they don't necessarily need the cool temperatures of the fridge because their fruit content gives them a fairly high acidity, which will keep them from harbouring and growing bacteria.

It's mainly meat, poultry and fish that become super dangerous if stored badly. Try to use up this meat right away to avoid any risks.

The short-term fix

The main items that will require cold storage should you find yourself without a fridge are dairy items. I'd advise buying meat as you go so you don't need to store it at all. It's too risky to use a makeshift fridge to store meat.

To fashion a temporary fridge you'll need:

- A cooler box
- Ice or ice packs (enough to rotate so someone like a neighbour or friend can freeze the spares while the others are in use)

Make sure your cooler box seals perfectly and you can pack it with ice or ice packs, replacing them as they thaw or melt. When you're without a fridge, the main thing is to shop smart. This doesn't just mean picking food that doesn't need to be stored in a fridge; it means buying food that comes in smaller packages so it can all be consumed almost immediately and not require storage afterwards.

Toilet Troubles

If you receive advance warning that your water supply is going to be interrupted – for example, during building works – fill the bath beforehand so you've got some water on standby. If you don't have a bath, store it in your metal bucket (see page 41).

If there's ever a water outage, the last thing people tend to think about is the toilet. This is usually because a cistern always has one flush's worth of water in it, so the toilet will go unnoticed. The thing to remember with flushing toilets is that it's basically all down to gravity, so you will be able to bucket flush until your water returns. The trick with the bucket flush is not to pour meekly. A strong flow of water is needed to create the 'flush', so make sure you literally dump the water in. Once the water in the toilet bowl is clear, you're sorted – don't overuse the water you've saved.

Washing Machine Woes

If your machine is temporarily out of order or you are waiting on a new one to arrive, it's time to go back to the old-school ways of hand-washing items.

What you'll need:

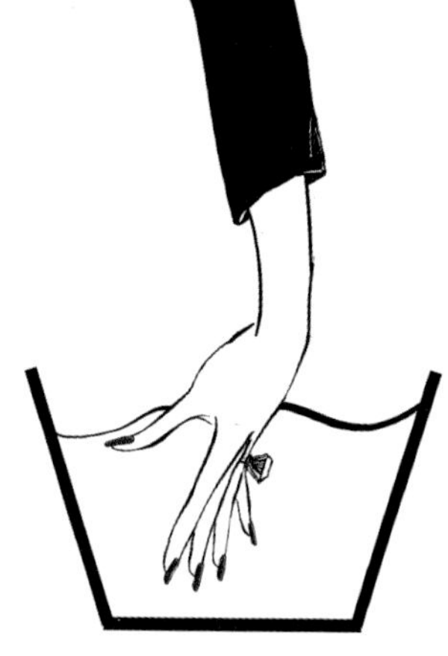

- Two large containers – I'd use your metal bucket (see page 41) and kitchen sink for ease instead of buying and storing plastic basins specifically for this purpose. Make sure they are both completely clean before use.
- Hand-washing detergent – make sure you use one that suits the items you're washing. Some fabrics, such as wool or silk, can't handle the enzymes that are found in some biological detergents and will damage the fibres, so it's important to check first.
- Rubber gloves – some detergents can irritate sensitive skin and it's less likely your nail varnish will lift if you remember to wear a pair.

#SAFEISCHIC

Always read the garment label on your clothes before you wash them. If something is dry clean only that may mean it's not OK to hand wash, so avoid doing so. Some items of clothing, particularly tailored pieces, can't actually handle a lot of water and agitation and so need to be dry cleaned only.

Step 1

Separate your load by colour, as you would when using a washing machine. When you begin washing, always start with the lightest colour items first. You wouldn't want to put something white into water that may have some dye in it.

Step 2

Fill your bucket with warm water – not too hot! The heat can damage fibres as well as harming you. Make sure it's about half to three-quarters full only. You'll be putting clothes in and also moving them around a lot so let's prevent overspill here.

Add as much detergent as is recommended on the packaging. Do not use an excessive amount, as tempting as it might be. Too much soapy water and you'll have to rinse a lot more, which can damage your clothes and wreck your head.

Now, fill the sink with cold water – again, about half to three-quarters full.

Step 3

Pop your first few items into the warm water and get ready to mimic a machine cycle. Move the items of clothing around so they gently rub against each other. If any are particularly badly stained, use another piece of the garment to rub against the stain, which will hopefully lift it. I'd then leave these items to soak for a maximum of 5 minutes.

Step 4

Squeeze each garment gently and pop them into the sink of cold water. Time to rinse! This next stage will remove the detergent from the clothes. To do this, I lift each garment in and out of the water a few times (but never by its hem or shoulders as this can stretch it). When you're happy the detergent is gone, gently squeeze the garment again. Never wring out the clothes as this will damage the fabric.

To remove any excess water, place each garment in turn on a clean towel and roll it up to press out the water. As hand-washed garments can be wetter than those that have been spun in a machine, allow them to dry flat, especially if they are made of a fabric with stretch in it, such as wool or jersey. The water will weigh the garment down and cause stretching if hung up.

Caring for your clothes

While I have you here, let's chat about some general care points.

Hanging knitwear and shirts

Never, ever, ever hang any of your knitwear items. When a knitted garment is hung up, this can cause the seams to stretch and literally grow on the hanger over time. Necklines and shoulders will also distort. Now that you know this, keep an eye out for chunkier knitwear in end-of-winter sales – these often have huge, surprising discounts and this is usually because they've grown and distorted while hanging all season. For this reason, always fold knitted items.

When hanging shirts or anything that ties at the neck, make sure you fasten them up beforehand. This will reduce the risk of the garment creating a new neck shape.

Clip hangers

These hangers are great for keeping skirts and trousers that are pleated or tailored crease-free. However, if the item is heavily embellished or made from a delicate material such as suede or leather, the clips on the hangers can cause permanent dents and marks to the fabric. To avoid this, place a folded piece of card in between the clip and the garment.

Dry clean only

Dry cleaning is a process that uses chemicals instead of water and agitation to clean garments. When something says dry clean only, this usually means it can't hack excess water or the levels of agitation, rinsing and spinning of a regular wash cycle. Obey the dry clean only advice.

When it comes to storing dry cleaning on its return to you, *always* remove the plastic cover the dry cleaner packs it in. These covers are for transport only and never for storage purposes. We usually wear dry clean only items the least, and this means we often hang them straight up once they're returned and don't look at them until we need to wear them again. Instead, we should:

DRY CLEAN

DRY CLEAN ONLY

DO NOT DRY CLEAN

THESE NOTES ARE FOR YOUR DRY CLEANER AND INDICATE WHICH CHEMICALS ARE OK TO USE

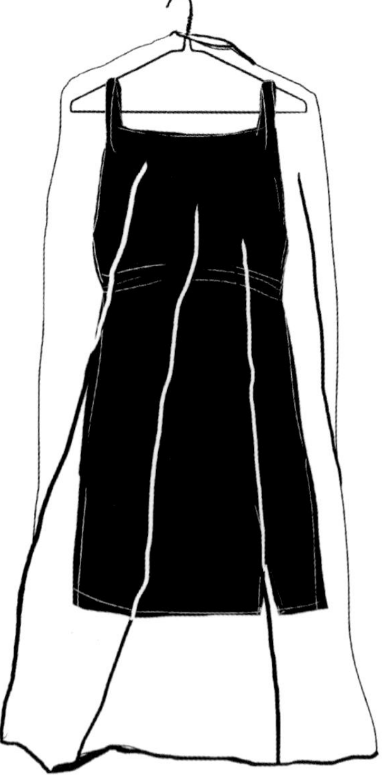

- Inspect the garment as soon as it's returned, or in the cleaner's if possible. There's usually a time limit on when you can raise an issue such as damage or fading with the company who carried out the work, so make sure you do it as soon as possible.
- Remove the clear plastic cover and store the item either without a cover or in a breathable clothing bag if needed. The plastic covers supplied by the dry cleaner actually trap moisture and don't let the clothing breathe. This means mildew and mould could begin to grow on your clothing without you noticing. As the item will also have been cleaned using chemicals, I always feel it's best to leave it to breathe afterwards, so the plastic is a no-go for me for more than one reason.
- If you want to protect your clothing using a clothing bag or cover, make sure whatever you use is designed for anti-mould, meaning it will be breathable and not trap moisture.

Mould

Mould, as we know, just happens. But when it appears on clothes … (shriek!) We can instantly think the piece is ruined for ever. Don't worry, though – you can easily remove the mould and next time, make sure you don't put away damp clothes.

Here's how to cure your mouldy clothes:

- If the fabric can withstand a gentle wash, pop the item in your machine on a warm cycle and keep an eye on it, so you know what stage it is at, and add 2 cups of distilled white vinegar to the rinse cycle. This should wash away the mould and then treat the fabric so that all mould spores are killed off. Let it dry completely before you inspect it to see if the mould has gone. If not, repeat.
- If you've discovered mould on a garment that can't go near water, fear not. Send it to the dry cleaner as normal and let them know the area affected. Dry cleaning uses so much heat it's effective at killing off the mould and they will also usually treat the area so not only will it be removed, it will be prevented from coming back. Some people say you can treat the area yourself, but I'd always advise sticking to the advice on the garment's care label – you never know if the fabric will take well to water and any other product you may use.

Although we're coming to the end of my tips and advice – *pats tear from cheek* – I know this is just the beginning for your inner Gaff Goddess! She's a state of mind, and one that is strong and powerful. She'll help you enjoy your space and will always see you right. To be handy in your home you don't need to be a DIY expert or have a shed full of tools, and I hope this guide has taught you just that. I also hope it's given you the confidence to approach repairs yourself, to know when to ask for help, to zone to perfection and to get the most out of your home and appliances. Remember #safeischic: *never* store your plunger by your toilet and always protect those beautiful hands. Most of all … don't forget, a red lip is always appreciated, approachable and appropriate, especially when indulging in some She-IY.

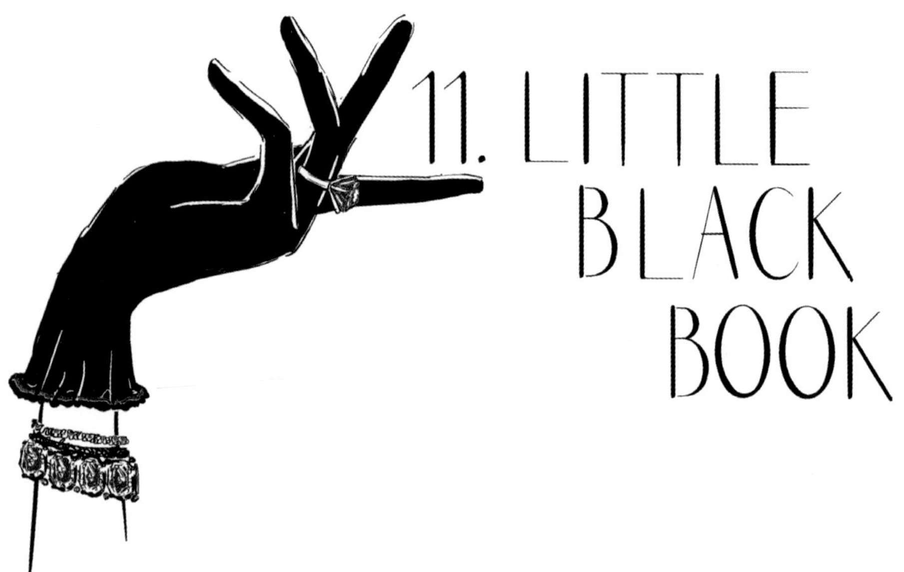

11. LITTLE BLACK BOOK

When it comes to hiring contractors, many people don't know where to start. You've probably heard so many horror stories about untrustworthy or unskilled tradespeople that the really good ones don't tend to get the airtime they deserve. A good contractor, to me, is worth their weight in gold. Next time you hear someone speaking about work they've had done (on their house, not their face – that's a whole different book!) in a positive way, ask them how they found their contractor and note down their details.

When I first started searching for contractors I had zero recommendations. At times, I was working in a new city with no contacts or price comparisons. On one project, I needed to get a quote for fitting new carpets, so I began my search by popping into local carpet shops and asking them if they had a list of fitters. They will always have a list of carpet fitters and they will never be the bad ones. This is because good contractors are in demand and will be buying lots of materials regularly. The stores therefore get to know them well and will usually have their contact details to hand.

Whether it's a carpet fitter, plumber, electrician or builder that you need, go to where they source their materials and those stores will almost always have some details for you. If I need a job done as low cost as possible, I'll always flag this during our initial conversation. The stores will usually give me the details of someone who works for property managers, as those contractors will always have the most competitive prices. Property management companies will usually choose something practical with good visual impact but the lowest price and so the contractors will be familiar with what materials and methods can achieve this.

Another way to find a good contractor is through one you already know. Birds of a feather will always flock together. If I work with a great contractor on a job, I'll make sure to ask them if they can recommend other contractors with different specialities. I usually ask whether they can recommend an electrician, carpet fitter, general handyman and a painter/decorator.

It's also worth bearing in mind that a contractor will have skills in another trade or two, other than that which you've hired them for – which is amazing because you've already built up a relationship with them. When I find out this info, I'll add these skills to their contact details in my book as well as any new contacts they've given me.

Apps and websites can be a good way of finding tradespeople, but I don't trust the results as much. I've hired people with great reviews who charge by the hour and take double the time to complete a less than satisfactory job, leaving me over budget and under pressure. On occasion I've found good local handymen through community apps, but I've had more success through word-of-mouth recommendations. It's always the best approach and this is why I've left some space at the end of this chapter for you to build your own little black book – just flick to page 268.

Once you've gathered some suitable contractors for the job in question, the best way to find a good price is by requesting quotes for the work. Make sure you get three for every job, if you can. If you've got someone particular in mind, who has been recommended, you can then use an app and website for an extra couple of instant free quotes. You'll be able to see if you're getting a deal from your chosen contractor, paying what you should be or being ripped off.

To ensure you're getting accurate quotes, send as much detail as you can in your query. Photographs can be incredibly useful here, and this also goes for one-off repairs. An image can give a solid idea of the job in question – the make and model of an appliance, for example, the type of light fittings or the size of lock and so on – so your contractor has as much info as possible. This should reduce the amount of add-ons to the quote, such as unexpected replacement parts, and saves everyone time because what is needed can be organized in advance.

Bear in mind the lowest quote won't necessarily be the best – be sure to check what's included in the price you've been given and take into account which contractor has the best skills for the job.

If you feel a quote you've been given is high, you should feel free to discuss this with the contractor. Whenever I've queried a price, I've come away from the conversation either happier to pay a greater sum (because I've learned that they're using high-quality products or there's more time involved than I thought), or I've been given info by the contractor on how I can reduce the cost, such as buying and delivering some materials myself for a lower price (tradespeople get the best prices on some things thanks to trade discounts, so this is never a guarantee) or cutting out some of the work I'm less fussed about, and so on.

If you're unsure about what's involved in the work that's being done – for example, if it's a new plumbing fitting going in – make sure to say you'd like a report and some pictures of the work carried out. Most contractors I work with will happily email me a light description and some images. I can't tell you how many times I've had contractors not carry out the work and then bill me for a fake repair, such as charging for new pipework when all that was fixed was a blockage. I now always take pictures before and after the job, just to be sure.

When it comes to decorating, contractors will always have images of their best work to hand, or available to view online, so have a look at these first. Not only can it ensure you're in safe hands, it can also be really inspiring!

Hiring a contractor can be daunting if you haven't done it before or if you've had a bad experience in the past. It's like trying to find a good hairdresser. What works for some might not be what you need or want, or you simply might not love their technique. It's always best to shop around and request images of previous jobs to decide whether the contractor is right for you.

Most will be more than happy to answer questions, explain their price and suggest better ways to achieve your desired look, so lean in to the process and don't be afraid to talk things through with them. It doesn't need to be a case of a stranger showing up, carrying out work you're clueless about, and billing you afterwards. It should be a process where you're involved, where your opinion matters, and where you know what you're paying for.

If it's something like an emergency repair, such as a leak or a breakdown, contractors will always be open to helping you understand why the incident happened and if there's anything you can do to avoid it happening again in the future. They're experts in their fields and their knowledge can help you run a better home.

Finally, always show anyone working in your home where the bathroom is and offer them something to drink. It's always best to get these things out of the way at the beginning. When I'm carrying out repairs for a tenant, nothing is more awkward than asking to use the bathroom, and when I have repairs carried out myself, I always find that offering a glass of water or a coffee can put us both at ease as it breaks the ice! Also, many appliance engineers work on back-to-back appointments, so you're pretty sound if yours is the one that they get a little break at.

Name:
Specialism:
Recommended by:
Contact Details:
Notes:
Name:
Specialism:
Recommended by:
Contact Details:
Notes:
Name:
Specialism:
Recommended by:
Contact Details:
Notes:
Name:
Specialism:
Recommended by:
Contact Details:
Notes:

Contractor Contacts

- NAME:
- SPECIALISM:
- CONTACT DETAILS:
- RECOMMENDED BY:
- NOTES:

- NAME:
- SPECIALISM:
- CONTACT DETAILS:
- RECOMMENDED BY:
- NOTES:

- NAME:
- SPECIALISM:
- CONTACT DETAILS:
- RECOMMENDED BY:
- NOTES:

- NAME:
- SPECIALISM:
- CONTACT DETAILS:
- RECOMMENDED BY:
- NOTES:

- NAME:
- SPECIALISM:
- CONTACT DETAILS:
- RECOMMENDED BY:
- NOTES:

- NAME:
- SPECIALISM:
- CONTACT DETAILS:
- RECOMMENDED BY:
- NOTES:

- NAME:
- SPECIALISM:
- CONTACT DETAILS:
- RECOMMENDED BY:
- NOTES:

- NAME:
- SPECIALISM:
- CONTACT DETAILS:
- RECOMMENDED BY:
- NOTES:

- NAME:
- SPECIALISM:
- CONTACT DETAILS:
- RECOMMENDED BY:
- NOTES:

- NAME:
- SPECIALISM:
- CONTACT DETAILS:
- RECOMMENDED BY:
- NOTES:

- NAME:
- SPECIALISM:
- CONTACT DETAILS:
- RECOMMENDED BY:
- NOTES:

- NAME:
- SPECIALISM:
- CONTACT DETAILS:

- RECOMMENDED BY:
- NOTES:

- NAME:
- SPECIALISM:
- CONTACT DETAILS:

- RECOMMENDED BY:
- NOTES:

- NAME:
- SPECIALISM:
- CONTACT DETAILS:

- RECOMMENDED BY:
- NOTES:

- NAME:
- SPECIALISM:
- CONTACT DETAILS:
- RECOMMENDED BY:
- NOTES:

- NAME:
- SPECIALISM:
- CONTACT DETAILS:
- RECOMMENDED BY:
- NOTES:

- NAME:
- SPECIALISM:
- CONTACT DETAILS:
- RECOMMENDED BY:
- NOTES:

Acknowledgements

Thank you to all of my loving family, Shane, my supportive and ever chic friends and the incredible, hardworking editorial team at Transworld (Fiona, you're one in a billion). A special, smaller, thank you is reserved for those who put me in positions where I was forced to understand the true power of self-belief, hard work, She-IY and a red lipstick. Who's laughing over an Old Fashioned now?

Index

About the Author

Laura de Barra is a Cork-born property portfolio developer and illustrator working in the competitive London rental market. She is a regular guest on RTE's *Today with Maura and Dáithí,* and also has a regular home-hack column with *thejournal.ie*. Her Instagram account @lauradebarra is a gold mine of clever repair, décor and She-IY inspiration, and her joyful passion for her work will inspire even the most hesitant tenant or homeowner to discover they really can do it for themselves.